AN UNSUNG HERO

TOM CREAN – ANTARCTIC SURVIVOR

Best-selling author **Michael Smith** is an established authority on Polar exploration. He has contributed to TV and radio, written for newspapers and magazines and lectured extensively on Polar history. His other books are *I Am Just Going Outside*, a biography of Captain Oates (2002), *Polar Crusader* about Sir James Wordie (2004), *Tom Crean – An Illustrated Life* (2006 and 2011), *Captain Francis Crozier – Last Man Standing?* (2006) and *Great Endeavour* (2010). Michael has also written two books for children, *Tom Crean – Ice Man* and *Shackleton – The Boss*.

Contact: michael.smith13@virgin.net

AN UNSUNG HERO

TOM CREAN – ANTARCTIC SURVIVOR

Michael Smith

The Collins Press

Published in 2009 by
The Collins Press
West Link Park
Doughcloyne
Wilton
Cork

First published in hardback 2000
First published in paperback 2001
First published in this format 2009
Reprinted 2010, 2011

British Library Cataloguing in Publication Data
Smith, Michael, 1946-
An unsung hero : Tom Crean - Antarctic survivor
1. Crean, Tom, 1877-1938 2. Explorers - Ireland - Biography
3. Antarctica - Discovery and exploration - British
I. Title
910.9'2
ISBN-13: 9781905172863

Typesetting by The Collins Press
Typeset in AGaramond 11 pt
Printed in Great Britain by CPI Cox and Wyman

Quotations/excerpts by Tom Crean are in bold text

Cover photographs:
Front: Tom Crean (Frank Hurley); *inside front*: Tom Crean on board
Discovery (Royal Geographical Society); *back*: the *Endurance* crew hauling
the small boats across the ice floe *(SPRI)*; *inside back*: Tom Crean outside the
South Pole Inn in the late 1930s.

To those who mean the most to me: Barbara, Daniel and Nathan

Contents

Acknowledgements

It would not be possible to thank everyone who contributed so thoughtfully to this book. But I owe a special debt to certain people without whom the story of Tom Crean's remarkable life would have been incomplete.

I am especially grateful to Tom Crean's daughters, Mary Crean O'Brien and Eileen Crean O'Brien, who readily agreed to allow themselves to be interviewed about their father. They were patient, helpful and most of all informative. Special thanks must also go to Crean's considerate and supportive grandsons, Brendan O'Brien and Gerard O'Brien, who provided important guidance and archive material, including Tom Crean's service records and other documents. Others who helped in the early stages included Dr Hugh R. Crean and Pat Crean.

A special mention must go to several others who were invaluable to my work. Judith Lee Hallock, the first person to write about Tom Crean, gave me very welcome support and considerable encouragement. I am also grateful for the patience and guidance of the Hon. Broke Evans, the son of Teddy Evans (Lord Mountevans), who allowed me access to his father's papers and permission to quote from *South With Scott* and *Adventurous Life*. The Hon. Alexandra Bergel, Sir Ernest Shackleton's granddaughter, was supportive of the book.

Tom Kennedy, who now owns the South Pole Inn, has been a great and valued friend of the project, who willingly provided many documents, great encouragement and valuable background knowledge of Anascaul. There was surely no more appropriate place on earth to discuss Tom Crean than over a glass of stout in the South Pole Inn.

Michael Costello at the Kerry County Library, Tralee, provided significant help and encouragement when I needed it most and I must acknowledge the support of Kathleen Browne, the County Librarian. I was also given many useful anecdotes and memories from those in Anascaul who remember Tom Crean, notably Dan Courtney, Mona Kennedy and Kathleen McCarthy. Father Tom Crean (no relation) of Anascaul willingly gave spiritual guidance. Comhlacht Forbartha Phobal Abhainn an Scáil Teoranta, the Anascaul Development Association, were equally helpful.

Dr Robert Headland, archivist and curator at the Scott Polar Research Institute, Cambridge, was a vital cog in the wheel and gave every assistance in producing original documents and offering friendly advice. Philippa Smith, also at SPRI, was especially patient and thoughtful in helping to trace photographs. I am indebted to SPRI for permission to quote directly from original material and reproduce photographs from their collection.

Jenny Wraight of the Admiralty Library, London, was endlessly patient on naval history. Gary Gregor, author of a book about Edgar Evans, provided useful guidance and Derek Phillips, Assistant Curator of the Cyfarthfa Castle Museum and Art Gallery in Merthyr Tydfil was enormously considerate concerning Crean memorabilia in south Wales. Thanks also to Trevor Cornford for permission to reproduce the photograph of Tom Crean and Bill Lashly on *Terra Nova*. Michael Murphy of University College Cork assisted with cartography.

I am also grateful to Spink & Co for assistance on the history of the Albert Medal and Chris Bates of Dunn Nutritional Laboratories for guidance on the characteristics of scurvy. I must also acknowledge the important contribution of C. Ian Purkis, who allowed me to quote from correspondence between Tom Crean and his grandfather, Captain R.H. Dodds.

I am especially grateful to those who gave their permission for me to use references from books and archive material. To Angela Mathias, who allowed me to quote from

The Worst Journey in the World written by her late husband, Apsley Cherry-Garrard; Dr Andrew Tatham, Keeper of the Royal Geographical Society, for permission to quote from archive material; Harding Dunnett for *Shackleton's Boat*; Oxford University Press for *Evans of the* Broke; Random House for *South* by Sir Ernest Shackleton and *The Life of Sir Ernest Shackleton* by Hugh R. Mill; C. Hurst & Co for *The South Pole*; Victor Gollancz for *Under Scott's Command: Lashly's Antarctic Diaries;* John Murray (Publishers) for *Birdie Bowers of the Antarctic*; Steve MacDonogh for permission to quote from *The Dingle Peninsula*; Bluntisham Books for permission to quote from *Antarctic Obsession, The Wicked Mate* and *The Quiet Land*; McManus Galleries, Dundee, for permission to quote from the diaries of James Duncan; the Alexander Turnbull Library, New Zealand, for permission to quote from the diaries of Harry McNeish; the County Archivist, West Glamorgan Archive Service, for *Swansea's Antarctic Explorer*; News International for permission to quote from an article by Duncan Carse, © Times Newspapers, 1956; Roland Huntford for permission to quote from *Scott & Amundsen* and *Shackleton*; Sue Limb for allowing me to quote from *Captain Oates, Soldier & Explorer*; Hermann Gran for permission to quote from *The Norwegian With Scott*; Faber & Faber for approval to quote from *The Waste Land* by T.S. Eliot.

I have made every reasonable effort to trace all the relevant copyright holders, although this has not been easy because much of the material was published so many years ago. I hope I will be forgiven if there are any unintentional omissions.

I was given a great deal of encouragement and advice from many other people in a variety of libraries and museums and I must record my gratitude to the secondhand book trade, which is a priceless and illuminating source of material for anyone with an interest in polar history.

The thoughtful contribution of my editor, Val Shortland, was important and welcome. My agent, Anne Dewe, offered sensible and valuable guidance for which I am very grateful.

Thanks are also due to Frank Delaney for much appreciated independent and critical advice. Frank Nugent and Paddy Barry were vocal and important supporters of the case for a book about Tom Crean's life and I would also like to record my thanks to the many other friends who believed in the book.

Finally, I must acknowledge the enormous support given by my wife, Barbara, who was always 100 per cent behind me and never doubted. Words cannot express how much I valued her support.

Notes

Temperatures used in this book, unless otherwise stated, are in Fahrenheit, the measurement used at the time. In many cases approximate conversion to the now widely used Celsius scale has been added in parenthesis. (To convert F to C deduct 32, multiply by 5 and divide by 9.) But, as guidance, the following useful examples may be helpful to those unfamiliar with Fahrenheit.

Fahrenheit	Celsius
98.4°	36.9° (body temperature)
32°	0° (water freezes)
0°	−18°
−10°	−23°
−20°	−29°
−30°	−34½°
−40°	−40°
−50°	−45½°

In line with the measurements used at the time, many of the distances are measured as geographical or nautical miles, which is 1/60th of a degree of latitude, or equal to 2,026 yards (1.85 kilometres). Others are stated as statute miles, which are equal to 1,760 yards (1.6 km). One yard (3 ft) is 91 centimetres. Some approximate conversions are provided.

Weights are given in the avoirdupois scale and approximate conversions are given in kilogrammes. One pound (1lb) equals 0.453 kg and one ton is 2,240 lb (1,016 kg).

Money is stated in the contemporary values and conversion to modern equivalents is based on information supplied by the Bank of England. This gives an approximate indication of the sums of money required in December 2007 to purchase the same goods as in Crean's time. Thus it would require £84 in 2007 to buy £1 of items in 1877, the year of Tom Crean's birth.

Preface

The Dingle Peninsula, Kerry, is one of Ireland's most beautiful spots, its rich mixture of rolling hills and rugged coastline jutting out into the Atlantic; nature at its best. Visitors today come from all over the world to admire the dramatic scenery.

About midway along the Peninsula, in a modest uncomplicated setting, sits the small village of Anascaul (*Abhainn an Scáil*). It is said that Ireland's last wolf was killed in the overlooking hills. But visitors passing through the main street of Anascaul are alerted by one of the last buildings they glimpse as they travel west towards the better-known town of Dingle and the Atlantic breakers. This is a small pub with a highly unusual name: the South Pole Inn – situated alongside a quietly flowing river and a charming stone bridge, nowhere on earth seems farther from the South Pole.

But it is impossible to arrive or leave Anascaul without catching sight of the little building and wonder how a public house in a rural village surrounded by endless green fields on the Dingle Peninsula came to be called the 'South Pole Inn'.

The answer, for those who linger, can be found in a small slate-grey plaque above the pub doorway. It reads:

Tom Crean
Antarctic Explorer
1877–1938

The South Pole Inn was the home of Thomas Crean, a local man who rose from the obscurity of a typical farming community in Kerry to become one of the greatest characters in the history of polar exploration at the turn of the century – the Heroic Age of polar exploration.

Few men made a greater contribution to the annals of Antarctic exploration than Tom Crean and few were more highly respected by his celebrated fellow explorers than the unassuming Kerryman. However, for too many years, Crean's contribution to the Heroic Age has been greatly underestimated, if not ignored.

The Heroic Age of polar exploration in Antarctica, which covers the first two decades of the twentieth century, produced some of history's most astonishing stories and some remarkable characters. Even today, almost 100 years after the event, people are still captivated by the tales of Scott or Shackleton, particularly the heroism and tragedies, the bravery and fortitude and the outstanding human sagas of achievement and failure which seem barely credible in modern times.

However, it would be wholly wrong to assume that all the great deeds and achievements of the Heroic Age in Antarctica were the sole preserve of Scott and Shackleton. The expeditions of the age were made up by equally important figures, not always from the officer or scientific ranks, who were vital to the success of these enterprises. But their valuable contribution has so far been mostly overlooked or at best unceremoniously lumped together with the deeds of others. Lesser known, perhaps, but no less important and certainly no less outstanding. Such a man is Thomas Crean.

Crean was a prodigious traveller who sailed on three of the four momentous expeditions of Britain's Heroic Age and at that time rightly won the highest possible recognition for his outstanding achievements. He was a colourful, popular character who was one of very few men to serve both Scott and Shackleton with equal distinction.

Crean was a simple, straightforward man with extraordinary depths of courage and self-belief who repeatedly performed the most incredible deeds in the world's most inhospitable, physically and mentally demanding climate. He was a serial hero.

Crean travelled further than most of the explorers traditionally associated with the Heroic Age and few left their mark as indelibly as the Irishman did. Appropriately enough, his name is perpetuated forever on the Antarctic Continent where he achieved his fame. 'Mount Crean', which extends to a height of 8,360 ft (2,550 m), stands at about 77° 53' S 159° 30' E in Victoria Land, Antarctica. The near 4-mile (6-km) 'Crean Glacier' runs down to the head of Antarctic Bay – 37° 01' W 54° 08' S – on the island of South Georgia, where the Irishman was to perform so nobly.

Tom Crean is not the only one whose adventures have been overlooked by Polar historians. History has also been unkind to men like Edgar Evans, William Lashly and Frank Wild, colleagues and friends of Crean in the South. It was men like these who provided the backbone for the great expeditions which lifted the veil from the Antarctic Continent, often at a terrible price. While these men were effectively second-class citizens at a time when the British class system was so prevalent, the Heroic Age would be incomplete without their contribution.

To be fair, it has not been easy for historians to chronicle the tale of Tom Crean, a semi-literate man who, unlike so many explorers of the age, did not keep a diary or maintain a prolific flow of correspondence with friends and family. Only a small amount of Crean's correspondence has survived and so, in order to piece together his life and times, we have to rely on the words and memories of his contemporaries. Fortunately, since he was a prominent figure of the Heroic Age, there are ample records of his exploits in the published and unpublished accounts of the three expeditions on which he excelled. It is no surprise, however, that much of the coverage so far has been inconsistent.

But with the combination of Crean's own writings, the works of his contemporaries and the invaluable recollections of his surviving family, for the first time an authoritative and accurate account of the life of a remarkable man can be constructed.

His contemporaries had few doubts about his special qualities. Frank Debenham, who served alongside Crean on Scott's fateful last expedition and later became the first director of the Scott Polar Research Institute at Cambridge, remembered the Irishman with special affection. He once wrote:

> 'Tom Crean was in his way, unique; he was like something out of Kipling or Masefield, typical of his country and a credit to all his three expeditions. One has only to close one's eyes for a moment to summon up his clean-cut features and his grin as he greeted one in the morning with: "Well fare ye, sorr".'

Since those momentous days, Tom Crean had sadly become a somewhat neglected figure, an unsung and largely unknown figure whose outstanding stories and achievements remained a closed book to modern generations. But, more than most, he deserves to have his story told.

All generations are hungry for heroes and Tom Crean is a hero for any generation.

1
A farmer's lad

Thomas Crean was born on 20 July 1877 at Gurtuchrane, a remote farming area a short distance to the west of the village of Anascaul on the Dingle Peninsula, in Ireland's County Kerry. The area is, even today, a quiet unassuming mixture of houses and farms surrounded by rolling green hills.

The contrast with the hostile, frozen Antarctic Continent where Crean would carve a remarkable career could hardly be more stark. By odd coincidence, Crean would later share his birthday with Edmund Hillary, the first conqueror of Mount Everest, renowned Antarctic traveller and one of the great adventurers of the twentieth century.

The Dingle Peninsula is rich in tradition, its origins easily traced back to the earliest European civilisations. It became a centre of Early Christian activity and despite conquest by both the Anglo-Normans and English, the area survived centuries of political and religious repression and persecution. The people were tough, resolute survivors and it is little surprise that Kerry was one of the areas which fought hardest to preserve the Irish language. To this day, the Dingle Peninsula is a *Fíor-Gaeltacht*, an Irish-speaking region.

By the late nineteenth century, it was in common use along the Peninsula and Crean's parents were part of the last generation of Kerry people who spoke Irish as a first language. As a young man, Crean was brought up speaking both Irish and English.

He was a member of a typically large Irish rural family which, like so many of the time, struggled against grinding poverty and the persistent fear of crop failure and famine. The name Crean is fairly common in the Kerry region and is thought to be derived from Curran. In Irish his name is written as *Tomás Ó Croidheáin* or *Ó Cuirín*.

His parents, Patrick Crean and Catherine Courtney, were farmers at Gurtuchrane who produced ten children during the 1860s and 1870s. Hardship was a way of life, with few if any luxuries and little prospect of any escape from the unrelenting battle to make ends meet and keep stomachs filled.

At the time of Crean's birth, Ireland itself was still recovering from the devastating effects of the Great Famine three decades earlier when between 800,000 and 1,000,000 people perished – one in eight of the total population at the time – after the disastrous failure of the potato crop. It was to have a searing effect on Ireland's soul, encouraging the mass emigration of perhaps two million people in the years immediately afterwards and greatly reinforcing the belief that Ireland should be master of its own affairs.

But by the end of the 1870s, famine once again threatened Ireland and inevitably reawakened in many fears of a repeat of the appalling horrors. The year of Crean's birth, 1877, was miserably wet in Ireland, which set off an unfortunate chain of events that led to a deterioration in the potato crop in the following years. At the same time, the collapse of grain prices meant many farmers were caught in a catastrophic poverty trap and were unable to afford the often exorbitant rents imposed by the hated absentee landlords. For many farmers, especially in the west of Ireland, the terror of famine was now matched by the fear that they might be evicted from their land and homes. These people would have known precisely what another Irishman, George Bernard Shaw, meant 30 years later when he wrote that poverty was the greatest of evils and worst of crimes.

It was against this background of impending famine, dwindling income and a growing family, that Patrick and

Catherine Crean struggled to provide a life for Tom and his five brothers and four sisters; an environment which inevitably helped shape and prepare the youngster for the hardships and privations which he would face during his lengthy spells in the Antarctic.

Tom was given a very basic education at the nearby Brackluin School, Anascaul – the local Catholic school – and like most youngsters of the age, probably left as quickly as possible. It was not uncommon for children to leave school at the age of twelve, although the majority stayed on until they were fourteen. Either way, the youngsters were given only a rudimentary education which provided them with little more than the ability to read and write. The need to help on the farm and bring in some meagre amounts of money to the family was overwhelming.

It is likely that events down the hill in the nearby village of Anascaul provided young Tom with his first taste for travel and adventure.

The village sits at the junction of a main road through the Dingle Peninsula and the Anascaul River, which flows down from the surrounding hills. It is a natural meeting place for travellers.

For centuries Anascaul had been the site of regular local fairs. In his book, *The Dingle Peninsula*, local author, Steve MacDonogh, said that for many centuries the Anascaul fairs were a 'vital focus' for the area. He recalled that the Anglo-Normans, who had established many commercial fairs across Ireland, settled around the Anascaul area in significant numbers. Tralee, one of Kerry's main towns, is known to have been established by the Anglo-Normans in the thirteenth century. Nearby villages, Ballynahunt and Flemingstown, are also said to be associated with the early Anglo-Norman presence.

Young Tom Crean grew up in this poor, rural community and must have drawn some relief from these regular fairs which punctuated the otherwise dreary routine. Anascaul played host to fourteen separate fairs a year, attracting a rich variety of locals and outsiders. The biggest occasions were the twice-yearly horse fairs in May and October, one of the oldest events in Ireland's long tradition of horse-trading and which attracted people from all corners of the land.

But the most regular event at Anascaul was the monthly fair, which cobbled together an unlikely mixture of commerce and trade and fun and entertainment. The entertainment, said MacDonogh, was not mere frills on a mainly commercial occasion but, in true Gaelic spirit, was essential to the proceedings. MacDonogh described a typical scene:

> 'The wheel of fortune, stalls selling humbugs, women in their best dresses and hats, men whose clothes echoed time spent in foreign parts, the three-card trickster, ballad singers, fiddlers, match-makers, peddlers and beggars – all combined to make a colourful social gathering as well as an occasion for business.'[1]

It was in the pubs and on the street corners that stories were told and in typical loquacious Irish fashion events were relived and the imagination of a young farmer's son was allowed to run wild. Against a harsh impoverished background of farm life, the tales of faraway places would have sounded all the more attractive to an inquisitive young man. The urge to travel must have been all too powerful.

Several of Tom's brothers emigrated from Kerry around this period and MacDonogh also notes that for some time there had been a tradition of Anascaul's sons moving away to serve in the British navy.

Tom's elder brother Martin found work across the Atlantic on the burgeoning Canadian Pacific Railway. Michael went to sea and was lost with his ship. Cornelius, who was six years older than Tom, grew up to become a policeman in the Royal Irish Constabulary and was later murdered during 'The Troubles'. Tom's sister, Catherine, also married a policeman. Two other brothers, Hugh and Daniel, remained behind to maintain the family tradition on the land. When their father

Patrick died, Hugh and Daniel split the family farm in two and remained at Gurtuchrane for the rest of their lives.

Growing up on the farm in the 1880s and 1890s was a huge challenge. It needed a strong sense of survival to co-exist in a home environment where the ten Crean children scrapped for supremacy and their parents' attention. Patrick Crean struggled to make ends meet and had little time to provide anything approaching today's level of parental guidance.

It was a severe upbringing which inevitably left the young Crean with a strong streak of independence. It was this independence which prompted the youngster to flee the family nest at the earliest opportunity.

It was customary at the time for the British navy to send its recruiting officers out to Irish villages to find new able-bodied men for the service. The navy was always on the lookout for fresh blood and the offer to swap the uncompromising life on the land for the apparent romance of the sea was a permanent feature of life in the area. Many young Irishmen were easily persuaded to sign up. At the time, the British navy boasted the world's most powerful fleet and its prestige was second to none. To young men like Tom Crean, the opportunity to escape from the bleak hardship of daily life must have been irresistible. The alternative of maintaining the unrelenting struggle was easily dismissed, and it is no surprise that Tom Crean left home when he did.

The background to his departure is far from clear, although it appears that Tom had a major row with his father when he inadvertently allowed some cattle to stray into the potato field and devour the precious crop. In the heat of the moment, Tom swore he would run away to sea.

Crean, still a fresh-faced fifteen years old, set off for Minard Inlet, a few miles southwest from Anascaul where there was a Royal Navy station. Crean and another local lad called Kennedy approached the recruiting officer and, suitably impressed by his patter, blithely agreed to join Queen Victoria's mighty Navy.

Although Crean was a fiercely independent young man, he was still unsure about the reception he might receive at home and did not immediately tell his parents about his new life. He chose not to inform them until after he signed the recruitment papers, which meant there was no chance of persuading him to stay on the farm. It was also an early indication of Crean's self-confidence and determination. And, if the two youngsters were looking for extra courage, they probably found it in each other's company.

But, after deciding to enlist, Crean had another problem. He was penniless and did not even possess a decent set of clothes to wear for the trip to a new life. He promptly borrowed a small sum of money from an unknown benefactor and persuaded someone else to lend him a suit. Tom Crean took off his well-worn working clothes in July 1893, squeezed into his borrowed suit and left the farm, never to return.

As he strode off, the young man had precious few possessions to carry with him as a reminder of his home and upbringing. But Crean did remember to put around his neck a scapular, a small symbol of his Catholic faith and a token souvenir of his roots. The scapular, which is two pieces of cloth about two and a half by two inches attached to a leather neck cord, contains a special prayer that offers particular spiritual relief to the wearer. As he set off into the unknown for the first time, Crean will have drawn special comfort from its fundamental tenet – that the wearer of the scapular will not suffer eternal fire. It was to remain around his neck for the rest of his life.

He travelled down to Queenstown (today called Cobh), near Cork on Ireland's southern coast with James Ashe, another Irish seaman from the merchant navy. Ashe was a close relative of Thomas Ashe from nearby Kinard, who was to become a leader of the Irish Republican Brotherhood and achieve martyrdom in 1917 by dying on hunger strike in Mountjoy Prison at the height of the war with the British.

Tom Crean was formally enlisted in the Royal Navy on 10 July 1893, just ten days before his sixteenth birthday.[2] Officially the lowest enlistment age was sixteen and the assumption is that the fifteen-year-old lad either forged his papers or lied about his age before signing up.

At this formative stage in his life, young Tom was not the tall, imposing figure well known on the polar landscape in later life. According to Ministry of Defence records of the time, the farmer's son, who had a mop of brown hair, stood only 5 ft 7¾ inches when he signed on the dotted line in July 1893 as Boy 2nd Class, service No 174699.[3]

His first appointment was to the boys' training ship, HMS *Impregnable* at Devonport, Plymouth in the southwest of England, where he served his initial naval apprenticeship.[4]

Life in the navy was tough, particularly for a young man away from home for the first time in his life. Discipline was strict and the regime harsh and unsympathetic. His initiation into naval life was perhaps the first test of the strength of character which was to become a hallmark of his adventurous life.

He survived his first examination and promotion of sorts came fairly quickly for the young man. Within a year Crean had taken his first step upwards and was promoted to Boy 1st Class. A little later on 28 November 1894 the Boy 1st class was transferred to HMS *Devastation*, a coastguard vessel based at Devonport.[5] Crean, for the first time, was at sea.

Little is known about Crean's early career in the Navy. It was, however, punctuated with advancement and demotion and it may not have been an altogether happy time for the youngster as he came to terms with the new life a long way from home. Some reports suggest that at one stage Crean became so disenchanted with the naval routine that he tried to run away. One writer claimed that Crean was so dismayed by the poor food and rough accommodation on board naval ships of the time that he threatened to abscond.[6]

The regime in the late Victorian Navy of the time was undoubtedly arduous and unforgiving. While the Royal Navy was traditionally the right arm of the British Empire, by the late Victorian era it had become smugly complacent, inefficient and out of date. It had more in common with Nelson and still lent heavily on rigid discipline and blind obedience. It required sweeping reforms by the feared Admiral Sir John 'Jackie' Fisher to eventually modernise the navy in time for the First World War in 1914.

But there is a strange inconsistency about a young man, fresh from a poor, undernourished rural community in the Kerry hills complaining about the quality of the food and bedding. It may be that Crean, like others at the time, had other grievances. Or it may well have been a simple case of a young man a long way from his roots who was homesick. In any event, he drew some comfort from the other young Irish sailors around him and decided that he, too, would stick it out.

On his eighteenth birthday in 1895, after exactly two years service, Crean was promoted to the rank of 'ordinary seaman' while serving on HMS *Royal Arthur*, a flag-ship in the Pacific Fleet. A little less than a year later, he advanced to become Able Seaman Crean on HMS *Wild Swan*, a small 170-ft versatile utility vessel which also operated in Pacific waters.

By 1898, Crean was apparently eager to gain new skills and was appointed to the gunnery training ship, HMS *Cambridge*, at Devonport. Six months later, shortly before Christmas 1898, he moved across to the torpedo school ship of HMS *Defiance*, also at Devonport. At the major naval port of Chatham, he advanced a little further by securing qualifications for various gun and torpedo duties.[7]

Crean was also developing a reputation for reliability and his career record is impressive. His conduct was officially described by the naval hierarchy as 'very good' throughout his early years in the service, despite occasional brushes with authority.

It was around this time – between 1899 and 1900 – that Crean began to rise up and down the slippery pole of naval ranking and he secured the only recorded blemish to his otherwise impressive career record. It may have reflected his discontent, or it may be that after six years 'below decks' Crean lacked any sense of purpose and felt he was going nowhere in this Englishman's navy. Or, more simply, it may have been that, like countless sailors before and since, Crean was a victim of excessive drinking, the traditional curse of the ordinary seaman. Drinking was a regular feature of a sailor's routine and shore leave was normally peppered with heavy and excessive bouts which easily got out of hand with predictable results. Crean liked a drink and as a gregarious, outgoing character would have been at his ease in the company of other heavy-drinking sailors.

At the end of September 1899, he was promoted to Petty Officer 2nd Class at the Devonport yard while assigned to *Vivid*. There followed a brief period on board HMS *Northampton*, the boy's training school before Crean made the move which would change his life.

The momentous move came on 15 February 1900, when PO 2nd Class Crean was assigned to the oddly-named special torpedo vessel, HMS *Ringarooma*, in Australian waters.[8] It was a move which introduced the strapping 22-year-old to a new and very different type of challenge – the rigours of polar exploration with the likes of Scott, Shackleton, Wild, Evans and Lashly.

2
A chance meeting

The year 1901 marked the end of the long Victorian era for Britain. Queen Victoria, who had presided over the country's most expansive age, died on 22 January after more than 63 years on the throne. It was also the year when Britain, under the leadership of Robert Falcon Scott, would launch the first major attempt to conquer the Earth's last unexplored continent – Antarctica.

At the time only a handful of people had visited Antarctica, which is the fifth largest continent with a diameter of 2,800 miles and an area of 5,400,000 square miles. It represents about ten per cent of the world's land mass and is larger than either America or Europe.

Antarctica is an island continent, totally isolated from the rest of the world's land masses and separated from civilisation by the violent Southern Ocean. It is 600 miles to South America and over 1,500 miles to Australia. Over 99 per cent of the land mass is permanently covered in ice and about 90 per cent of the world's fresh water is locked up in the icecaps. Wind speeds have been recorded at close to 200 mph (320 kph) and Antarctica has yielded the lowest temperature ever recorded on Earth, –129.3 °F (–89.6 °C).

There are no Eskimos from which to learn the art of survival in Earth's coldest and most inhospitable environment and there are few indigenous inhabitants, though it is visited by varieties of penguins, seals and whales. There are very few other living things beyond some algae, lichens and mosses, so all food and equipment has to be transported to the continent and carried along on any journey. Antarctica is also a land of extremes. Despite the ice sheet covering, it rarely snows and for much of the year the continent is either plunged into total darkness for 24 hours a day or bathed in full sunlight.

People down the ages had believed in the existence of Antarctica, or the Southern Continent, for perhaps 2,000 years before its presence was finally established. Long before its discovery, the 'unknown southern land' – *Terra Australis Incognita* – had entered mythology. Greek philosophers claimed that a giant land mass was needed to 'balance' the weight of the lands known to exist at the top of the earth. Since the Northern Hemisphere rested beneath Arktos (the Bear), the general belief was that the southern land had to be the opposite – Antarktikos.

Great sailors like Magellan and Drake flirted with the unknown southern land in the sixteenth century and two intrepid French explorers – Jean-Baptiste Bouvet de Lozier and Yves Joseph de Kerguelen-Tremarec – discovered some neighbouring sub-Antarctic islands in the eighteenth century. But it was Captain James Cook, arguably the greatest explorer of all time, who first crossed the Antarctic Circle on 17 January 1773, in his vessels, *Resolution* and *Adventure*. Cook never actually saw Antarctica – he sailed to within 75 miles of land – and was doubtful about the value of any exploration in such a frigid and hostile environment.

The earliest people to see Antarctica travelled on the expedition led by the Russian, Thaddeus von Bellingshausen, which on 27 January 1820 recorded the first known sighting. But Bellingshausen was unsure about his sighting and it was not until January 1831, that sealing captain John Biscoe circumnavigated the continent.

Sir James Clark Ross penetrated the pack ice which surrounds the continent for the first time in 1841 and sailed alongside the frozen land mass in his ships, *Erebus* and *Terror*. He gave the names of his two ships to two of Antarctica's most prominent mountains which stand guard over the entrance to the area that was to be frequented by several British expeditions around Ross Island in the Ross Sea.

An international expedition, led by the Belgian, Adrian de Gerlache, took the ship *Belgica* deep into southern waters between 1897 and 1899. His ship became stuck fast in the ice in the Bellingshausen Sea off the Antarctica Peninsula, which extends like an outstretched finger from the continent up towards the tip of South America.

Reluctantly and with great trepidation, de Gerlache and his crew were the first humans to spend the winter in the Antarctic, where the sun vanishes for four months. The hardship, bitter cold and endless gloomy months of total winter darkness took a heavy toll on the crew. One man died and two others were declared 'insane'.

The survivors included a 25-year-old Norwegian, Roald Amundsen, and a 33-year-old American, Frederick Cook. Amundsen, the finest polar explorer of all time, would later complete the first ever navigation of the North West Passage across the frozen top of the North American Continent, and he would reach the South Pole a month before his ill-fated British rival, Captain Scott. Cook, a flawed but undeniably gifted character, would falsely claim until his dying day that he had beaten Robert Peary to become the first man to reach the North Pole.

The first landing on the Antarctic Continent outside the Antarctic Peninsula is thought to have taken place on 24 January 1895 when an eight-man party from the whaler, *Antarctic*, landed at Cape Adare. The identity of the first person to make the landfall has never been accurately established because of a series of disputes. But the naturalist, Carsten Borchgrevink, claimed to have leaped out of the rowing boat ahead of others to gain the honour of being first to place his feet on the Continent. Borchgrevink later went on to secure the significant distinction of leading the first expedition to deliberately overwinter in Antarctica.

Borchgrevink, a Norwegian, landed near the entrance of Robertson Bay at Cape Adare on the Adare Peninsula in 1899 and erected two small prefabricated huts where his ten-man party was the first to spend winter on the Antarctic Continent. One hut, the party's living quarters, still stands today. However, Borchgrevink's exploratory deeds were modest and confined to a short trip onto the Ross Ice Shelf, or the Great Ice Barrier.

The first major attempt to explore Antarctica was conceived some years earlier by a remarkable English naval figure, Sir Clements Markham, who had made a brief trip to the Arctic decades before. Markham, an ex-public-school boy who entered the Navy at thirteen years of age, was on board the *Assistance* in 1850–51 during one of the many fruitless searches for Sir John Franklin's party, which had tragically disappeared in search of the North West Passage in 1845 with the loss of all 129 lives.

It was an episode which shaped Markham's colourful life and had profound consequences for Britain's role in polar exploits, first in the Arctic and later in the exploration of the Antarctic Continent. Britain's memorable part in the 'Heroic Age of polar exploration' would have been entirely different without the driving influence of the formidable bewhiskered Victorian patriarch, Markham.

Markham, a brusque and stubborn man who has been likened to a Victorian Winston Churchill, adopted polar exploration as a personal quest which bordered on obsession. There was a fanatical zeal about the way he manoeuvred, cajoled and expertly used his influence to ensure that Britain should undertake new expeditions south at a time when there was little support elsewhere for the idea. Moreover, Markham ensured that future exploration to the South would be a naval affair, when Britain could once again demonstrate its manhood and superiority to a slightly disbelieving world.

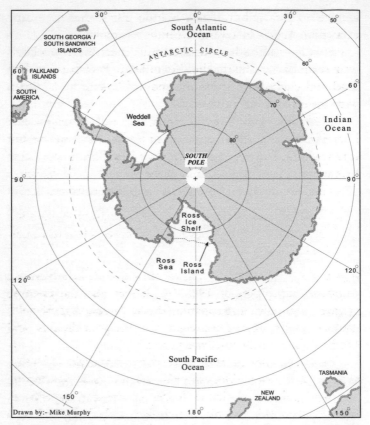

The Antarctic: the fifth largest continent was largely unexplored at the start of the twentieth century.

In particular, he was determined that the expedition would use traditional British methods of travelling, which meant man-hauling sledges across the ice, rather than the more suitable and modern use of dogs and skis. Dogs were quicker, hard working and at worst, could be eaten by the other dogs or the explorers themselves to prolong the journey or ensure safe return.

Markham, however, was typically sentimental towards dogs and implacably opposed to using them as beasts of burden at a time when others – notably the Norwegians – used the animals to great effect. There is little doubt that he greatly influenced Scott's lukewarm attitude to animals on both his journeys to the South, with the result that British explorers were destined to suffer the dreadful ordeal of man-hauling their food and equipment across the snow. The beasts of burden were the explorers themselves.

Markham, who loved intrigue, successfully engineered himself into the position as unelected leader of the venture but it took almost two decades to bring the first British expedition to Antarctica into fruition. In his celebrated *Personal Narrative* of events leading up to the *Discovery* expedition, he recalled:

'In 1885 I turned my attention to Antarctic exploration at which I had to work for sixteen years before success was achieved.'[1]

It was the first tentative step towards the British National Antarctic Expedition of 1901–04. It was also the opening chapter of Britain's participation in the Heroic Age of polar exploration. Tom Crean was eight years of age at the time and Scott, Markham's protégé, was sixteen.

Markham plotted and planned his Antarctic adventure with great determination, especially when it came to selecting his own preferred choice as leader of the first expedition. Although probably not his first choice, he had alighted on a young naval officer who was destined to carry his banner into the South – Robert Falcon Scott, or as he has become known, 'Scott of the Antarctic'.

Markham had been 'talent spotting' in the Navy for some years and finally selected Scott towards the end of the century, helped by a chance meeting near Buckingham Palace in June 1899. Writing in his famous book, *The Voyage of the Discovery*, Scott remembered:

'Early in June I was spending my short leave in London and chancing one day to walk down Buckingham Palace Road, I espied Sir Clements on the opposite pavement, and naturally crossed, and as naturally turned and accompanied him to his house. That afternoon for the first time I learned that there was such a thing as a prospective Antarctic expedition.'[2]

Two days later Scott formally applied for the post as commander of the expedition, though he must have been given some indication from Markham that at the very least he was likely to travel with the expedition. In any event, Scott was not officially appointed until a year later on 30 June 1900 at the age of 32. It was the beginning of the Scott legend.

Markham, meanwhile, was busily trying to arrange the sizeable sum of £90,000 (equivalent to £8,000,000 at today's purchasing prices) to pay for the expedition – the largest amount ever raised in Britain for a polar journey. This was a prolonged and frustrating exercise and only after lengthy debate and political manoeuvring was the cash found. Markham's dream had become a reality.

The British National Antarctic Expedition was under way, complete with a new, purpose-built ship, the 172-ft long *Discovery* which boasted a steel-plated bow and 26-inch thick sides to combat the ice. It was to be a mixture of exploration and scientific research, although this, too, caused considerable friction between the sponsors, the Royal Geographical Society and Royal Society. Although there was some dispute over the expedition's priorities, Markham's will prevailed. Markham was unequivocal and insisted that the great object of the expedition was the 'exploration of the interior of Antarctic land'.

Crucially, it was Markham who decided that Scott should explore the Ross Sea area which had been discovered 60 years earlier by Sir James Clark Ross and was to become forever associated with Britain's polar exploration exploits during the Heroic Age.

Markham schemed and plotted at every turn, imposing his influence right down to the smallest details of the expedition. He even designed individual 3-ft long, swallow-tailed flags or pennants which would be carried by the sledging parties on their journeys across the ice into the unknown.

With most squabbles now settled, *Discovery* left London on 31 July 1901 for the short trip to the Isle of Wight to participate on the fringe of Cowes Week and receive a royal farewell. The country was still coming to terms with the loss of Queen Victoria after her long reign and the new, but uncrowned monarch, Edward VII and his wife Queen Alexandra, came on board *Discovery* on 5 August to bid the expedition a royal farewell. Scott was impressed and recalled:

> 'This visit was quite informal, but will be ever memorable from the kindly, gracious interest shown in the minutest details of our equipment, and the frank expression of good wishes for our plans and welfare. But although we longed to get away from our country as quietly as possible, we could not but feel gratified that His Majesty should have shown such personal sympathy with our enterprise . . .'[3]

Discovery, the fulfilment of Markham's obsessive ambition and the opening chapters of both Britain's Heroic Age and the Scott legend, sailed slowly away from the Isle of Wight at noon on 6 August 1901. She would not return home for almost three years.

On the other side of the world, Tom Crean was in the middle of a period of almost two years on board HMS *Ringarooma*, the P-class special torpedo vessel of 6,400 tons which formed part of the Royal Navy's Australia–New Zealand squadron. *Ringarooma*, with the unlikely sounding name, was to be the unexpected launching pad for his remarkable Antarctic career.

The odd name for a ship in the Royal Navy arose from a special arrangement struck between Britain and Australia in the late Victorian age. Under the Imperial Defence Act of 1887, the Australians agreed to pay for the building of five warships for the Navy on condition that they were deployed in the seas around Australia and New Zealand. *Ringarooma*, built in 1890, was crewed by Royal Navy personnel, but the Australians were given the right to choose their own names for all five ships.

Crean had joined *Ringarooma* on 15 February 1900 but before long had suffered an unfortunate brush with naval authority. On 18 December he was summarily demoted from PO to Able Seaman for an unknown misdemeanour, a rank he would retain for exactly twelve months.[4]

By November 1901, Scott's expedition was in open water heading for New Zealand, the last staging post of civilisation before setting off into the unexplored region. Unknown to either of them, Able Seaman Tom Crean would be waiting for *Discovery*.

Some confusion has surrounded the circumstances of Crean's introduction to the polar landscape. Almost every mention of Crean in books, magazines and newspapers over the years has linked his arrival on the Antarctic scene with the untimely and widely reported death of another seaman, Charles Bonner, at Lyttelton, New Zealand, where *Discovery* was being resupplied before departing for the South at Christmas 1901. However, Crean's elevation from the obscurity of the naval mess deck to a high-profile place on the *Discovery* expedition had nothing to do with the death of Bonner. Crean was already on board *Discovery* when Bonner died, having signed up with the expedition two weeks earlier. His arrival on the Antarctic scene was due to an entirely different act of fate which has received very little attention over the years.

Crean's contact with the expedition arose because *Ringarooma* and another man-of-war in the New Zealand squadron, HMS *Lizard*, had been instructed by the Admiralty to lend every possible assistance to Scott in New Zealand before the party set out on the journey into the unknown. *Ringarooma's* log reported its first sighting of *Discovery* off New Zealand at 4.45 a.m. on Friday, 29 November,[5] and doubtless Crean would have been as eager as his messmates to catch sight of the historic vessel as it headed for one of the greatest journeys of the age.

The *Discovery* expedition to one of the world's last unconquered spots had aroused huge interest in the English-speaking world. It was regarded by many as something of a virility symbol for Britain at a time when the Victorian age had finally drawn to a close and the Empire was under severe strain in places like South Africa and Ireland.

A little later that day, *Discovery* arrived at Lyttelton Harbour, just to the south of Christchurch and *Ringarooma*'s Captain Rich wasted little time carrying out Admiralty orders to help the explorers. He immediately provided Scott with some extra manpower to assist with his preparations for the journey. This included extensive overhauling and refitting to *Discovery*'s rigging and a trip into dry dock to trace a persistent leak which had badly damaged some provisions since leaving London.

The *Ringarooma* log records that the first working party was despatched to *Discovery* on 3 December 1901.[6] It seems probable that Crean was a member of that and other teams of men who were sent across the harbour to the *Discovery* over the following two and a half weeks while the ship was docked at Lyttelton. From 3 December to 20 December, the ship's log details an almost unbroken daily routine of crew members leaving the ship in the morning and returning in late afternoon after a stint on *Discovery*'s decks.

As a member of these working parties, Crean quickly gained some knowledge of *Discovery* as a working vessel and the mood on board. It also helps explain why he volunteered to join a ship making ready to sail into largely unexplored territory for perhaps two or three years.

However, it needed another intervention of fate to bring Crean onto the Antarctic stage alongside the likes of Scott, Shackleton, Wilson, Lashly, Evans and Wild, some of the most famous names from the Heroic Age of polar exploration who were all together on board *Discovery* that day in Lyttelton.

Crean's opportunity came when Scott encountered an ugly problem with a member of the *Discovery* crew, seaman Harry

J. Baker. Surprisingly, the Baker incident has been widely overlooked in chronicling events at this time.

Baker, who appears to have been a troublemaker, struck a Petty Officer for some unknown reason and promptly deserted. This left Scott with an unexpected vacancy to fill only days before he was due to sail south and he went straight to Captain Rich on the *Ringarooma* for help.

Scott chose not to mention the Baker incident in his best-selling book on the expedition and Markham provided only scant information about the seaman. Indeed, Baker does not warrant a single mention in the lengthy Scott tome, even in the list of crew members. It is as though he did not exist. However, it was the little-documented desertion of Harry J. Baker which was directly responsible for introducing Tom Crean to polar exploration.

Seaman Baker, who was 25 years of age and came from Sandgate in Kent, appears to have caused problems on the *Discovery*'s long journey from England and was not popular. But the only formal record of Baker's misdemeanours can be found in a handwritten letter from Scott to the Royal Geographical Society dated 18 December 1901 as *Discovery* was preparing to leave New Zealand for the last time.[7] It was also written three days before Bonner's fatal accident and the subsequent desertion of another seaman, Sinclair, who felt responsible for Bonner's death and also fled.

Scott hinted at earlier difficulties with seaman Baker when he confided to the RGS:

> 'Baker was a good seaman but unpopular with his messmates.'[8]

Striking a PO was an offence regarded as very serious in the Royal Navy at any time and Scott immediately ordered Baker's arrest. In his letter to the RGS, Scott dutifully reported:

> 'He [Baker] struck a Petty Officer and learnt from me that I could not afterwards keep him in the ship – in

consequence of which, he ran away. I immediately issued a warrant for his arrest and offered a reward for his apprehension, but he has not yet been found.'[9]

Sir Clements Markham, presumably acting on Scott's information, later wrote his own truncated version of events in his *Personal Narrative*. He described the Baker incident in the following way:

'Discharged at Lyttelton as objectionable. He ran. Messmates did not like him.'[10]

Markham later amended his initial entry with a more abrupt verdict on Baker, striking out the original comments and writing:

'Ran at Lyttelton. Objectionable.'[11]

Nor does *Ringarooma*'s log provide any further background into the circumstances of Crean's appointment and transfer to *Discovery*. But it does show that Crean was assigned to *Discovery* before Bonner's death. The final entry in the log on 9 December, some eleven days before Bonner's death, simply records:

'Discharged Crean AB to SS *Discovery*.'[12]

Records of the *Discovery* expedition at the RGS show that Crean was recruited on 10 December 1901. Scott merely recorded in his letter to the RGS:

'By permission of the Admiral, Captain Rich of the *Ringarooma* was able to fill this vacancy [Baker] with one of his men named Crean.'[13]

The farmer's-son-turned-sailor had now graduated to exploration and for his troubles Crean was paid the going rate for an able seaman, some £2 5s 7d per month (£2.28 or the equivalent of £201 a month at today's prices). The general assumption has always been that Crean volunteered for *Discovery* in those days before Christmas, 1901, although there is no conclusive evidence either way. However, it seems inconceivable that

Captain Rich would have ordered the seaman to join the expedition, given the hazardous nature of the journey. It was also consistent with Crean's nature to volunteer.

One popular anecdote claims that a shipmate of Crean's heard him offering to volunteer for the expedition and declared: 'I didn't think you were crazy enough for a mad trip to the end of the world.' Crean responded: 'Haven't I been mad enough to come from the other end of the world?'

Crean's daily trips to *Discovery* as a member of the auxiliary working parties obviously would have alerted him to the vacancy caused by Baker's assault on the Petty Officer. But there were other issues. Any seaman who did answer the call for volunteers for such a journey would have earned considerable respect and admiration on the lower decks. Any sailor with a knowledge of history would also have known that exploration had been a well-trodden route to promotion in the British navy since the days of Cook and others.

But the decision to volunteer also reflected an early indication of Crean's innate self-confidence and inner belief in his own ability. This, allied with the sense of independence which he had developed during his tough upbringing, had created a formidably strong character.

The likely voluntary nature of Crean's secondment to *Discovery* also underlines the essential haphazard nature of the early days of polar exploration. Like the vast majority of the *Discovery* party, Crean had no experience of the polar environment and had received no training for the rigours ahead. The basic qualification for so many on board was a strong sense of adventure and the promise of travel into the unknown. In Crean's case, there was the added factor that he happened to be in the right place at the right time.

The average age of the men in the *Discovery* party was only 27 and Crean at 24 would have been entirely comfortable with his new messmates. For someone who had lied over his age to join the Navy at fifteen in the quest for adventure, volunteering for a trip into the unknown for an unknown duration would have represented a new and exciting challenge.

Crean had become a popular figure among the seamen on the *Ringarooma* during his near two years' turn of duty. His messmates confirmed his popularity by arranging a collection to buy a small parting gift for the Irishman before his journey. The small token of friendship was a photo album with a simple inscription which provides a clear indication of the high regard in which he was held. The inscription with the album reads:

> 'This was presented to Thos Crean by his shipmates of HMS *Ringarooma* as a true token of respect and good wishes for his future welfare and safe return on his departure to the Antarctic Regions as a volunteer in the British ship, *Discovery*. December 20, 1901.'

Another personal possession he took on his way south was the little scapular, still tied round his neck by the leather cord.

3
Into the unknown

Preparation for the send-off from New Zealand quickened and Scott planned to sail from Lyttelton, the port of Christchurch, on 21 December 1901, before making one brief final stop at Port Chalmers, Dunedin, to take on the last few supplies of coal for the trip across the treacherous Southern Ocean. However, the great adventure did not get off to a very encouraging start because of the fatal accident to seaman Charles Bonner.

Departure day had begun well, in almost festive mood. The arrival of *Discovery* in New Zealand had aroused tremendous local interest and thousands flocked to the modest little port to bid Scott's party farewell. The clamour to catch a final glimpse of the explorers was such that special trains packed with well-wishers were chartered from the centre of nearby Christchurch. On arrival they found bands playing, whistles hooting and the enthusiastic crowds cheering and waving.

The Bishop of Christchurch came on board and ceremoniously blessed the explorers after a short service on the mess deck. Soon afterwards, the warship, *Lizard*, and Crean's former vessel, *Ringarooma*, led the heavily-laden *Discovery* slowly out of Lyttelton Harbour and Scott reported another five gaily dressed steamers, crowded with passengers who accompanied them on the initial stage of their long journey. Scott noted:

'Wharves and quays were packed with enthusiastic figures. It was indeed a great send off.'[1]

William Lashly, the stoker who was to become so closely linked with Crean in the annals of Antarctic folklore, said there were 'hundreds' on the quays to hail *Discovery* and added:

'Our stay in Lyttelton has been a busy but pleasant one. I think the people are very nice in every thing and every way. They really seem to think we want a little enjoyment before we leave here. We had a splendid send-off – all the ships in harbour came out to the heads and wished us God speed and safe return . . .'[2]

But at this point, death struck Bonner, the young seaman. Bonner, who was 23 years of age and hailed from Bow in London's East End, had joined *Discovery* in June 1901, from HMS *Jupiter*. He was one of Scott's earliest recruits for the expedition.

Unfortunately, the celebratory mood proved too much for the seaman, who had been drinking heavily and rashly climbed above the crow's-nest to the top of the mainmast in his eagerness to gain the best view of proceedings below as *Discovery* began to move gently out of Lyttelton Harbour. Scott remembered the sorry episode in his book:

'There, seated on the truck, he had remained cheering with the rest until in a moment of madness he raised himself into a standing position, supported only by the slender wind vane which capped the mast. Precisely what happened next will never be known; possibly the first of the sea swell caused him to lose his balance; we below only know that, arrested by a wild cry, we turned to see a figure hurtling through the air, still grasping the wind vane from the masthead. He fell head foremost on the corner of an iron deckhouse and death was instantaneous.'[3]

Lashly, never a man for over-embroidery, wrote in his diary:

'He lost his balance when the ship met the first swell and fell to the deck still clutching the weather vane.'[4]

Edward 'Bill' Wilson, the surgeon and zoologist on *Discovery*, remembered that many of the hardened sailors were affected by the tragedy. His diary records that some of the men 'wept like children' and James Duncan, the shipwright, said the accident had 'cast a gloom over the ship's company'.[5] Seaman Sinclair, who is thought to have given Bonner a bottle of whisky before he climbed the mainmast, later stole some civilian clothing and disappeared. Scott described the incident as 'one of those tragedies that awake one to the grim realities of life' and explained that 'sadness and gloom' descended on the ship. Bonner was buried shortly after arrival at Port Chalmers on 23 December. And as a bleak reminder of the 'grim realities' of the meagre life below decks in the Royal Navy in the early Edwardian era, Scott's report to the RGS reveals that Bonner's 'few clothes and belongings' would be sold on board the *Ringarooma*. The proceeds, he noted, would 'probably be very small'.

Bonner's replacement was not Crean, but Jesse Handsley, a native of Gloucester and a former shipmate of Crean from the *Ringarooma* who had also volunteered to join the expedition.

The final send-off from Port Chalmers on Christmas Eve, 1901, was noticeably more restrained than the scene at Lyttelton three days earlier, with events undoubtedly overshadowed by the tragic loss of Bonner. The ship, weighed down with coal, provisions and livestock, steamed ponderously away from civilisation at 9.30 a.m. Louis Bernacchi, who was physicist on the expedition, said every hole and corner of the ship was utilised for something '. . . until the Plimsoll line had sunk so deep it was forgotten'. He described the send-off as a 'most un-ship-shape confusion'.

Although the second send-off was a muted affair, *Ringarooma* was nearby and Crean was able to bid his own personal farewell to former comrades. It would be almost two and a half years before *Discovery* returned from the South and once again berthed at Lyttelton.

Christmas Day, 1901 was not what Crean or the rest of the crew might have expected as the *Discovery* moved slowly south – the first British expedition to sail to the Antarctic since Sir James Clark Ross 60 years earlier. There seems to have been little celebration and the mood on board was more pensive. The death of Bonner was still fresh to the memory and some among the traditionally superstitious sailors may have felt it was a bad omen for the expedition.

Scott, contemplating at least one year out of contact with civilisation, wrote:

> 'Christmas Day, 1901 found us on the open expanse of the Southern Ocean, but after such a recent parting from our friends we had none of us had much heart for the festivities of the season and the day passed quietly.'[6]

The traditional Christmas dinner was postponed because of the death of Bonner and not eaten until 5 January when *Discovery* had crossed the Antarctic Circle. Shipwright Duncan, who came from *Discovery*'s home town of Dundee, summed up the melancholic mood on board as the new year, 1902, dawned with the ship ploughing through the Southern Ocean. He wrote:

> 'New Year's morning broke fine, bringing back memories of old, turning my thoughts to My Dear Loved ones at Home, we being about 14,000 miles from them and in Latitude where there has not been any ships for a century and I may say cut off from the civilised world but return as yet being doubtful. Hoping for the best.'[7]

Nonetheless, *Discovery* enjoyed very good weather which was enormously fortunate in view of the heavily over-laden decks and the notorious reputation of the stormy Southern Ocean. It is the most ferocious stretch of water on earth and a strong gale would have posed a serious and potentially catastrophic threat to the ship. Scott admitted that the consequences of gales would have been 'exceedingly unpleasant' and accepted that the expedition would have lost its deck cargo – a jumble of provisions cases, heaps of coal, 45 terrified sheep and 23 howling dogs.

The *Discovery* party sighted its first iceberg on 2 January 1902 at latitude 65½° south. A day later, *Discovery* slipped across the Antarctic Circle – 66° 33' south – and Bernacchi recorded a peculiar sea-going custom in which ordinary seamen are permitted to drink a toast with both feet on the table. It is possible to visualise the ample frame of Crean indulging in this odd ritual for the first of many times he would cross the Circle.

The *Discovery* party recorded their first sight of Antarctica at 10.30 p.m., 8 January 1902. Scott wrote:

> 'All who were not on deck quickly gathered there, to take their first look at the Antarctic Continent; the sun, now near the southern horizon, still shone in a cloudless sky, giving us full daylight.'[8]

Bernacchi, whose family originated in Italy, was more expansive, even though he alone of the *Discovery* party had sailed south before. Bernacchi was physicist on Norwegian Carsten Borchgrevink's *Southern Cross* expedition, which in 1899 had been the first to deliberately spend a winter in the Antarctic. Now, as he saw the familiar landscape a second time, he was captivated:

> 'It was a scene of fantastic and unimagined beauty and we remained on deck till morning.'[9]

Bernacchi's book, *The Saga of the Discovery*, paints a glowing picture of life on the lengthy expedition, though others tell a slightly different tale. Bernacchi said:

> '*Discovery* throughout the whole of her three years' commission was what is known as "A Happy Ship". One cannot recall a serious quarrel either among the officers or the men. She was a floating abode of harmony and peace.'[10]

However, it was not a view shared throughout the ship and the crew below decks were beginning to complain. For the men the rigid, mind-numbing routine and discipline of naval life remained constant, regardless of the icy conditions. One of Crean's fellow seamen, Thomas Williamson, writing at the time, painted a different picture to Bernacchi when he said:

'. . . this monotonous idea of scrubbing the decks every morning in the Antarctic, with the temperature far below freezing point, is something terrible; it seems as though they cannot forget the Navy idea or commandment (thou shalt not miss scrubbing decks no matter under what circumstances) . . . as soon as you turn the water on it is frozen and then you have to come along with shovels to pick the ice up which the water has made.'[11]

Frank Wild, who was to serve both Scott and Shackleton with great distinction, gave a clear signal that *Discovery* had been a troubled ship right from the start off the coast of the Isle of Wight. He wrote bluntly in a letter home:

'The voyage out to New Zealand was neither eventful nor happy.'[12]

Another incident recorded by Reginald Skelton, the chief engineer, also typified the men's unhappiness. Two stokers had their grog and tobacco stopped because of what Skelton described as 'discontented language' about their food. Scott's biographer, Roland Huntford, believed that *Discovery*'s sailors were depressed by the unnecessary naval routine and felt uninformed and nervous. No one, he wrote, had bothered to tell them where they were going, nor for how long.

While this was the best-equipped expedition the British had ever sent south, there was a conspicuous lack of knowledge and understanding about polar matters among the officers on *Discovery*. Only three men had been to the ice before. Bernacchi had travelled South with Borchgrevink, while Lieutenant Albert Armitage and the doctor, Reginald Koettlitz, had both been on the Jackson–Harmsworth expedition to the Arctic some years earlier.

Crean's colleagues on *Discovery* were a mixed bunch but, under Markham's influence, they inevitably had a heavy bias towards the navy.

Scott's deputy was Albert Armitage, a merchant officer with the P & O. Two of Scott's former officer colleagues from HMS *Majestic* were in the party: Lieutenants Michael Barne and Reginald Skelton. Another, Lt Charles Royds, could boast that his uncle, Wyatt Rawson, had once been to the Arctic. The remaining officer was another from the merchant ranks, Ernest Shackleton, a colourful and popular character who was born in Ireland's County Kildare but moved to London at an early age.

There were two doctors, Koettlitz and Edward Adrian Wilson, known to one and all as 'Bill' and soon to be a close friend of Scott. Geologist was Dublin-born Hartley Ferrar and the biologist was Thomas Hodgson, later to become curator of Plymouth Museum.

Below decks, the men were largely drawn from the Royal Navy, including experienced sea-dogs like the boatswain Thomas Feather, the second engineer James Dellbridge and Petty Officer Jacob Cross. There was also a group of men who would become celebrated polar veterans during the Heroic Age – men like Edgar 'Taff' Evans, Ernest Joyce, Bill Lashly, Frank Wild and Thomas Williamson.

As a group, they were united by their lack of polar experience. Few, if any, had shown any great interest in polar matters prior to the expedition. Nor was there any obvious reason why, for example, Scott should lead the expedition other than as a means of his personal advancement in the Navy. He had previously displayed no particular interest in the Antarctic and had no experience of the demands which the cold and ice place upon even the most resolute of people. It is unlikely that Scott had bothered to read very many books on the subject.

What is undeniable is that Scott sailed south clinging to the discredited methods of survival and travel promoted by the obsessive 70-year-old Markham which, in turn, were based on his own brief experience in the Arctic 50 years earlier.

Polar survival and travel had made great strides since the 1850s, particularly through the advances made by the proficient and innovative Norwegian Fridtjof Nansen. The American Robert Peary was also developing into a first-class polar explorer at the time and had published several books detailing his methods and experience in the Arctic North.

But the British expedition was poised to enter unknown and hostile territory without taking a great deal of notice of these advances and with an inexperienced and largely untried group of sailors and scientists.

Discovery sailed closer to land and on 9 January 1902, anchored at Robertson Bay near Cape Adare, where Borchgrevink – and Bernacchi – had wintered in 1899. Some made a brief visit to Borchgrevink's hut and Lashly added a homely touch to proceedings:

'I have also left a letter to my wife – she may get it some day if the postman should happen to come this way.'[13]

More important for the safety of the expedition, a note was left in a tin cylinder recording *Discovery*'s position. Scott had sailed south with comparatively vague instructions about a landing and wintering site and if the *Discovery* was crushed by the ice, search parties would have great difficulty locating the lost party. The note in the tin box was their only communication with the outside world if they became lost.

After some weeks sailing along the coast, new territory was discovered on 30 January 1902, and Scott named it Edward VII Land in honour of the new King. It was the expedition's first new discovery in Antarctica.

On 3 February Crean was chosen for the expedition's first brief sledging journey across the ice into the unknown hinterland. The Irishman joined Armitage, Bernacchi and three others on a brief trip to the south to examine the immediate surroundings, notably the area where the Ice Barrier meets the land. The six men spent an uncomfortable night cramped in a tent made for only three, before returning to *Discovery* the following afternoon. However, the close quarters did at least keep the men warm and their first significant discovery of the expedition was the uncomfortable fact that temperatures on the Barrier were significantly lower than on the ship. It was a painful early introduction to the rigours of the Antarctic climate.

Another 'first' for the party was achieved while Crean's party was away when two ascents were made in a balloon. Sir Joseph Hooker, the elderly Arctic veteran, suggested that the party could obtain a better view of the unknown landscape if they ascended in a hydrogen-filled balloon. Scott elected to climb into the cramped little basket and go up first and he came perilously close to achieving another notable 'first' – the first man to be killed in a balloon over the Antarctic.

After climbing slowly to 500 ft, Scott threw out the sandbag weights and the balloon shot upwards to about 800 ft. Fortunately, the weight of the chain halted the upward climb and Scott slowly began to descend. Despite the hair-raising escapade of his captain, the impetuous Shackleton immediately climbed into the basket and began his ascent. He took the first aerial photographs of Antarctica but neither saw anything useful. Wilson, irritated by the whole dangerous episode, said it was 'perfect madness' to allow novices to risk their lives. Fortunately for Wilson's peace of mind, the balloon developed a leak after Shackleton's ascent and was never used again.

But there was also some anxiety at the increasingly urgent need to find suitable wintering quarters before the season closed in and, worst of all, that *Discovery* might became stuck fast in the ice. By 8 February, Scott had reached the head of McMurdo Sound in the Ross Sea, close to the imposing volcano Mount Erebus on the edge of the Great Ice Barrier. It was decided to establish the expedition's base camp at this spot and soon after, a shore party landed. The group immediately began to erect a wooden hut on a rocky promontory, which became known as 'Hut Point'.

Originally, it had been intended that *Discovery* would return to the safety of New Zealand for the winter, leaving a landing party to overwinter and prepare for exploration in the following Antarctic spring and summer. But Scott changed his mind after finding a snug sheltered harbour in which the ship was expected to moor safely during the bitter Antarctic winter. Although the ship would be frozen in for the winter, the belief was that the spring and summer thaw would free her. He was wrong and it would be exactly two years before *Discovery* was freed from the grip of ice.

Parties of men worked flat out to bring provisions ashore to the newly erected hut and make the ship ready for its winter hibernation. It was long, heavy work but somehow they also found time for play and Scott recorded:

> 'After working hours, all hands generally muster on the floe for football. There is plenty of room for a full-sized ground in the bay and the snow is just hard enough to make a good surface.'[14]

Scott also sent his novices out onto the ice in an early training session designed to get them accustomed to travel over unfamiliar terrain. Although Scott had consulted the expert Nansen before leaving England, he was blissfully ignorant of the skills of ski travel or dog-sledging. They made an inauspicious start to polar exploration when Charles Ford, the ship's steward, slipped and broke his leg.

It was an unhappy start and Crean's messmate, Williamson, dolefully recorded:

> 'So, here we are, doomed for at least twelve months.'[15]

Shortly afterwards, the party began to dig in and prepare for the dreaded Antarctic winter.

4
A home on the ice

Hut Point, the site of *Discovery*'s winter quarters, is a small volcanic promontory which lies at the southern end of Hut Point Peninsula on Ross Island in McMurdo Sound. In the distance stands the towering, smoking volcanic beacon of Mount Erebus, which rises 12,400 ft (3,779 m) above the frozen sea level and stands imperiously as the world's most southerly volcano.

The narrow peninsula reaches out to touch the very tip of the Great Ice Barrier – the vast sheet of floating ice which is up to half a mile thick and covers an area larger than France. The Barrier is 400 miles long and almost 500 miles across at its widest point and in a warmer climate it would be an enormous triangular-shaped bay, lined on one side by an imposing chain of mountains, which point towards the South Pole. Now known as the Ross Ice Shelf, it is the flat, forbidding and hostile gateway to the Transantarctic Mountains, which ultimately lead 10,000 ft up (over 3,000 m) to the Polar Plateau and South Pole itself.

The Barrier was named after Sir James Clark Ross, who was awestruck when he first encountered the formidable sight 60 years earlier. As he sailed alongside, the Barrier loomed higher than his ships' masts and Ross said that he might as well try to 'sail through the cliffs of Dover'.

There was plenty of work for Crean and his colleagues before the sun finally disappeared for four long months and the officers, scientists and men had little time to waste on idle thoughts about the rigours ahead. Provisions for up to three years were landed, including 42,000 lb (over 19,000 kg) of flour, 3,000 lb (1,360 kg) of roast beef, 800 gallons (3,636 l) of rum and the 45 sheep who had managed to survive the horrendous trip south. There was also an endless supply of equipment, including extra clothing, tents, sledges and a windmill to power a dynamo for lighting. The party also carried a modest printing press on which the *South Polar Times* was published – the first journal to be published in Antarctica.

Although the hut had been erected, it was decided to spend the winter on board *Discovery*. Crean had quickly established himself as a popular and adaptable member of the party, capable of turning his hand to most tasks and with a great appetite for work. Armitage, the navigator and Scott's second-in-command, was obviously fond of the Kerryman and had spotted a character in the making. In his book, *Two Years in the Antarctic*, Armitage wrote:

> 'Crean was an Irishman with a fund of wit and an even temper which nothing disturbed.'

Crean was in his twenty-fifth year as *Discovery* sailed south and physically in his prime. He was a big, broad-shouldered man, taller than average, although not as tall as is often depicted. He had grown since enlisting in the Navy eight years earlier and Crean's naval records show that he stood 5 ft 10 ins (almost 1.8 m), although some contemporary references described him as being well over 6 ft. It may be that his deep chest and broad shoulders conveyed the impression of greater height and at 5 ft 10 ins he would have been taller than many others at the turn of the century. He was a cheerful-looking soul, with dark brown hair and clear hazel eyes. His trademark was the broad, welcoming grin and a warm 'open' face.

Crean was quickly recognised as a thoroughly dependable and stalwart member of the *Discovery* party. He soon adapted to life on the ice, developing into a highly capable sledger who was disciplined and never afraid of hard work. Doubtless his upbringing on an Irish farm had acclimatised him to hard work but it was his adaptability, reliability and enduring sense of humour which probably marked Crean out from the bunch. The officers also discovered that he was someone who obeyed orders.

His selection for the first sledging party immediately after landing had shown that he quickly picked up the knack of man-hauling sledges quicker than most. It was an unlikely talent for a man from the splendid green fields and rolling hills of southwest Ireland.

It is full testament to his rapid progress that he became one of the most consistent ice travellers of the entire party. The expedition records show that Crean amassed a total of 149 days man-hauling sledges in just over two years with the *Discovery* in the South. Only seven of the 48-man party spent more time than Tom Crean in the sledging harness during the expedition. He was behind only Scott with 193 days, Taff Evans' 173 days, Skelton's 171 days, Albert Quartley's 169 days, Barne's 162 days, Wilson's 158 days and Handsley's 153 days.[1] But it ranked him many weeks ahead of Lashly and Wild, two men who were to establish their own formidable reputations as sledge travellers in the South.

Crean accompanied Lt Barne on three notable sledging trips, which were a mixture of exploration and depot laying of supplies for other parties. These trips also provided early examples of the difficulties of sledge travel in the South and the serious dangers posed by the hostile polar climate, which brought him several narrow escapes. Crean endured a tough test of character in those early days on the ice as the party struggled to come to terms with the environment – and he passed with flying colours.

He also formed a close friendship with Evans and Lashly, two fellow sailors who, with Crean, were to become an influential triumvirate in the Age of Polar Exploration. Crean, Lashly and Evans, with their background in the navy, formed a strong bond as soon as fate threw them together at Lyttelton in New Zealand and before long the trio were inseparable. In time they would become the backbone of Scott's sledging parties.

Crean remained unflappable and phlegmatic in most situations, even though he had an unhappy reputation for accidents and mishaps. But the imperturbable Irishman was rarely shaken despite finding himself in some nasty and potentially fatal tight spots on all three expeditions on which he sailed. Throughout his career in the South, colleagues remarked on his unending cheerfulness and constant habit of launching into a song at the slightest excuse. One fellow traveller said he had the 'heart of a lion'.

The *Discovery* expedition was Crean's Antarctic apprenticeship and there is little doubt that without the experience of those early years he would never have made the outstanding contribution to polar exploration which was to become so apparent in later journeys. Both Shackleton and Scott clearly recognised the Irishman's qualities even at this early stage in his polar career and both readily took the Irishman on subsequent trips south.

Ice anchors had secured the *Discovery* in its temporary berth, but as an insurance against the threat of being crushed by the ice, the ship's boilers were kept permanently lit. The theory was that, in the face of any threat from the ice, the ship could make a quick getaway. The reality was different. *Discovery* became trapped and would remain a prisoner of the ice.

However, Wilson said that *Discovery*'s winter quarters were the 'most perfect natural harbour', helped by the abundant stocks of Weddell seals. Wilson's hope was that the regular supply of fresh meat would eliminate scurvy, the debilitating disease which is caused by lack of vitamin C and for centuries had plagued sailors on long voyages. But, rather like the wishful thinking over *Discovery*'s quick getaway from the ice,

Wilson's hope of avoiding scurvy was to prove optimistic. Indeed, it is likely that even in their winter quarters, the *Discovery* party suffered from the early effects of scurvy because they did not get enough fresh meat or vegetables. The men disliked the strong fishy taste of seal meat and instead preferred tinned meat. It is likely, therefore, that the party was weakened even before it began exploring.

Meanwhile, two observation huts were erected nearby and the men began the necessary but bloody business of slaughtering seals and penguins to provide food for the winter, despite their misgivings about the taste. Short reconnoitring trips across the ice were undertaken as the party began to familiarise themselves with the surroundings. Ski practice continued, although even at this early stage in proceedings Scott doubted their value. By contrast, some of the party had adapted well and Scott noted that Skelton, the chief engineer, was by far the best of the officers. He added that 'some of the men run him close' but he curiously did little to encourage their use. Scott's discomfiture with skis may have been further hardened by a slight accident when he fell and damaged a hamstring.

Nor was there any real progress made in mastering the teams of dogs who had been taken south with the express purpose of pulling the party's supplies as far as possible and saving the terrible toil of man-hauling sledges. As we have stated, dogs were to become the key method of travel across the ice, most notably by Amundsen, the finest of all polar explorers. But Scott, taking a lead from Markham's antiquated methods, was already warming to the laborious and monotonous task of man-hauling sledges.

Man-hauling, the system of placing groups of men in harness and dragging heavy sledges on foot across the ice, is probably the most physically demanding form of travel anywhere on earth. The painfully slow, back-breaking work of hauling an 800-lb (360-kg) sledge over uneven and broken ground strewn with hidden crevasses is an exhausting exercise. But it becomes a debilitating ordeal in temperatures of –40 °F

(–40 °C) and in the face of biting winds and a swirling blizzard.

The principal strain is taken on the waist but when the sledge became stuck fast, it requires a succession of heavy jerks to jolt the dead weight out of its imprisonment. On soft snow, the physical exertion is immense, reminiscent of pulling a dead weight across sand. It was one area of activity where class and rank did not matter, with officers and men in the same harness engaged in the same exhausting struggle, each man desperate to pull his weight.

The system also demanded that the haulers had to be well fed to compensate for the heavy work. But there were no seals, penguins or birds to yield fresh meat for hungry men once they left the shore-side base, so the long-distance travelling parties had to carry every ounce of food with them on any long journey.

Man-hauling over a long distance, therefore, became a vicious circle for the men, involving a life-or-death equation of weight versus distance. The farther they travelled, the more food they had to drag and the more food they had to haul, the weaker they became and the less they travelled. It became a delicate balancing act to measure the amount of food against the prospective distance to be travelled.

Although explorers developed a system of leaving depots of food brought out by supporting parties, it meant that man-hauling parties could only travel as far as the supplies of food they could carry on sledges weighing 700 or 800 lb. Each person in a typical four-man team was regularly pulling the equivalent weight of 200 lb (90 kg) a head across soft snow, occasionally sinking up to their midriffs and constantly battered by bitter, bone-chilling winds. Even worse was the fear that the fragile ice might crack, sending a man crashing to his death down a crevasse to a concealed abyss below.

However, successive expeditions underestimated the need to refuel the men with adequate amounts of food, and with the understanding of diets and vitamins still in its infancy, they also failed to ensure that the men ate the correct types of food.

In addition, the men rarely consumed enough liquid because ice had to be melted in the primus stove to produce drinking water. But the precious fuel had to be carefully rationed to cook hot meals, which meant they rarely bothered to stop, pitch a tent and rig up the primus simply for a mug of tea.

Man-haulers during this era were plagued by the intense cold, frost bite, blizzards, hurricane-force winds, snow blindness, life threatening crevasses and one final indignity – they were always thirsty and hungry.

The British, influenced by Markham, took special pride in the ability to cope with hardship, the test of real men pitted against the worst the elements could throw at them. Men battled against each other in silent resolution to ensure that their own piece of the harness did not slack. They gloried in the hardship and seemed unable or unwilling to adapt to more modern, less arduous methods of travel, such as dogs and skis.

Amundsen, who would become the greatest of all polar explorers, mastered the art of dog travel and skis long before travelling to Antarctica. He had travelled extensively in Norway and elsewhere in the frozen North, observing and learning the techniques and survival skills of the local people.

The preparation paid handsome dividends and during his successful journey to the South Pole in 1911, his party on occasions covered up to 60 miles (96 km) a day in ideal conditions. Overall, the Norwegian party averaged 23 miles a day while by contrast the man-hauling British explorers, Scott and Shackleton, covered the ground far more slowly. A distance of 12 or 13 miles (20 km) was considered very good going and 15 miles (24 km) a day was rarely exceeded.

At worst, British explorers of the Age covered only 3 or 4 miles a day after exhausting labour. Equally, the British parties were in their harnesses pulling about 200 lb per man for ten to twelve hours a day, sometimes even longer. It also meant that British teams had precious little strength left at the end of a day. The men were frequently only capable of erecting a tent, cooking a quick meal and collapsing into their sleeping bags.

In contrast, Amundsen and his dog teams generally ran for only about five hours a day which meant longer breaks and a greater margin of time to cope with emergencies. The difference in the scale of work and the amount of rest between the British and Norwegians in the Heroic Age was enormous.

Bernacchi, writing in the late 1930s, said that even by 1902 the man-hauling of sledges was 'an out-moded idea'. But the *Discovery* expedition was already unloading its equipment and preparing for a season of sledging journeys into the unknown. And the sledges would be largely man-hauled by men like Tom Crean.

The expedition, which had got off to an unhappy start with the death of seaman Bonner at Lyttelton, was struck by a second tragedy only weeks into its stay in the South. A simple journey across the ice rapidly deteriorated into a nightmare ordeal and another loss of life. It was an early and dire warning of the party's vulnerability.

Crean was not in the party of twelve asked to travel 40 miles across the Barrier in early March to leave a note at Cape Crozier, a pre-arranged spot for any relief expedition to learn of *Discovery's* winter position. It was to prove a costly postal delivery.

The Cape Crozier party was divided into two, with each pulling a single sledge and each helped by four dogs. But the men had picked up very little experience of ice travel and, to make matters worse, even the basic preparation was hopelessly inadequate. Scott confessed to being 'ashamed' by the inefficient way the sledges had been packed and the clothing worn by the men.

Although Scott was indisputably in charge, he somehow managed to assume a lofty detachment from overall responsibility, almost as though someone else was carrying the can. In his book, written after the expedition had returned home, he wrote a damning assessment of his own shortcomings:

'But at this time our ignorance was deplorable; we did not know how much or what proportions would be required as regards the food, how to use our cookers, how to put up our tents, or even how to put on our clothes. Not a single article of the outfit had been tested and amid the general ignorance which prevailed the lack of system was painfully apparent in everything.'[2]

Despite the obvious dangers, the party set out on 4 March 1902. A blizzard struck soon afterwards and visibility was reduced to nil. The party's inexperience and lack of control began to emerge with fatal consequences.

Although the tents had been pitched, the men, who were frightened at their vulnerability, panicked. It was the first time that many of them had been caught out in the open and they decided against sitting tight and allowing the blizzard to blow itself out. In their panic, they abandoned their tents and gear and blindly set out on foot to reach the ship. The party found itself on a steep icy slope, which ran down to a precipice overlooking the forbidding icy waters of the Ross Sea below. They began to slip and slide on the glassy slopes and soon realised that someone could slip and crash over the edge to a certain death.

George Vince, a seaman whose fur boots did not have spikes or modern day crampons, lost his footing with fatal consequences. He slipped and shot past his startled and helpless shipmates over the steep edge and down to a freezing, watery grave. Wild watched his messmate slide to his death and said it was a 'straight drop of 300 ft into the sea'. His body was never found.

Far worse catastrophe threatened. The party, by now even more frightened and in disarray, was scattered across the swirling Antarctic landscape, with no one quite sure of their location or whether others had also been lost. Crean joined the search parties who soon came across Barne, Evans and Quartley dazed and wandering aimlessly about the slopes of nearby

Castle Rock. By late evening Royds had somehow returned with most of his party, which left only two lost souls – Clarence Hare, the steward, and George Vince, now presumed dead.

Scott said it was 'one of our blackest days' and, like everyone else at Hut Point, assumed that Hare had died alongside the hapless Vince. But at 10 a.m. the next day a lone figure was seen approaching, crawling down a nearby slope. It was Hare. The young steward had survived some 36 hours in the open and had not eaten a hot meal for 60 hours. He had wandered around in confusion and eventually curled up in the snow and dropped off to sleep. According to Wilson, Scott looked as though he felt 'the dead was really walking in'.

There is little doubt that Hare was extremely lucky. But the rest of the party had been given a very early and brutal lesson in the hazards of the Antarctic landscape and the rapid way in which the weather can change and bring catastrophe. A far worse disaster had only been narrowly averted and at least half the party had suffered bad frostbite.

Wild conceded that Evans had been 'lucky not to lose an ear' in the escapade. But the warning signs were starkly apparent and seaman Frank Plumley summed up the mood of the wintering party by reporting that all hands were 'despondent'.

It was becoming colder as winter began to set in and on 23 April the sun disappeared for four months. But Bernacchi, who had seen it all before, was concerned about the experiences of the expedition so far and wrote:

> 'Autumn was at an end. Sledging has been a failure. Food, clothing – everything was wrong. There would be much to think about and much to rearrange during the long winter night.'[3]

Scott insisted that naval routine and naval discipline would be maintained throughout the stay in the South, notably the forced separation of officers and men. The officers, for example, ate at different times from the men. The pettiness, particularly the unbending insistence on enforcing traditional rigid naval practice, irritated the men and seaman Williamson reported a 'lot of discontent' on the cramped mess deck. Only weeks after his remarkable survival in the snow, steward Hare complained in his diary about the monotony and low spirits.

Duncan also complained about the 'sufficating' sleeping accommodation and said the men were often kept standing out on deck in freezing temperatures for routine inspections. On one occasion his diary recorded:

> 'All hands are swearing at being kept in the cold for 2 hours & it blowing a gale. (Temp) –23°. We are treated just as if we were children.'[4]

A typical day involved parties of men rising early and quarrying chunks of ice for melting as drinking water. They assembled for breakfast at 8.30 a.m., which was a major meal of the day, usually starting with lashings of hot porridge and dollops of treacle. Seal's liver was a typical fare for those who fancied it and there was an endless supply of fresh-baked bread and sticky jam.

The men ate and slept together in close confinement with their hammocks strung across the mess deck. There was no privacy. In contrast, many officers and scientists enjoyed the privacy of their own small rooms and dined together around a delightful mahogany wardroom table adorned with silver cutlery and fine wines. In the corner was an Edwardian piano.

Prayers followed soon after breakfast and the men were then employed in groups to repair and maintain equipment. Lunch followed at 1 p.m. when the men were also allowed a daily ration of rum and tobacco. Routine for the scientists included regular readings of the extensive meteorological, magnetic and other instruments, while others were busy on geology, biology, botany and physics. Supper was at the early time of 5 p.m. and the rest of the evening was free for sedate parlour games, such as 'shove ha'penny', chess or cards.

There was a permanent fog of smoke from the coarse, rough-cut Navy shag which, contrary to traditional regulations, the men were allowed to smoke at any time of the day. Crean, a pipe-smoker all his life, was in his element, though some non-smokers complained about the stifling atmosphere.

Some wrote letters home or filled in diaries, while others preferred conversation or, in typical naval style, the spinning of a yarn. It was cheerfully estimated that the 'thrilling experiences' of the cook, Charles Clark, in many parts of the world before the *Discovery* expedition alone would extend over a period of 590 years!

The monotony was occasionally broken by a lecture from one of the scientists or officers, while some seaman earned a few extra pennies by doing the weekly washing of the odd idle officer. Sundays saw a regular religious service, but Crean as a Catholic was excused and allowed to make his own private arrangements.

People ventured outside at their peril, although the reading of scientific instruments was maintained throughout the winter. The cold was bad enough. But the biggest danger was the constant wind and swirling, engulfing blizzards. Bernacchi said the combination was 'blinding and deafening' and people could become lost and disoriented within yards of the safety of the hut or ship.

The great event of the winter was Midwinter's Day, which was celebrated as a form of Christmas Day without the religion. Bernacchi mentioned feasting 'like old time pagans'. Streamers decorated the separate messes and the party enjoyed a splendid menu of best turtle soup, New Zealand lamb, plum pudding and mince pies. Champagne flowed, followed by port. The men were served a slight variation of turtle soup, boiled ham, kidney beans and potatoes, followed by plum pudding and brandy sauce. Gifts were exchanged, including a present for every man on board from Mrs Royds, the mother of the first lieutenant, Royds.

Spirits picked up considerably on 22 August when the sun made its reappearance after four months' total darkness. But the return of natural daylight also meant that the months of inactivity were now over and the real work of the expedition about to begin.

5
Into the wilderness

S cott planned a series of sorties into the unknown land, climaxing with his own bid to establish a new record for travelling further south than anyone else and possibly, even a tilt at the Pole itself. This was to be the centrepiece of the *Discovery* expedition, though no one on earth at this stage knew what lay beyond the immediate horizon of the Barrier.

Crean was involved in two notable firsts in the opening skirmishes with the Antarctic hinterland. He was a member of the party which by mid-November 1902 had duly achieved a record of travelling further south than anyone before. On a more trivial note, he also became one of the first humans to celebrate Christmas in a tent on the great ice sheet.

Initially Crean was in the team of men who were called upon to support the first major journey onto the Barrier. The three-man team for the main southern journey was made up of Scott, Wilson and Shackleton, and the supporting parties intended to place supply depots on the featureless landscape, which the trio would pick up on the return trip.

The twelve-man supporting party, led by Barne, set out on 30 October amid great enthusiasm and ringing cheers from their colleagues. The sledges each flew colourful pennants and a Union Jack, while one rejoiced in the British penchant for deliberately making hard work of things by carrying a banner which read: 'No dogs need apply.'

Crean's sledge carried his own distinctive trademark, an Irish flag. Barne recorded a 'fine show of bunting' at the send-off and made particular note of '. . . an Irish ensign belonging to Crean AB, consisting of a green flag with a jack in the corner and a gold harp in the centre'.[1] In what was overwhelmingly an English occasion, Crean felt it necessary to demonstrate that he had not lost touch with his roots.

The depot-laying support party would be gone for 35 days and return in time to set off again on 20 December for a unique Christmas on ice. Before that the men would face a desperately hard struggle to overcome their own inexperience of polar travel, poor equipment and the first sustained journey over the ice. However, they completed their journey and were back in time to set off again shortly before Christmas.

Scott, Wilson and Shackleton began their march on 2 November 1902, to another rousing send-off from their colleagues, with five heavily-laden sledges pulled by nineteen energetic dogs and with their pennants flying stiffly in the wind. In total the sledges weighed 1,852 lb (839 kg), with the heaviest 450 lb and the lightest 177 lb. But while Scott was initially preparing to rely on the dogs to cross the Barrier, it was clear that none of the men had so far mastered the art of leading and controlling the animals. Nor were the three men anywhere near to getting to grips with their skis, despite the practice sessions.

In reality, all the men setting out for a hazardous journey into the unknown were complete novices and had mostly failed to come to terms with the two best methods of transport for the job – dogs and ski. Before long they would fall back on the outdated ordeal of man-hauling.

It soon turned into a dreadfully hard slog, with the men sinking up to their knees in soft snow and the heavy sledges frequently getting caught up in the broken ice. Six of the supporting party turned for home on 13 November and two days later the remainder stopped at 79° 15', the furthest south ever travelled. It was a hard-won, but notable achievement.

But as Barne, Crean and the others turned northwards, Scott warned that the southern party faced 'extreme toil' to make fresh progress. It was a prophetic remark because the three men would take 30 days to cover the first 109 miles onto the Barrier, or a weary plod of under 4 miles a day. This was partly because of the heavy weights and poor handling of the dogs, but largely because Scott resorted to relaying the sledges. This meant that for each mile they travelled south, the tired men had to cover three – taking a share of the load one mile ahead, walking a mile back to pick up the remaining load and then retracing their steps for another mile back to the original spot.

It was soul-destroying and doubly exhausting labour which lasted for up to ten hours a day. On 14 December, barely five weeks into the journey and still supposedly fit, they covered only 2 miles 'by the most strenuous exertions'.

The men were also getting hungry as the work became heavier. Even more worrying, they were developing early signs of scurvy. The first of the rapidly weakening dogs died on 10 December and Scott had to reconsider how far they would get if, as expected, others died. The dogs, who were also poorly fed, were ceasing to be of much value.

Despite their deterioration, the three men made some progress and each day brought sightings of new land and mountains. On 28 December, weakened by lack of adequate food, heavy pulling and developing scurvy, the party pitched camp at 82° 11' south and Scott wrote:

'We have almost shot our bolt.'[2]

Shackleton was feeling the effects more than the others and on 30 December, Scott and Wilson left him behind in the tent with the dogs and equipment and skied south for a few miles. Observations placed them at between 82° 16' and 82° 17', a new record 'furthest south' and about 480 statute miles from the Pole itself. Shackleton never forgot the slight at being left behind and not sharing the honour.

The journey home became a desperate race against time, with the trio constantly hungry and scurvy beginning to take a grip. There is little doubt that they had underestimated the strain of the heavy work and their need for food. Food and supply depots, on which their lives depended, were poorly marked and difficult to spot. One lengthy blizzard at this critical stage, confining them to their tent, would probably have killed them.

Disaster threatened when Shackleton's health deteriorated and he came close to breaking down. Two exhausted, hungry men would have to haul about 500 lb (225 kg) meant for three. Scott jettisoned everything he could and killed the remaining dogs. Shackleton was forced to stumble alongside the sledges, gasping for breath while Scott and Wilson man-hauled for their lives. Significantly, Scott jettisoned all but one pair of skis.

Shackleton, who was coughing blood, collapsed and was placed on the sledge and pulled by the two weary haulers. It was readily apparent to Wilson, as the doctor, that the pair could not possibly survive if they continued to haul the extra weights and carry the burden of their sick companion, Shackleton. At one point Wilson told Scott he did not expect Shackleton to survive the night. Shackleton overheard and remembered that conversation years later when both Scott and Wilson had perished not far from the same spot on the Barrier on their way back from the South Pole.

However, Shackleton's phenomenal strength and mental resolve, which were to be a feature of his later exploits, surfaced and he somehow managed to get through the ordeal. He may have been driven by a growing dislike of Scott, who had reacted badly to Shackleton's illness. Scott was irritated by Shackleton's 'failure' and Wilson had to intervene to prevent Scott from berating the sick man, even though all three faced a race for their very lives.

On 3 February, still 11 miles from the safety of *Discovery*, the party unexpectedly ran into Bernacchi and Skelton. After three months on the Barrier, undernourished and struck with scurvy, the three men were almost unrecognisable. Scott wrote:

'There is every reason to think however that our return was none too soon.'[3]

While the southern party ordeal was unfolding, Barne's party, including Crean, enjoyed a tough but manageable exploratory trip to the southwest. The party, pulling almost 1,200 lb (543 kg) on two sledges, set off on 20 December 1902, with five weeks' supply of food and six weeks' supply of oil. Five days later, the six men were crammed into their little tents for the first recorded Christmas party on the Barrier.

Shipmates from *Discovery* had thoughtfully written greetings cards which were dutifully carried across the ice by Williamson and the men were happy to improvise, even in the coldest conditions, to ensure that the celebrations did not falter. After dinner, the six men somehow crowded into one three-man tent for what Barne described as a 'concert'. Barne said each man did a 'turn', which would have suited the big Irishman.

Crean was well known for breaking into song even under normal circumstances and now his voice was lubricated by a special gift which had been smuggled onto one of the sledges. Barne revealed:

'Our efforts were stimulated by a bottle of port which had been brought for the purpose.'[4]

Barne was fulsome in his praise of his fellow travellers, helped by the fact that no one had suffered any ill health which would have severely hampered the trip. He wrote to Scott:

'I cannot speak too highly of the sledge crew, all of whom, during the entire trip, were in good spirits and from whom did I not hear a word of complaint, or notice a sign of dissatisfaction.'[5]

Barne's team returned to the mother ship on 30 January to learn that *Discovery* remained stuck fast, still trapped by about one mile of ice in McMurdo Sound. Unless the ship suddenly broke free, it would mean another year in the South.

A relief ship, *Morning*, under Captain William Colbeck had arrived while the southern party had been away. But Colbeck was concerned that the ice might seize his ship, trapping them for another twelve months. Colbeck had been with Borchgrevink and Bernacchi on the *Southern Cross* expedition and was well aware of the hazards of the ice and was not prepared to take the risk.

Also on board the *Morning* was a young naval Lieutenant, Edward 'Teddy' Evans. It was the first time that Evans – later to be Lord Mountevans – met Scott and the seamen Crean and Lashly, all of whom were to become significant figures in his life.

Scott realised the vulnerability of their position and immediately began preparing for a second winter, stocking up the larder with fresh supplies of seal, skua gulls and lamb brought down from New Zealand. He also decided to send back eight men with Colbeck, mostly those from the merchant service. Significantly, the list of men returning home on the *Morning* included Shackleton.

Shackleton, who felt slighted at not being invited to share in the prestige of the 'furthest south', was now further insulted at being invalided home. He felt the rebuke deeply and as the *Morning* slipped out of McMurdo Sound on 2 March 1903, and headed north, Shackleton broke down and wept.

At Hut Point, the feelings were equally despondent as the *Morning* disappeared over the northern horizon and the party began to contemplate another year of isolation. On 13 March 1903 Scott wrote:

'I have abandoned all hope of the ice going out.'[6]

The winter months were spent much as the previous year, with various scientific duties and improvised games to keep the men as busy as possible. On one day a football match – 'Married & Engaged versus Single' – was played in a temperature of –40 °F (–40 °C). The result is not recorded, but the intense cold restricted the play to 30 minutes each way.

The weather throughout the winter was colder than the previous year but the men had learned some valuable lessons. Bernacchi admitted that the second winter was 'wearisome' but explained:

> 'In fact, knowledge gained by experience, particularly in relation to food, made us more fit when summer dawned in 1903 than had been the previous year.'[7]

Lashly, too, longed to get back to civilisation 'just for a change' and wrote in his diary on 1 April 1903:

> 'The worst time of the year is just coming on. In three weeks time we shall lose the sun, then for the darkness. But we shall be all right as long as we continue in good health.'[8]

Scott said the winter passed away in the 'quietest and pleasantest fashion' despite the weather. But inside the living quarters, plans for another season of sledging were also under way. Scott intended to lead a party across the Ferrar Glacier and Royds and Wilson were setting out for Cape Crozier to collect eggs from the colony of Emperor penguins. Barne, assisted by Crean, was due for a run towards the mountains first sighted on Scott's southern journey.

But this time there was a renewed urgency about the preparations because Scott was clearly concerned about freeing *Discovery* from the ice to avoid the grim prospect of a third winter in the South. As a result, he ordered all sledging trips to be completed by mid-December so that each and every man would be available for the essential work of breaking *Discovery* out of its captivity. A third year of captivity was too much to contemplate.

In mid-September Crean was in Barne's party to lay a depot to the southeast of White Island on the Barrier, which was very early in the season and left the men highly vulnerable to severe weather. In the event, the conditions were worse than anyone imagined and the party suffered badly.

The six man team – Barne, Lt Mulock (who had replaced Shackleton), Quartley, Smythe, Joyce and Crean – met temperatures of –40 °F (–40 °C) as soon as they left the ship and conditions deteriorated badly as they made painfully slow progress dragging their sledges onto the Barrier. As conditions worsened, it was evident that the harsh lessons of the previous year, particularly the suffering endured by Scott's 'furthest south' party, had not been fully learned.

Temperatures plunged to more than 100° of frost and one member of the party was lucky to survive without losing some toes. Scott pointed out that a mere tent and sleeping bag had never before afforded protection to men in such extreme circumstances. He recounted the harrowing tale in his diary:

'The temperature was well below –40° when they left the ship; it dropped to –50 °F (–45 °C) as they reached the corner of White Island and a little beyond to –60°; but even at this it did not stop, but continued falling until it reached and passed –65°.

At –67.7 °F (–55 °C) the spirit column of the thermometer broke and they found it impossible to get it to unite again; we shall never know exactly, therefore, what degree of cold this party actually faced but Barne, allowing for the broken column, is sure that it was below –70°.

Joyce was the only one who suffered seriously from these terribly severe conditions. After his features had been frostbitten several times individually, they all went together and he was seen with his whole face quite white. Though, of course, it is in a very bad state now, the circulation was restored in it at the time without much difficulty; but worse was to follow, for on the march he announced that one of his feet was gone and, having pitched the tents, Barne examined it, and found that it was white to the ankle. It was quite an hour before they could get any signs of life in it, and this was only accomplished by the officers taking it in turns to nurse the frozen member in their breasts.

All the party, and especially the owner of the frozen foot, seem to regard this incident an excellent jest; but for my part I would be slow to see a joke when I had a frost-bitten foot myself, or even when I had to undo my garments in a temperature of $-70°$ to nurse someone else's. It appears that those who were giving the warmth found that they could keep the icy foot in contact with their bodies for nearly ten minutes, but at the end of that time they had to hand it on to the next member of the party; they own that it was not a pleasing sensation, but think that it increased their appetites. However their ministrations have brought Joyce safely back to the ship with his full allowance of toes, which is the main point.'[9]

Fortunately, the men were out on the Barrier for only eight days. But it had been a harrowing experience and another reminder of the risks. Nevertheless, within days of their return, Crean and his colleagues prepared to launch themselves on a fresh trip to the area around what is now called the Barne Inlet, a little over 200 miles across the Barrier to the south. Once again, though, the weather, driven by a southerly gale, was appalling.

The party of six left the ship on 6 October and was provisioned for 70 days. In the event, they were out for 69 days which in the context of the poor weather suggests the party cut things pretty finely. A lengthy blizzard at the wrong time would have trapped the men in their tents with disturbing consequences. As it was, the bad weather forced the party to remain in their tents for nine whole days when supplies were plentiful. On another fourteen days, they either started late or were stuck in their tents for half the day. Further hold-ups would have eroded their margin of safety.

Barne was unhappy at not making better progress but Scott fully understood the severity of the weather and later recalled that 'ill fortune dogged this party from the start'. The party was also hampered by numerous 'undulations and disturbances' where the Barrier joins the frozen inlet at the bottom of what is today known as the Byrd Glacier in the Britannia Range.

It was the most testing journey Crean undertook on the *Discovery* expedition. The party had to cross steep crevasses and ridges but there was some reward for the risks and hard slog of dragging sledges across the uneven landscape. Against the odds, they managed to chart accurately for the first time the mountain coastline running down to the Barrier, which in itself was a creditable performance.

However, the party's most significant contribution to the entire *Discovery* expedition was made purely by chance as the men were trudging northwards back to the safety of the ship. The returning party came across Depot A, which Scott had laid down and accurately fixed thirteen months earlier at Minna Bluff alongside Mount Discovery on the very edge of the Barrier. But to everyone's astonishment, the depot had moved 608 yards (556 metres) in thirteen months, or more than 4 feet a day. Although scientists with the expedition believed that the Barrier was moving, the accidental discovery of the depot's movement enabled them to measure for the first time the speed at which it was travelling. Scott described the news as 'one of the most important results of the expedition'.

Despite the hardships and lack of progress, Barne was pleased with his party and reported back to Scott:

> 'With regard to the conduct of my party, I can only say that those with me are deserving of all praise. They all

used their utmost endeavours to make the journey a success.'[10]

The round trip for Crean and his colleagues was a little short of 400 miles (640 km), but the poor weather and heavy work meant it had taken 69 days to cover the distance – an average of less than 6 miles a day. Even after taking account of the time spent confined to the tent because of blizzards, the party travelled at a rate of only $7^1/2$ miles a day.

In contrast, Scott's party to the west during much the same time had travelled 1,098 miles (1,750 km) in 81 days which showed that the leader himself had learned at least one important lesson from his last lengthy trip on the 'furthest south' journey a year earlier. This time he had sensibly opted for proven man-hauling quality from the ranks of the seamen and had taken Evans and Lashly, two of the most formidable sledgers of the Heroic Age. On his 'furthest south' journey with Wilson and Shackleton, admittedly the first major expedition into the Antarctic hinterland, Scott had covered only 960 miles (1,500 km) in 93 days. The improvement was dramatic.

Scott returned to *Discovery* on Christmas Eve, 1903, to find only four men on board. The others, including Crean, were busy with the laborious task of trying to free *Discovery* from her imprisonment in the ice.

To the party's deep dismay, there were now about 20 miles (32 km) of ice separating *Discovery* from open sea and freedom. There was a growing realisation that either *Discovery* would need a miraculous escape or that the ship would have to be abandoned and the men carried home on the relief ship.

The men threw themselves into the task of freeing the ship, desperately trying to saw through 20 miles of 7-ft (2-m) thick ice in a vain attempt to carve out a channel. But after twelve days' hard labour, the men had made pitifully small progress, slicing two parallel cuts of only 150 yards (137 m) each. To continue was futile and Scott called a halt. He wisely began to make preparations for another winter and the men began earnestly searching the horizon for the relief ship, *Morning*, which was expected at any time.

On 5 January 1904 the men were astonished to see not one, but two ships sail into view – the *Morning* and the Dundee whaler, *Terra Nova*. The stranded party, already two years into their sojourn, were understandably delighted. Williamson said the party started 'jumping around like wild men'.

But Scott had reason for dismay. The relief ships had brought the unequivocal message that unless *Discovery* was freed within about six weeks, she would have to be abandoned.

Sailors, by tradition, regard abandoning ship as the last resort and Scott believed he and his men had been placed in a 'very cruel position'. Leaving *Discovery* to be crushed by the ice on her maiden voyage would have been a severe blow to Scott's credibility and to him abandonment was unthinkable. It would also have exposed the folly of his original decision to allow the ship to become frozen in.

Nevertheless, there was some sympathy for the Captain among the officers and men. Charles Ford, the ship's steward, said that never had orders been framed which gave an officer less option. Scott was obviously deeply affected by the decision and his concern was readily apparent. Ford wrote:

> 'The Captain is very much cut up and says that he cannot yet realise abandoning the ship. He thanks everyone for the way they had stood by him loyally. Men gave him three cheers.'[11]

Colbeck's reports on *Discovery* a year earlier, in 1903, had caused some alarm back in London. Although there was praise for the achievements so far, there was concern about the safety of the men if *Discovery* had to endure another winter in the South. The mood was not helped by the eccentric behaviour of Sir Clements Markham, who still acted as though it was his personal venture.

Markham, who was now 73, simultaneously managed both to celebrate *Discovery*'s achievements and cause concern about the men's safety. He demanded that a relief ship be sent, but overlooked the fact that very little money remained in the kitty. He became almost hysterical in his attempts to rally support for a relief vessel, warning about a 'terrible disaster' if *Discovery* was not relieved and arguing that it was now a 'matter of life and death'.

There was also continuing friction between the expedition's original sponsors, the Royal Geographical Society and the Royal Society. Markham eventually went directly to the Balfour Government with a plea for £12,000 (today: over £1,000,000).

But to Markham's chagrin, ministers took the matter out of the two societies' hands and set up their own Antarctic Relief Committee under the chairmanship of Sir William Wharton, a leading hydrographer at the Admiralty. The Government, it emerged, would finance a rescue if the societies handed over the *Morning*; a second ship would also go on the relief expedition. It may be that the Government wanted to keep a closer eye on proceedings than Markham had managed previously with the *Morning* relief.

Time was marching on and a frantic search began to find and refit a suitable vessel to accompany *Morning*. The Committee trawled the leading British whaling fleets and the Norwegian explorer, Nansen, was also approached. By early July, the Committee had alighted on the *Terra Nova*, a whaler in the fleet of C.T. Bowring, which it bought for £20,000 (today: over £1,750,000). Together with the refitting of the *Morning*, the relief of *Discovery* was to cost the tax-payers around £35,000 at 1903 prices, or the equivalent of nearly £3,000,000 at current purchasing power.

It soon became clear that it would be impossible to refit the *Terra Nova* in time for her to leave England by early August, the latest possible date for her to make the 14,000 mile journey to McMurdo Sound. However, Wharton was determined and decided to have the *Terra Nova* towed most of the way across the globe by a series of Royal Naval vessels.

By a supreme irony, one of the men called upon to help rush through the refitting of *Terra Nova* was Ernest Shackleton, who had only recently returned to Britain after being sent home on the *Morning* by Scott six months earlier.

The *Terra Nova*, under the seasoned Scots whaling veteran, Captain Henry Mackay, duly reached Hobart, Tasmania, for rendezvous with Colbeck and the *Morning*. They reached the ice edge in McMurdo Sound on 5 January 1904, three weeks earlier than *Morning* had arrived the previous year.

The three ships' parties were organised into a single company working up to eighteen hours a day with one simple task – to free *Discovery*. With ice sawing ruled out, the men turned to explosives. Blasting began on 15 January but, frustratingly, progress was negligible and the mood blackened. Scott began transporting valuable scientific instruments and records to the relief ships, while everyone tried hard to keep up their spirits. Arrangements were made for most of the wintering party to return onboard the larger vessel, the *Terra Nova*.

But the work to free the ship was not without danger and Crean came perilously close to losing his life after plunging through the ice near Hut Point twice in a single day. On the first occasion, he returned to the ship and sensibly changed his wet clothes. He immediately went out again on skis and promptly fell through the ice a second time with near fatal results.

The steward, Ford, was on hand and recorded the Irishman's narrow escape. He reported to his diary:

> '[Crean was] unable to help himself out, it being all he could do to keep himself from being dragged under the ice by the current.
>
> Fortunately, some men working there heard his shouts for assistance and after some difficulty (for he was numbed with the cold and unable to help himself) a noose was put round him and he was dragged to safety and assisted to the ship.'[12]

Without his quick-thinking comrades, Crean, weighed down by the extra polar clothing, would certainly have perished in the freezing waters. For Crean it was the first of many narrow escapes from death in the hostile Antarctic environment. But he seemed undisturbed by the life-threatening incident and Scott noted that Crean was 'very cheerful' about his ducking.

Although some movement in the ice was apparent, on 13 February there remained still two frozen miles between *Discovery* and the relief ships. Abandoning the ship was looking more likely and Scott was gloomy:

> 'Thick weather again today; have seen or heard nothing from the ice edge. Very anxious for a clearance.'[13]

But 24 hours later, as if in answer to the silent prayers of everyone on board, the ice suddenly broke up. Chunks of ice drifted out to open sea and *Morning* and *Terra Nova* came sailing alongside. It happened very quickly and *Discovery* was free at last.

A night of celebration and wild cheering followed. The men on shore ran up a Union Jack and Colbeck observed that there was not a happier man living than Scott that night.

Final preparations were made for a swift exit, including the removal of the last traces of ice encasing *Discovery*. An explosion on 16 February did the trick and the ship swung around, 'with blue water lapping against her sides', as Scott put it. He added an emotional postscript which probably summed up the feelings of all onboard:

> 'I wish I could convey some idea of our feelings when the *Discovery* was once more floating freely on the sea, but I doubt if any written words could express how good it was to walk up and down the familiar bridge, to watch the gentle movement of the ship as she swung to and fro on the tide, to feel the throb of the capstan engine as we weighed one of our anchors, to glance aloft and know that sails and ropes had now some meaning, to see the

men bustling about with their old sailor habit, and to know that our vessel was once more able to do things for which a ship is built. It is sufficient to say that it would have been hard to find a prouder or happier ship's company than we were that day.'[14]

The next day the party carried out one final solemn duty when they erected a simple white painted hardwood cross on the summit of Hut Point, 300 ft from the *Discovery* hut in memory of their fallen comrade, seaman Vince. His colleagues stood bare-headed while Scott read a prayer. Vince was the first person to die at McMurdo Sound and the simple inscription on the cross remains clearly visible to this day.

The trio of ships finally left Antarctica on 19 February 1904, two years and six weeks after the *Discovery* first caught sight of the Continent. Scott spoke of his feelings of sadness at leaving familiar sights, but after two years of enforced captivity the men were utterly delighted to be on the high seas and heading back to civilisation.

Six weeks later, on 1 April 1904 the three ships sailed quietly into Lyttelton. It was Good Friday, the weather was pleasantly warm and the reception given by the generous people of New Zealand was even warmer. Scott said they showered the party with a 'wealth of hospitality and kindness'. Relieved at touching dry land again, the party settled down for two months of well-deserved rest and recuperation before heading back home to England.

Discovery reached Spithead in the Solent on 10 September, before finally berthing at East India Docks on the Thames on 15 September 1904. They had been away for three years and one month. In their absence, the Boer War had come to an end, the Wright brothers had made man's first powered flight and war had broken out between Russia and Japan.

6
South again

om Crean arrived back to greenery and civilisation in
September 1904 having exceeded even his wildest
expectations. He had established himself as a
thoroughly dependable and valuable member of the polar
team, which was a notable achievement in an age when class
distinction and rigid lines of demarcation above and below
decks made it difficult for ordinary seamen to gain the
attention of the officers.

For the first time in his life the modest Irishman would be
elevated above others. Only a very small exclusive band of men
had been to Antarctica by 1904 and the 27-year-old Kerryman
was now among the select few. For the first time he had truly
achieved something and in naval terms was a 'cut above the rest'.

His popularity with the officers and men of the expedition
was a tribute to his enthusiasm as was the speedy way in which
he had so easily adapted to the hostile environment of the
South. His work, especially in the man-hauling harness, had
caught the eye of his team leader, Barne. Scott, too, had
recognised the worth of the genial Irishman. Notably, he was
also a team player, which was an important consideration in
the South where men came to rely upon each other for support
at critical moments.

Before his chance meeting with the *Discovery* expedition
three years earlier, Crean had been going nowhere fast, drifting

aimlessly through the unappealing and unrewarding life in the British navy towards the end of the Victorian era and with no particular purpose or direction. He was just another sailor, working slowly towards his pension.

But that had all changed now and Antarctica, the most unforgiving place on earth, had given him that purpose and direction. He had made the transition from boyhood to manhood in the navy and had matured into a responsible and capable polar figure during his spell in the Antarctic. Crean, by chance, had found his true calling.

It was no surprise that Scott and Shackleton recognised his qualities and that the Irishman was one of the first people they sought when they went South again. Nor that he would go back to Antarctica again without hesitation.

Crean's wages for well over two and half years' hardship and privation in the South was the sum of £55 14s 11d (£55.74 or about £2,850 at today's equivalent).[1] But his contribution to the *Discovery* expedition was formally recognised and placed on the record by a grateful Scott. He recommended that Crean should be promoted to the rank of Petty Officer 1st Class and that the promotion – and the extra pay – be backdated to the day *Discovery* arrived home. Scott's judgement, written in early September 1904, made impressive reading for the Irishman and provided its own testimonial. He said Crean should be:

> 'Specially recommended for continuous good conduct and meritorious service throughout the period of the Antarctic Expedition 1901–4.'[2]

Like all members of the expedition, Crean was also awarded the Antarctic Medal for his services in the South. He was also given the special Royal Geographical Society Medal for his part in the *Discovery* adventure and Scott's earlier praise was echoed by Sir Clements Markham, the 'father' of the expedition. Writing after *Discovery*'s return to England and doubtless after consulting Scott, Markham provided his own idiosyncratic and slightly offbeat assessment which surprisingly compared the

Kerryman with one of England's most famous heroes of an earlier age. Crean, he said, was:

> 'An excellent man, tall with a profile like the Duke of Wellington, universally liked.'[3]

However, Crean had arrived back in New Zealand to learn that his mother, Catherine, had died while he was out of contact in Antarctica. According to Markham, he was immediately offered a free discharge from the navy. But in the circumstances there was nothing Crean could do about the loss and so he elected to remain in the service. He had, after all, been away from home for more than eleven years and developed a new life entirely apart from the farming community in the Kerry hills.

However, Markham's private comments on the death of Crean's mother lacked understanding and portrayed the insensitive side of the old man's nature. He wrote:

> 'He received a free discharge as his mother had died; but he thought better of it and came back to the Navy.'[4]

His appointment as Petty Officer 1st Class took effect on 9 September 1904 and he was soon back in the familiar naval ranks, where his exploits would have been a major topic of conversation and the subject of friendly banter among fellow seamen. However, he was a typically loquacious Irish character and would have had no difficulty holding his own against the mess-deck ribaldry.

Crean's first appointment after *Discovery* was something of an anticlimax after the adventures in the South. He was sent to the naval base at Chatham, Kent, where for accounting purposes, he was assigned to HMS *Pembroke* on 1 October 1904. The naval routine may have been somewhat drab and unexciting after the more colourful two and a half years in Antarctica and he was doubtless keen for a return to more active duties. However, he did not have to wait very long before he was reunited with Scott, a relationship which would continue almost unbroken until the explorer's death in 1912.

Initially, he transferred to the torpedo school of HMS *Vernon* at Portsmouth and the following February he ran into an old *Discovery* friend, Taff Evans, now PO 1st Class at the gunnery school. Doubtless they shared a drink or two and talked over old times, plus the prospects of going South again. They made a formidable pairing, both tall and broad shouldered, seasoned and respected naval men in their late twenties with the proud record of having served in the famous *Discovery* expedition.

Scott wanted Crean back under his wing. Scott, not an easy man to get close to, was evidently much impressed with the work of Crean on their first visit to Antarctica and had earmarked the Irishman as a prime candidate for his inevitable return to the South. However, for much of 1905, Scott was immersed in the arduous task of writing his book, *The Voyage of the* Discovery, which finally appeared on 12 October 1905.

Shortly before publication, he sent a copy of the book to all members of the *Discovery* crew. But inserted in Tom Crean's copy was a personal request that Crean rejoin his former leader as coxswain as soon as Scott managed to get back to sea. Crean was delighted and eager to team up with Scott again. On 10 October, the day before he was transferred to duties at the Harwich naval base, Crean wrote back to Scott:

> **'I am very thankful for you being so good as to let me have your well written book on the Voyage of the Discovery. It will remind me of being on the Veldt again. I am very glad to have the chance of becoming your Cox. Thanking you very much sir for all you have done for me.'[5]**

In September 1906, precisely two years after *Discovery* had returned to England, he was duly reunited with Scott and the prospects of returning to the South had suddenly brightened. Scott had requested that the Irishman join him on board the battleship HMS *Victorious* in the Atlantic Fleet.[6]

Although Tom Crean was never a close friend to Scott, it is clear that the Irishman was held in particularly high regard. In-built class distinction and social barriers ensured that a personal friendship was unlikely, and they were also two entirely different characters. Scott was an introverted, moody man who did not make friends easily, whereas Crean was a large, outgoing, gregarious, self-confident character at home in the company of others.

Scott was attracted by the Irishman's unshakeable loyalty and reliability, particularly in the forbidding Antarctic climate where these qualities were even more important. Crean, Scott felt, could be trusted and wanted him alongside for the return to the South.

Scott, a navy man through and through, saw great strengths in the ordinary seaman and regarded Crean and the two other *Discovery* veterans, Taff Evans and Bill Lashly, with particular affection. The three men represented what Scott saw as the finest qualities of the navy ranks and he came to trust and rely upon them, giving them considerable responsibilities and influence. Indeed, he saw them almost as talismanic.

After the near disaster of his 'furthest south' journey in 1902–3, Scott never again went on a major polar sledging journey without at least one member of the Crean–Evans–Lashly triumvirate in the harness alongside him.

By the beginning of 1907, Crean and Scott had joined HMS *Albermarle*, also in the Atlantic Fleet. Crean was coxswain and Scott flag captain of the battleship, which had a full complement of 700 men. He was already planning a second voyage to Antarctica and in the light of his work on *Discovery*, had already pencilled in the Irishman's name as a member of the next team. There was little doubt Crean would be asked to go and little doubt that he would say yes.

Their relationship – overwhelmingly a working relationship – continued to grow and expand. Crean also followed Scott to HMS *Essex* and HMS *Bulwark* in 1908. One of the naval surgeons on board was George Murray Levick, who would later find himself alongside Crean on Scott's fateful last expedition to the Antarctic.

By spring 1909 Crean was back at the Chatham naval barracks, assigned to HMS *Pembroke*. This was the defining moment for Scott, when after much personal debate and deliberation, he finally decided to go South again. And, with fortunate timing, Crean was present when the historic and, for Scott, fateful, decision was taken to seek the South Pole.

The occasion was March 1909, when the news broke that Shackleton had returned from the Antarctic in *Nimrod* after smashing Scott's 'furthest south' record and coming within striking distance of the Pole. Shackleton and three companions – Jameson Adams, Eric Marshall and Crean's former *Discovery* colleague, Frank Wild – had suffered terrible hardship and overcome dreadful travelling conditions to reach 88° 23' south. It was a tantalising 97 miles (155 km) from the Pole but it might as well have been 97,000,000 miles.

Shackleton could have made it over those remaining few miles and achieved lifelong fame by becoming the first man to reach the South Pole. But the four-man party would almost certainly have died on the appalling journey home, struck down by a combination of scurvy and starvation. Shackleton had to make the heartbreaking and very brave decision to turn his back on fame and glory and struggle back to base camp with the prize within his grasp. As it was, the four men survived by the narrowest of margins.

Shackleton was deeply disappointed and knew that, with Scott's own plans coming to fruition, the glory of being the first to reach the South Pole would inevitably be snatched from him. But in a memorable remark to his wife, Emily, he said that 'a live donkey is better than a dead lion'.

Scott learned about Shackleton's achievement when he and Crean, then coxswain on HMS *Bulwark*, were travelling by train to London in spring 1909. Scott bought a newspaper at the station with news of the remarkable journey and ran along the platform to tell Crean: 'I think we'd better have a shot next'.[7] Some years later, Dr Edward Atkinson, who was to become a key figure in the subsequent expedition, would declare that this unheralded and insignificant event '. . . settled the moment of the commencement . . .' of Scott's last expedition.[8]

Crean was barely four months away from his thirty-second birthday.

News of Shackleton's near-miss in the South came in the same year as the Americans Robert Peary and Dr Frederick Cook had each claimed to have reached the North Pole. It helped ignite a growing international interest in conquering the South Pole, by now the last unexplored spot on the globe.

The lurid stories of Shackleton's memorable journey and his penchant for publicity had effectively turned the South Pole challenge into a race. The Americans were rumoured to be interested in a dash to the Pole; so, too, the Germans and Japanese. But little was heard about any interest from Norway, the most seasoned and highly respected of polar travellers.

Scott took up the challenge and set about what for him was the uncomfortable task of raising funds for the British Antarctic Expedition, as it was formally called. Scott disliked the fund-raising element of his expeditions, which was a combination of begging and cajoling from governments, institutions, private companies, wealthy benefactors and public subscriptions.

Scott was no rabble-rouser and he lacked the charm and wit of Shackleton to handle an audience at fund-raising events. Shackleton, in turn, did not possess the administrative ability of Scott.

But throughout his life Shackleton enjoyed good fortune at important moments, whereas Scott did not. For example, Shackleton returned home from his *Nimrod* expedition saddled with debts of £20,000 (equivalent to over £1,700,000 in today's money) and no obvious method of redeeming them. It was typical of his luck that the Government came to his rescue, awarding him a knighthood and wiping out his debts.

In the event, Scott struggled to raise the £40,000 (today: £3,400,000) he needed. It eventually came from a mixture of government grants, donations from wealthy private individuals and earnings from the sale of publishing rights, plus public subscriptions. The Liberal Government of Herbert Asquith donated £20,000 but, disappointingly, the Royal Geographical Society and the Royal Society, who had sponsored the *Discovery* expedition, contributed only £750 (today: £63,000) between them for Scott's bid to conquer the Pole.

Scott went on a whirlwind tour of the country, drumming up money from public subscriptions, sometimes without much success. At one gathering in Wolverhampton he raised the tiny sum of £25 (today: £2,000). Some members of the expedition also chipped in with personal contributions, either with direct donations or by accepting nominal sums in wages. The cavalry captain, Lawrence 'Titus' Oates, donated £1,000 (today: £85,000) to the enterprise which was to cost him his life.

The ship presented a further problem, partly because the natural choice, *Discovery*, was unavailable. It had been chartered to the Hudson's Bay Company in Canada, so Scott turned to the Dundee whaler, *Terra Nova*, which had been on the 1904 relief expedition and was fairly well known to him. It was bought with a down-payment of £5,000 (today: £425,000) and the promise of a further £7,500 when funds became available.

Terra Nova was eminently suitable, a veteran of the whaling fleet and the trip to McMurdo Sound some years earlier to rescue *Discovery* had proven her worth. Built in the Dundee shipyard of Alexander Stephens in 1884, *Terra Nova* was 187 ft long and registered at 749 tons. Experienced sailors said she was 'an easy ship'.

But while the money-raising campaign plodded along very slowly, there was no problem raising a party of men to go South. Scott set up an office in London's Victoria Street and was promptly deluged with applications from 8,000 willing volunteers drawn from all walks of Edwardian life. Scott's *Discovery* expedition a few years earlier had alerted the public to Antarctica, but Shackleton's heroic failure had aroused a more popular response and the public now wanted the South Pole to be conquered.

Scott wanted to surround himself with tried and trusted people, including a few carefully chosen men from the *Discovery* years such as Tom Crean. He was helped by the Admiralty's slightly unusual decision to allow him to choose his own team, although unlike *Discovery*, this was not to be a Royal Navy-dominated expedition.

Crean, after spending the past two and a half years working alongside Scott, had been selected even before the expedition had been formally launched. From places like the Chatham barracks and in the Atlantic fleet, Scott had confirmed what he had initially found on the *Discovery* – that Crean was the type of reliable, trusted character who would be invaluable to the venture.

Although no record exists of earlier conversations, it is safe to assume that the matter was discussed at considerable length during the years Crean and Scott spent together in uniform. The appointment was made official when he wrote to the Irishman at Chatham from the offices of the British Antarctic Expedition in Victoria Street on 23 March 1910:

'Dear Crean

I have applied for your services for the Expedition and I think the Admiralty will let you come. I expect you will be appointed in about a fortnight's time and I shall want you at the ship to help fitting her out. Come to this office when you are appointed and I will tell you all the rest.'[9]

Crean, now approaching his thirty-third birthday, joined the *Terra Nova* on 14 April 1910, as a Petty Officer at a salary of 15s (75p) a week. The monthly pay of £3 (today: £255 per month) was somewhat better than the £2.5s.7d (£2.28) he received on *Discovery* and, of course, he was going back to his adopted home. He would be gone for another three years.

Scott also signed up the two other veterans from *Discovery*, Taff Evans and chief stoker, Lashly, who with Crean were to become the expedition's most influential figures 'below decks'.

Others on board from the old ship were PO Williamson and William Heald. Scott also recruited his friend, Dr Wilson, as head of the large and diverse scientific team. After *Discovery*, Wilson had undertaken a major study of a mysterious disease which was killing large numbers of grouse and by coincidence, in 1905, had visited Crean's hometown of Anascaul on the Dingle Peninsula.

The purpose of the expedition was primarily to reach the South Pole, but Scott was also anxious to complete a wide range of scientific work which would add a large degree of academic credibility to the mission. Under the guidance of Wilson, he took meteorologists, geologists, biologists, physicists, a motor engineer and Herbert Ponting, the 40-year-old photographer, or 'Camera Artist', who was to capture some unforgettable photographs and moving film footage of Antarctica.

Scott's Number Two was to be Edward 'Teddy' Evans, who had sailed on the first *Discovery* relief expedition in 1903 and knew Antarctica. A place was also found for Henry Robertson Bowers, a small, squat man of only 5 ft 4 ins with a beak-like nose and enormous strength who boasted a 40-inch chest measurement. Inevitably, Bowers was known as 'Birdie'.

Transportation was to be a key element of the *Terra Nova* expedition and Scott appointed the taciturn ex-English public schoolboy and cavalry officer, Lawrence Edward Grace Oates, to look after the Siberian ponies. The intention was that the ponies would carry essential supplies onto the Barrier and avoid too much man-hauling of the sledges. A slightly eccentric global traveller, Cecil Meares, was hired to look after the dog teams and Bernard Day, a member of Shackleton's recent

Nimrod party, was appointed to take care of the motor-driven tractors. Scott agreed to take along a tall, dashing 21-year-old Norwegian ski expert, Tryggve Gran, after consulting Nansen in Norway shortly before the expedition sailed.

The polar landing party, 31 in all, was rounded off by two Russians, Anton Omelchenko and Dimitri Gerof, hired to groom the ponies and help drive the dogs. It also included a six-man party, under the leadership of Captain Victor Campbell, which would explore the coast of King Edward VII Land.

Crean joined *Terra Nova* and immediately bumped into several familiar faces like Evans and Lashly and soon began to get acquainted with the others as they came aboard over the next few weeks. He was on hand to record the party's first meeting with the ill-fated Oates, who arrived on the *Terra Nova*, which was berthed at South-West India Docks on the Thames, in May. The arrival of Oates, a cavalry captain with a distinguished record from the Boer War, was eagerly awaited by the naval men who were keen to indulge in customary inter-service rivalry and banter.

But as he stepped onto the ship, the 30-year-old Oates was wearing a battered bowler hat and a scruffy looking raincoat buttoned up to the neck, which was hardly the typical attire of a stiff-backed, cavalry captain. The seamen were astonished and according to later recollections from relatives of Oates, Crean observed:

> 'We could none of us make out who or what he was when he came on board – we never for a moment thought he was an officer, for they were usually so smart. We made up our minds he was a farmer, he was so nice and friendly, just like one of ourselves, but oh! he was a gentleman, quite a gentleman and always a gentleman.'[10]

Oddly enough, Oates, who became known as 'Soldier', had once ridden at the Tralee races in Ireland, only a few miles from Crean's home along the Dingle Peninsula in Kerry. Although they came from very different social and cultural backgrounds, the men would develop a mutual respect for one another.

There was feverish activity in and around South-West India Docks in the spring of 1910 as *Terra Nova* prepared to set sail. Gran, the Norwegian, arrived in mid-May, and reported men tearing about 'like busy ants'. An endless supply of equipment boxes were stowed away as the party tried to find suitable space on the crowded holds and decks for the sailing party of 60 men, 30 dogs, 19 ponies and countless boxes of stores and equipment for at least two years.

Preparations were eventually complete and at 5 p.m. on 1 June 1910, *Terra Nova* finally slipped away from the wharf and onto the Thames. Some of those onboard were struck by two odd coincidences as *Terra Nova* moved slowly along the Thames. First, the nation was again mourning the loss of a monarch, King Edward VII who had died three weeks earlier after only nine years on the throne. As *Discovery* left the same port in 1901, Britain was still coming to terms with the death of Queen Victoria after 63 years on the throne and was preparing for the coronation of Edward. Second, *Terra Nova* had to sail past *Discovery*, now in the merchant fleet of the Hudson's Bay Company, which happened to be berthed in the same dock.

Terra Nova headed first to Greenhithe near Dartford and then round to Spithead and on to Cardiff, where she was to take on 100 tons of free coal and a large donation for the expedition's kitty from generous public subscriptions in South Wales. *Terra Nova* had caught the imagination of Wales and the people of Cardiff alone raised around £2,500, (today: £212,000) the largest single donation of the £14,000 (today: over £1,200,000) which the expedition raised through public subscription.

There was one other sober duty to perform before the ship left Britain. On the way to Cardiff, Scott mustered the entire party at the stern of the ship and quietly suggested that each man should make out a will before travelling South.

At Cardiff, a banquet was held for the officers at the Royal Hotel, while the men were entertained at nearby Barry's Hotel. After dinner, Scott asked the men to join the officers and Taff Evans, a native of South Wales, was given pride of place between Scott and the Lord Mayor. Unfortunately, the burly Evans got so drunk that it took six fellow sailors to help him back on board *Terra Nova*.

Finally, on 15 June 1910, *Terra Nova* was ready to bid farewell to Britain and set sail for the Antarctic. A large and boisterous crowd had gathered to cheer the expedition off, mindful that they would be gone for at least two years, perhaps more. Public hopes were high and there was a feeling that capturing the South Pole, the last geographic prize, would provide a boost to the country's confidence. Britain, after seeing the end of the long Victorian age and the brief Edwardian era, was undergoing considerable social change under the Liberal Government of Asquith and was more uncertain than it had been for a very long time. For some, the prize of capturing the South Pole would be a symbol of the country's strength, particularly at a time when the threat of war with Germany was looming ever larger.

The departure was strongly reminiscent of *Discovery*'s farewell almost a decade earlier. Like *Discovery*, the *Terra Nova* made a slightly unhappy start as she slipped through the lock gates. In the excitement, a member of the crew was accidentally knocked overboard. But unlike the incident involving the unfortunate Bonner on *Discovery* nine years earlier, the mishap was not fatal. The seaman managed to clamber back on board and the vessel moved slowly out into the Channel flanked by a flotilla of crowded small pleasure craft. On board one vessel, the Cardiff Artillery band energetically played 'Auld Lang Syne'. Lt Evans yelled a grateful thanks to the crowds through a handy megaphone and *Terra Nova* was finally on her way.

The first stop was to be Madeira, next Simonstown, South Africa, and then on to Melbourne, Australia, before leaving for the final staging post of Lyttelton in New Zealand, as *Discovery* had done nine years before.

As they crossed the equator on the way to South Africa on 15 July, Crean was at the centre of the traditional festivities and an initiation ceremony for those, mainly the young scientists, who were 'crossing the line' for the first time. Taff Evans was dressed as Neptune, the strapping Petty Officer Frank Browning an unlikely sea goddess Queen Amphitrite and Williamson and Crean were the two policemen who man-handled the victims to their ritualistic ducking. Gran was ducked with some relish on the dubious basis that he had never before crossed the line in a British ship.

Scott had remained behind in Britain to complete fund-raising engagements and would travel independently to South Africa. He finally caught up with *Terra Nova* at Simonstown and set off to slowly cross the Indian Ocean for Melbourne.

No one on board *Terra Nova* was prepared for the shock that awaited them.

Terra Nova reached Melbourne on 12 October 1910, and Scott found a telegram waiting for him. It was sent from Madeira on 3 October when *Terra Nova* was in the middle of the Indian Ocean and simply read:

'Beg leave to inform you *Fram* [his ship] proceeding Antarctic. Amundsen.'

7
South in a hurricane

Roald Amundsen, who came from a Norwegian family in a small rural community a few miles south of Oslo, was born to be a polar explorer. Amundsen was the consummate professional at a time when the British were still effectively amateurs and from the moment he decided to challenge Scott in the race to the reach the South Pole, it was an unequal struggle.

It was typical of Amundsen's single-minded devotion to his calling that at an early age he slept with his bedroom windows open during the freezing Norwegian winter nights to help toughen himself for the challenges ahead.

He sailed on the *Belgica* in 1897–8, the first expedition to overwinter in Antarctica. Between 1903–6 he achieved everlasting fame when his tiny 47-ton ship, *Gjoa*, became the first to sail through the North West Passage across the top of the North American Continent, achieving something which navigators, particularly the British, had struggled to do for over three centuries.

After *Gjoa*, his ambition was to become the first to set foot on the North Pole. But he was thwarted by the Americans, Peary and Cook, who each claimed to have landed the big prize in 1909. Amundsen, irritated by the news, immediately set his sights on the South Pole, even though he knew of Scott's

Tom Crean, photographed by Herbert Ponting, Cape Evans 1911. Ponting, who called himself a 'camera artist', captured the essential Crean – cheerful, optimistic and ready. (SPRI)

> *I immediately issued a warrant for his arrest and offered a reward for his apprehension, but he has not yet been found.*
>
> *By permission of the Admiral, Captain Rich of the Ringarooma was able to fill this vacancy with one of his men named Crean.*
>
> *I would ask you to inform the*

Extract from Scott's letter to the Royal Geographic Society, dated 18 December 1901.

Crean's first taste of polar exploration. The Discovery *party poses for photographers at Lyttelton, New Zealand, after returning from Antarctica in 1904. Crean sits in the back row (8th from the left).* Discovery *brought together for the first time many famous names from the Heroic Age of polar exploration. Robert Scott (front 8th left), Ernest Shackleton (front 5th left, arms folded), Edward Wilson (front 6th left), Frank Wild (back row 3rd left), William Lashly (back 7th left) and Edgar 'Taff' Evans (back 10th left). (SPRI)*

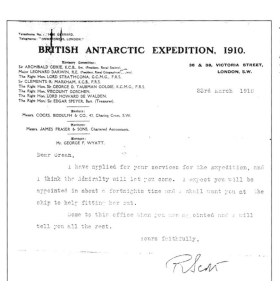

Scott's letter to Crean appointing him to the Terra Nova *expedition.*

Telephone No. : 1400 GERRARD.
Telegrams : "ONWARDNESS, LONDON."

BRITISH ANTARCTIC EXPEDITION, 1910.

Advisory Committee :
Sir ARCHIBALD GEIKIE, K.C.B., &c. (President, Royal Society).
Major LEONARD DARWIN, R.E. (President, Royal Geographical Society).
The Right Hon. LORD STRATHCONA, G.C.M.G., F.R.S.
Sir CLEMENTS R. MARKHAM, K.C.B., F.R.S.
The Right Hon. Sir GEORGE D. TAUBMAN GOLDIE, K.C.M.G., F.R.S.
The Right Hon. VISCOUNT GOSCHEN.
The Right Hon. LORD HOWARD DE WALDEN.
The Right Hon. Sir EDGAR SPEYER, Bart. (Treasurer).

36 & 38, VICTORIA STREET,
LONDON, S.W.

23rd March 1910

Bankers :
Messrs. COCKS, BIDDULPH & CO., 43, Charing Cross, S.W.

Auditors :
Messrs. JAMES FRASER & SONS, Chartered Accountants.

Manager :
Mr. GEORGE F. WYATT.

Dear Crean,

I have applied for your services for the Expedition, and I think the Admiralty will let you come. I expect you will be appointed in about a fortnights time and I shall want you at the ship to help fitting her out.

Come to this office when you are appointed and I will tell you all the rest.

Yours faithfully,

R Scott

Mr. T. Crean,
P.O.1. R.N.
R.N. Barracks,
Chatham.

Crean (left) and his friend, Edgar 'Taff' Evans, mending sleeping bags at Cape Evans, winter 1911, before embarking on the Polar journey. (SPRI)

Ponting persuaded Scott's party to pose before the camera shortly before embarking on the fateful dash to the Pole. Back row standing left to right: Griffith Taylor, Cherry-Garrard, Day, Nelson, Teddy Evans, Oates, Atkinson, Scott, Wright, Keohane, Gran, Lashly, Hooper, Forde, Anton and Dimitri. Sitting left to right: Bowers, Meares, Debenham, Wilson, Simpson, Taff Evans and Tom Crean. Only the injured cook, Clissold, and photographer, Ponting, are absent. (SPRI)

Crean and 'Bones', the pony he led on the 400-mile march across the Great Ice Barrier, pictured before departure, October 1911. (SPRI)

Crean (right) and Taff Evans after a Polar march, April 1911. (SPRI)

Dear Sir, I received your
letters on the 25th and
was very pleased to get my
letters. I returned on the
24th from sledging, after
being 4 months away. It was
very trying indeed. If anyone has earned fame, it is
your own County. Kerry man.
There were 3 of us returning
after being 140 miles from the
Pole.   Lieut. Evans was
taken bad, and we had

to drag him 90 miles on the
sledge. Then we had got to
go to our hut, and we were
in a bad way regarding
food, and our patient got
very bad. So it fell to my
lot to do the 30 miles for
help, and only a couple
of Biscuits and a stick
of Chocolate to do it. Well
Sir, I was very weak when
I reached the hut. It's
a fine record for us. But
I & J. know how things will
turn out until the Captain
returns. You may say for
certain the Pole is reached.

this time. Well. Sir. I must change the subject. But I must ask you not to say anything about it, as I am not suppose to give any news. Well. James I must congratulate you on the increase in the family. I hope this will find the child, Yourself and all the family in perfect ord. How is my little Jimmy now or Remember me to them all I am afraid I chan't be able to stand a treat as regards God. Father for another 18 months, as I am down here for another year. But I am doing very well I am very thankful to you for what you have done for me regarding myself and Hannah. I P. I hope the good things will turn out all right. I must thank you very much James for being so good as to break the ... to her Father any how and with the help of God we shall have a time at ... Please God I must ... for me ... Dr. ... buddy ... will Know me in this ... yours

Crean's letter to a friend describing his ordeal, 26 February 1912.

The effect of Crean's heroic trek to save Evans is clearly evident in this picture taken soon after he came back to Cape Evans in February 1912. (SPRI)

well-publicised plans. In his book, *My Life as an Explorer*, Amundsen would later write:

> 'This was a blow indeed! If I was to maintain my prestige as an explorer, I must quickly achieve a success of some sort. I resolved upon a coup.'

He kept his plans highly secret, even from Nansen, the father figure of polar exploration who lent him his specially-built ice ship, *Fram*, ostensibly for a journey to Arctic waters. Even the small party of tough Norwegians who signed up to go with Amundsen thought they were heading north to the Arctic as the *Fram* sailed away from Oslo, then known as Christiania. He further blotted his copy-book in the eyes of the British by furtively slipping out of Christiania under the cover of darkness at midnight on 6 June 1910. Coincidentally, 6 June was Scott's birthday.

Amundsen was hugely ambitious and entirely focused on his goal. Whereas Scott's expedition was a wide-ranging mixture of exploration and various scientific studies, Amundsen had only one target in mind – to reach the South Pole and get home again with the news in the fastest possible time. There was little academic or scientific work to hamper proceedings and his single-mindedness was reflected in the small group of trained specialists he took on the historic South Pole journey.

Sverre Hassel was an expert dog driver, Helmer Hanssen an experienced navigator and first-rate dog driver, Oscar Wisting was another fine dog driver and utility man and Olav Bjaaland was a champion cross-country skier and ski-jumper. Others in the party included Hjalmar Johansen, who had been with Nansen on his epic 'furthest north' fifteen years earlier.

The drama of the most famous and tragic race in the history of exploration was under way in earnest.

Scott had initially shown very little sign of emotion as he digested the news of Amundsen's challenge. The introverted explorer bottled up his anger and apprehension at facing what he knew would be a formidable and highly skilled opponent.

Instead of displaying outward signs of concern, Scott plunged himself deeper into the organisation of the expedition, including launching several last minute attempts to raise more money.

On 28 October 1910, *Terra Nova* sailed into another warm welcome at the small New Zealand port of Lyttelton, where by chance Crean had launched his polar career. It was almost nine years since *Discovery* had first landed at Lyttelton and a little more than six years since Crean, Evans, Lashly, Wilson and Scott had left there.

Lyttelton is the port of Christchurch, New Zealand's most English of cities whose very name derives from Christ Church College, Oxford. It sits beneath impressive mountains and has been linked with Antarctic discovery since the 1840s when James Clark Ross and the American, Charles Wilkes, visited the area before going south.

The little port had changed very little in the years since the explorers had last set foot there and the party was at ease as they completed the last-minute preparations for the coming journey south. Some even took time off for long walks to feel the final tread of grass under their feet for some time to come.

Another month would pass while *Terra Nova* was prepared for the trip across the stormy Southern Ocean and all the final farewells were delivered. The wives of Scott, Wilson and Teddy Evans had travelled to New Zealand to see their husbands off, a luxury not afforded to the men. Instead, the sailors bade farewell in their own inimitable style and Taff Evans went on a drunken spree and fell into the harbour. Scott, still unhappy about Evans' behaviour in Cardiff, promptly dismissed the Welshman, sending him 200 miles by train to Port Chalmers to cool off.

At 3 p.m. on 26 November, *Terra Nova* left Lyttelton for its last brief port of call, Port Chalmers at Dunedin. Apsley Cherry-Garrard, the young Oxford graduate who was an assistant to Wilson, recalled that telegrams were sent from all over the world to wish the party good luck and the people of

Lyttelton once again rallied to provide a colourful send-off for the explorers. In a scene strongly reminiscent of *Discovery*'s departure in 1901, excited crowds gathered on the quays to wave their enthusiastic farewells, gaudily decorated steamers packed the harbour and bands played stirring and patriotic tunes.

Terra Nova made a slow passage to Dunedin's Port Chalmers where they would take on board their final supplies of coal and a contrite Evans. Scott forgave the Welshman and in the process angered his Number Two, Teddy Evans, who saw the reinstatement as bad for discipline. But Scott was not prepared to jettison one of his three talismen.

Finally, weeks later than expected, *Terra Nova* pushed off from Port Chalmers at about 2.30 p.m. on 29 November 1910, to another enthusiastic farewell. It was a moment for reflection and Teddy Evans admitted to having 'a heart like lead'. Gran said that 'all links with civilisation are cut . . .'

The ship, dangerously weighed down with equipment, food and a menagerie of dogs and ponies, was an ungainly sight. The Plimsoll line, it was said, had been painted out to avoid any embarrassing brushes with authority. Teddy Evans said the *Terra Nova* looked like 'a floating farmyard', while below decks the men from the sailing and landing parties were squashed together like sardines. Part of the mess deck had been given over to accommodate the Siberian ponies with the result that men frequently shared a hammock – one climbing in as the other left to take his watch. In the wardroom there was not enough room for all the officers and scientists to sit down together for a meal.

Lt Campbell, an expert sailor, was already worried about the vessel's seaworthiness. He wrote:

> 'We must hope for a fine passage as besides being as full as we can cram her below hatches we have 3 motor sledges, the ice house is full, about 40 tons of coal, 2,000 gallons of petrol, pony fodder, etc, etc, all on the upper deck.'[1]

Campbell's concern was well placed. Shortly after leaving New Zealand, *Terra Nova* ran into a full-blown gale which raged for 36 hours and came very close to capsizing the fragile vessel. It was the first of many near and actual disasters on the expedition.

The ship's log recorded a Force 10 gale, which on the Beaufort Scale puts the wind at between 55 and 63 mph. An officer estimated that the waves were up to 35 ft high and in one remarkable incident, one of the dogs was blown overboard by one mountainous wave and washed back on board by the next.

The over-laden ship pitched and rolled alarmingly and during the night the *Terra Nova* looked a doomed vessel when the main bilge pump became choked. Water poured in and the handpump, the only remaining defence against the flood, was woefully inadequate against the tidal waves of water. Officers, scientists and the men grabbed buckets and the party baled for their lives in the gathering storm.

Bowers said the storm force increased to 11, which is up to 72 mph and only marginally below the official 75 mph rating of a hurricane. He described the scene below as like a swamp and said the men were dependent for their lives on each plank of the little ship standing the strain. 'If one had gone we would all have gone . . .' he added.

Yet, at the depths of the crisis, Scott reported that the crew could be heard above the roar singing sea shanties. A heroic ten-hour ordeal by the crew working up to their chests in water had managed to repair the pumps and mercifully the gale abated soon afterwards. But two ponies and two dogs had died in the storm and the party had lost 10 tons of coal and a valuable quantity of petrol. Oates had struggled vainly for many long hours to keep the ponies alive and many of the exhausted men had worked virtually without a break for 48 hours. *Terra Nova* had come narrowly close to disaster but, miraculously, had survived.

As the gale abated, *Terra Nova* plodded southwards, crossing the Antarctic Circle on 10 December and making good progress as the days passed. Christmas was marked by a major addition to the Crean family. The Irishman, who was fond of animals, had taken a pet rabbit on board the *Terra Nova* in New Zealand and Christmas Day turned out to be a day of celebration. Scott recorded in his diary:

> 'An event of Christmas was the production of a family by Crean's rabbit. She gave birth to 17, it is said, and Crean has given away 22! I don't know what will become of the parent or family; at present they are warm and snug enough, tucked away in the fodder under the forecastle.'[2]

Land was finally sighted on New Year's Eve, 1910, much to the excitement of those seeing Antarctica for the first time. Scott had wanted to build his base at Cape Crozier, the eastern extremity of Ross Island, but landing was impossible and so they returned to McMurdo Sound, where *Discovery* had spent over two years.

This time the party chose a headland about 14 miles to the north of *Discovery*'s Hut Point, a little closer to the towering, smoking Mount Erebus. A piece of flat, firm ground was selected and work began to erect a hut where the party of 25 men would spend the Antarctic winter. In 1902, it had been called the Skuary because so many skua birds had been found there but Scott thoughtfully renamed the site 'Cape Evans' after his deputy, Teddy Evans.

There was precious little time to dwell on the new home because *Terra Nova* had not reached land until 4 January, which was comparatively late in view of the preparatory work that had to be completed before the winter season closed in. The first consideration was to offload supplies and equipment and then erect the hut before winter and darkness set in. Equally, Scott wanted to lay down some supply depots on the Great Ice Barrier for next season's assault on the Pole before the weather deteriorated and travel became impossible.

In the flurry of activity, the landing and ship's parties worked for up to seventeen hours a day hoisting supplies off the *Terra Nova* and carrying them a mile or so across the ice to the slowly emerging hut. Both the dogs and ponies were put to work and seemed to revel in the energetic activity after the ordeal of the dreadful journey across the Southern Ocean. Crean was put in charge of one of the ponies, each journey to the hut ferrying 1,100 lb of precious supplies for the wintering party.

But another catastrophe struck when one of the three motor tractors, which Scott saw as vital for carrying tons of supplies across the Barrier, suddenly plunged through the ice into 120 fathoms of freezing water. The three tractors bore a strong resemblance to the tanks which would be used in the First World War and were capable of hauling a ton of equipment at a top speed of 3½ mph. Although this was very slow, the hope was that the tractors would cut down the amount of work that men would be forced to do, man-hauling supplies across the Barrier in freezing temperatures. Scott said it was a 'day of disaster' and promptly ordered that the two remaining vehicles should not be used on the ice until far later in the season when the sea was firmly frozen.

Finally, on 18 January, the party began to move into the hut which was to be their home for the next two years. Cherry-Garrard said it was 'beautifully warm' and soon after in a pleasant homely touch, the metallic, crackling sounds of a gramophone could be heard drifting across McMurdo Sound.

The 25 officers, scientists and men of the landing party were crammed together in the 50 ft x 25 ft hut which, in typically British fashion, was divided between the gentlemen and the players. The sixteen officers and scientists were separated from the nine 'men' by a purpose-built bulkhead of provision boxes, and the former occupied about two-thirds of the tiny hut, including two laboratories and a darkroom for the photographer, Ponting.

The most striking symbol of the segregation were separate mess deck and wardroom tables for meals, as though one side of the bulkhead would be offended by eating alongside the other. However, neither side objected to the barricade, regarding it as a normal slice of both naval routine and social distinction in the late Edwardian era.

Crean slept in a row of four bunks, flanked by his old *Discovery* friend, Taff Evans on one side and Patsy Keohane, another Irishman from Cork, on the other. Next to Keohane was Robert Forde, another Irishman. Close by was the party's sewing machine where Crean and Evans were to be found during the dark winter months mending the reindeer skin sleeping bags, preparing the sledges, overhauling tents, repairing foot-gear and other items of clothing, and stitching an endless number of provision bags for the coming journey.

They were two of the dominant personalities on the mess-deck at Cape Evans; tall, experienced, hard-working and full of stories and idle chatter. The backbone of Scott's Antarctic mess-deck was completed by Lashly, a quiet man with the unusual naval characteristic of being a non-drinker and non-smoker. Although a totally different character, he, too, was impressed with Crean. His published diaries describe Crean as a 'strong, healthy, utterly dependable sort of man with a great zest for life'. Crean described himself to Lashly as being like 'the wild man from Borneo'.[3]

The hut was cramped but more comfortable than *Discovery*, where the men had to make do with a hammock slung across a crowded mess-deck. At Cape Evans, each man had his own bunk and the galley stove kept the inhabitants reasonably warm at around 52 °F (11 °C). The hut was double-glazed and the floors, walls and roof were insulated with dried seaweed sewn into quilts and a layer of ruberoid felt which helped to keep out the bitter Antarctic winter.

With the unloading of supplies and equipment now largely complete, attention switched to the two important tasks which had to be wrapped up before the severe Antarctic winter took grip. First was an important journey to lay down depot supplies for the spring march to the Pole. Second, the *Terra Nova* was to carry a party of six men under Lt Campbell to undertake exploratory and scientific work to the east past the Barrier onto King Edward VII Land.

However, what was supposed to be a straightforward scientific outing had a couple of major surprises in store. Campbell's party – geologist Raymond Priestley, surgeon Murray Levick and the seamen, George Abbot, Frank Browning and Harry Dickason – sailed eastwards along the Barrier, reaching a place called the Bay of Whales. Suddenly and unexpectedly, they caught sight of another ship. It was Amundsen's *Fram*.

Campbell, a cultured man who spoke Norwegian, strode across the ice to meet Scott's rivals. After a while, three of the English party went aboard for breakfast and Campbell returned the favour by inviting Amundsen and two others onto *Terra Nova* for lunch. They were both rather stiff, formal occasions with each side politely attempting to learn details about the other's plans but without resorting to the vulgarity of a direct question. Half an hour after lunch *Terra Nova* sailed back towards Cape Evans with the news of the remarkable meeting.

After they had left, Amundsen reported that some of the *Fram* party had caught irritating colds.

Campbell promptly abandoned the eastern option and switched his attention to Cape Adare and Terra Nova Bay to the north and the six men were duly landed. However, 30 miles of ice later wrecked plans for the *Terra Nova* to lift them off the land and the six-man party was forced to spend the winter in a 12 ft x 9 ft cave, eking out a survival by killing seals and penguins. But, as if to remind even stranded sailors that naval discipline was inviolate, Campbell drew a line in the snow-filled cave to signify separate 'quarters' for the officers and men.

The achievements of Campbell's party should not be under-estimated. If they had not been overshadowed by the tragedy of Scott's march to the Pole, the ordeal of the Northern Party in that tiny cave would undoubtedly have been regarded as one of the great endurance and survival stories of polar history.

The journey to lay depots for the following season was vital and Crean was an obvious choice for the mission, his experience on *Discovery* giving him a significant lead over most of the others who prepared for the first major trip of the expedition. He cheerfully worked alongside Taff Evans in preparing sledges for the thirteen-man party and Scott was relieved to have such a reliable, hard-working back-room team.

The intention was to carry a large amount of supplies and equipment to three depots out on the Barrier which would be picked up by the party returning from the Pole a year later in 1912. The depots were the vital supply links.

The first depot, to be called 'Safety Camp', was barely 2 miles onto the Barrier and was thought to be a region of firm ice which would not disappear with the regular seasonal break-up of the sea-ice. The second depot was 'Corner Camp', some 35 miles from Hut Point, *Discovery*'s old base and situated at the place where travelling parties would turn away from the base camp region to head due south across the Barrier for the Beardmore Glacier and the Pole itself.

Finally, the most important depot would be laid some 170 miles from Cape Evans at 80° S. The cache, which became known as 'One Ton Depot' because of the large amount of supplies and equipment it would hold, was to be the crucial link in the supply chain for the returning polar party. But no one at this stage realised how crucial.

The thirteen-man party set out on 24 January 1911, with Crean leading a pony called Blossom, one of the eight animals which each carried around 570 lb of supplies. The others in the party were Scott, Lt Evans, Wilson, Oates, Bowers, Meares, Cherry-Garrard, Gran, Atkinson, Forde, Keohane and the Russian Dimitri, plus 26 dogs. The group, which was hauling a total of 5,385 lb, carried fourteen weeks' food and fuel. Only Crean, Scott and Wilson had any real experience of polar travel, though Gran was an expert skier and was therefore somewhat accustomed to the environment.

The routine was briefly interrupted when Crean and some of the party broke off to visit the old *Discovery* hut at Hut Point, which was a nostalgic detour for the Irishman. It was seven years since he had last seen the old hut.

The depot-laying party, which began with great expectations, soon ran into difficulties and Scott immediately turned to Crean's experience to solve the problem. Edward Atkinson, the surgeon, had developed a suppurating heel caused by chaffing soon after leaving Cape Evans. The heel was lanced when the party reached Safety Camp but his condition did not improve.

Scott decided to leave Atkinson behind and turned to Crean as one of the most trusted and dependable members of the party to look after the dispirited surgeon. Scott's diaries recorded the incident:

> 'Atkinson and Crean remained behind – very hard on the latter. Atkinson suffering much pain and mental distress at his condition – for the latter I cannot have much sympathy, as he ought to have reported his trouble long before. Crean will manage to rescue some more of the forage from the Barrier edge – I am very sorry for him.'[4]

Gran, with classic understatement, said:

> 'It isn't funny to be ill here.'[5]

Crean was obviously disappointed at missing out on the expedition's first important mission and Cherry-Garrard recognised it. He recalled:

> 'Poor Crean was to spend his spare time in bringing up loads from the Fodder Depot to Safety Camp and, worse from his point of view, dig a hole downwards into the Barrier for scientific observations!'[6]

A spare tent and primus stove was found for the two men but a disappointed Crean was forced to watch the party break camp and disappear slowly southwards on 2 February. The depot journey, which was to have been a fairly routine affair, ran into considerable difficulties that would have tragic consequences.

The weather deteriorated and the ponies, on whom Scott had placed such faith, suffered badly. Despite the exemplary care of Oates, the ponies were weaker than expected and, without equine snow shoes, they frequently sank deep into the soft snow surface, making their task a terrible ordeal. The realisation was dawning on the party, particularly the horse-flesh expert Oates, that the ponies were not adequate for the planned task of carrying large quantities of supplies across the Barrier.

Although doubts about the ponies began to grow, Scott was equally unconvinced about the dogs. He had never quite come to terms with the difficult task of driving and handling the beasts. Indeed, his weakness with both the dogs and the ponies was to prove a serious flaw in his overall management of both expeditions.

Scott had great hopes that the ponies would be vital in hauling tons of supplies across the Barrier, thus saving the men from the back-breaking work of man-hauling. But, misguidedly, he despatched Meares to Russia to buy the animals. Meares was no expert on horse-flesh and he had purchased a poor bunch. Oates, the real expert, was not even consulted about the animals and instead was employed humping boxes around *Terra Nova* on the Thames like an ordinary docker when he might have served the expedition more profitably buying the right type of ponies. Significantly, Oates was appalled when he saw the beasts, dismissing them as a bunch of 'wretched old cripples'.

Scott had a further difficulty with animals. He was squeamish and could not tolerate what he saw as cruelty or unnecessary blood-letting. It was an attitude that would prove costly because he could not bring himself to shoot the weaker dogs and ponies, leaving the meat as food for the men and animals on their return journey. It was precisely this method of killing off dogs as he travelled which helped Amundsen to move so efficiently across the ice.

However Scott rejected the idea and complained to a dismayed Oates about unnecessary 'cruelty to animals'. Despite protests from Oates, he decided to halt the harrowing pony marches and place One Ton Depot at 79° 28½' S. It was about 30 miles north of where he planned, enough to make the difference between life and death.

Scott hurried back to Hut Point, losing two more dogs in the process. At Hut Point he was reunited with Teddy Evans who had returned early with three of the weaker ponies. There was a double dose of bad news. Evans had lost two ponies on his return journey and there was a letter from Campbell informing Scott about Amundsen's camp 400 miles away at the Bay of Whales. Scott conceded that Amundsen's plan was a 'very serious menace' to his ambitions and noted that the Norwegians were camped 60 miles nearer to the Pole. Scott, once again showing little understanding of utilising animals in polar travel, even wondered how Amundsen had got his 120 dogs onto the ice.

Crean had been busy carrying pony fodder and seal meat up to Safety Camp. He and Atkinson had also gone back to Hut Point and cleared the snow which had built up inside the familiar old *Discovery* hut.

On 24 February Crean was back in harness alongside Scott as they travelled back to Corner Camp, where they were to meet Bowers and Cherry-Garrard. Crean's experience of the ice was invaluable to Scott and both agreed that travelling by foot was harder than using skis. But Scott persevered with foot-slogging and the men prepared to head back for Hut Point.

The simple return to Hut Point, which almost turned into a disaster, was to be the first of Crean's many acts of heroism on the expedition.

Bowers, who was on his first polar journey and was under-standably inexperienced, had been ordered to start back alone to Hut Point on 28 February with one of the remaining ponies. Soon Scott ordered Crean and Cherry-Garrard to take three more animals and catch him up. Scott remained behind with Oates and Gran to nurse another sickening pony.

Bowers, as a marine lieutenant, held the senior rank and was an immensely enthusiastic and well-meaning character. But Crean knew far more about the ice and had developed into an accomplished traveller in these treacherous conditions. His experience was to prove invaluable.

The trio marched across the remaining miles of the Barrier and eventually stepped down onto the sea-ice adjacent to Cape Armitage, close to Hut Point. But they soon came upon ice which was moving, a dangerous sign that it was breaking up all around them. Crean, aware of the dangers of falling into the freezing water, suggested that they push farther west to where he had previously seen firmer ice, but the inexperienced Bowers was unsure. Although the ice was 5–10 ft (1.5–3 m) thick, water was squelching through in some places and they could feel the disturbing swell of the sea beneath them, which indicated that the ice was breaking up.

The ponies were close to exhaustion, darkness was descending and a mist was swirling around the three men. Bowers, nominally in charge, decided to camp for the night and lit the primus stove to make a drink of hot cocoa. It took one and a half hours to heat the water alone and in the misty darkness, Bowers mistook a small bag of curry power for the cocoa bag. Unwittingly, Crean drank his mug of boiling curry before discovering that anything was wrong.

But, barely two and a half hours later at 4.30 a.m., the three men were woken by strange noises and appalled at what they saw. The ice had broken up around them, one of the ponies had disappeared, two of the sledges were on another floe and then suddenly their own floe split in two.

The men were stranded on a 30-ft floe in misty semi-darkness and dangerously low temperatures, floating menacingly towards open sea and certain death. Cherry-Garrard recalled that it looked a 'quite hopeless situation'.

The trio leapt up and began their desperate fight for survival, with the men jumping from one moving floe to another, dragging their sledges and enticing the three terrified ponies to join them. They desperately needed to find a larger, more solid piece of ice.

Crean, summoning up his *Discovery* experience, was a tower of strength and offered considerable reassurance to the two inexperienced men. Bowers observed that the Irishman behaved 'as if he had done this sort of thing often before' which, of course, he had. Bowers and Cherry-Garrard, who were suffering their first ordeal in the ice, could not have chosen a better companion for the occasion.

When the men had gained some confidence in their ability to leap across the moving ice floes, another serious threat emerged with the sudden appearance of killer whales. It is not unusual for these whales to attack an ice floe in search of a meal, deliberately tipping a seal or penguin into the sea and its waiting jaws.

After about six hours of aimless drifting, with the killer whales still circling the marooned party, their floe came floating up close alongside the Barrier itself. It was only a small comfort since the Barrier presented a sheer cliff of ice some 15 or 20 ft high (4.5–6 m) and it was impossible to haul the ponies and sledges to safety.

At one stage there was a lane of open water between them and the Barrier about 150 ft (45.6 m) wide which Cherry-Garrard said was a 'seething cauldron'. Bergs were falling off the Barrier and killer whales filled the rest of the lane. At one point, Cherry-Garrard recalled seeing at least six whales crammed into a space between two floes which was no larger than normal room-size.

Crean showed great composure, despite the grave danger and the rawness of his colleagues. He bravely volunteered to go for help, hoping to climb aboard any passing ice floe which floated close enough to the Barrier that would allow him to climb up with the improvised aid of a ski stick. It was a desperate gamble.

Bowers stuffed Crean's pockets with food and a note to Scott. The two men watched as Crean boldly jumped from one floe to another, eagerly looking for the one which would carry him closer towards the Barrier. But this was no instant rescue. Crean spent many hours waiting for the right floe to drift by and Bowers, writing afterwards, described the scene:

> 'Crean was hours moving to and fro before I had the satisfaction of seeing him upon the Barrier. I said: "Thank God one of us is out of the woods, anyhow". Crean had got up into the Barrier at great risks to himself as I gathered afterwards from his very modest account.'[8]

Luckily, Cherry-Garrard took the trouble to record Crean's 'modest account' of the hair-raising escapade in his famous book of the expedition, *The Worst Journey in the World*, which was published many years afterwards.

In the semi-darkness, Crean had made for the Barrier over the best path of the ice, but was soon forced to retrace his steps and make for nearby White Island, jumping from floe to passing floe. A single slip on the ice would have killed the Irishman and possibly spelt death for the stranded Bowers and Cherry-Garrard. Crean himself took up the story:

> 'I was pretty lively and there were lots of penguins and seals and killers knocking around that day.
>
> [One of the ski sticks] was a great help to me for getting over the floes. It was a sloping piece like what you were on and it was very near touching the Barrier, in one corner of it only. Well, I dug a hole with the ski stick in the side of the Barrier for a step for one foot, and when I finished the hole I straddled my legs and got one on the floe and one in the side of the Barrier. Then I got the stick and dug it in on top and I gave myself a bit of spring and got my outside leg up top. It was a terrible place but I thought it was the only chance.

I made straight for Safety Camp and they must have spotted me; for I think it was Gran that met me on skis. Then Scott and Wilson and Oates met me a long way out; I explained how it happened. He was worried-looking a bit, but he never said anything out of the way. He told Oates to go inside and light the primus and give me a meal.'9

Scott was full of praise for the Irishman and remembered to record the incident in his diary. He wrote:

'He [Crean] travelled a great distance over the sea ice, leaping from floe to floe and at last found a thick floe from which, with the help of a ski stick, he could climb the Barrier face. It was a desperate venture, but luckily successful.'10

Wilson, who was at Safety Camp with Scott, said Crean had considerable difficulty and 'ran a pretty good risk' in undertaking the solo walk to alert the others. Gran was despatched to run out on his skis and meet the lonely figure seen from a distance walking across the ice. He was the first to reach the weary Crean and in the circumstances feared the worst:

'He was tired and looked done in, and I was afraid to ask about the party's fate. I ask carefully and am answered robustly, "All right, sir". The answer was encouraging in a way, but unfortunately it was clear, after some probing, that the situation was not quite all right.'11

Crean, a Catholic, may have appreciated the irony of the occasion. It was Ash Wednesday – the first day of Lent and the start of the 40 days of penitence.

Bowers admitted that he had underestimated the danger signs on the sea-ice but did not forget to mention the 'splendid behaviour of Cherry and Crean'. Teddy Evans, who was later to be the ultimate beneficiary of Crean's courage, said the Irishman had acted with 'great gallantry'.

In retrospect, it seems likely that the two stranded men could easily have abandoned their ponies and equipment and scrambled up the Barrier in the same fashion as Crean. However, this should not diminish the courage which he showed in setting out alone, without shelter in sub-zero temperatures, to bring help for his comrades.

Crean's journey to alert Scott to the plight of Bowers and Cherry-Garrard was the first recorded occasion when the Irishman undertook a solo journey across treacherous terrain to help rescue stricken comrades. It displayed the first clear signs of Crean's great physical and mental strength under pressure and showed the value of the Irishman's fortitude and ability to improvise in the most testing circumstances. The incident also demonstrated that Crean had great confidence in his own ability and was not afraid to take risks.

It was also a foretaste of the heroics which Crean would perform on the Barrier a year later with an even more memorable solo escapade.

The rescue of his comrades also provided an early insight into the modest and unassuming nature of the Irishman. Frank Debenham, who wrote an appreciation of Crean's life for the Scott Polar Research Institute in Cambridge, remembered chatting to the Irishman about his exploits on the ice floes. He recalled:

> 'As always he made light of his feats in extricating himself from trouble and all I ever got out of him about that trip was, "*Oh I just kept going pretty lively, sorr, them killers wasn't too healthy company*".'[12]

Meantime, Bowers and Cherry-Garrard spent an anxious few hours awaiting rescue before Crean, having recovered from his ordeal, reappeared with Scott and Oates. An alpine rope was used to drag the two men to the surface. But, despite intense efforts, the three remaining ponies were lost.

Crean's reward, typical of the unforgiving Antarctic climate, came a few days later when he was struck by a severe case of snowblindness, a painful and debilitating experience for even the toughest of individuals which is caused by too much white light entering the eye. Before the arrival of effective sunglasses, polar travellers were frequently struck by snowblindness and in Crean's case he was so incapacitated that he could only hold the reins while the others struggled to rescue a pony which had fallen into the freezing waters.

Soon afterwards, the bulk of the depot-laying party reassembled at Hut Point. But the short journey back to base was impossible because the sea between the old *Discovery* quarters and Cape Evans had not yet frozen over. To add to their general discomfiture, their numbers were soon swollen to sixteen with the arrival of Griffith Taylor's geological party from the western mountains.

On 16 March, Crean was in the eight-man party, the last of the season, which sledged out to Corner Camp, some 35 miles away, in poor weather. Temperatures had soon plunged to –40 °F (–40 °C), visibility was down to 10 yards and winds reached over 30 mph. The season was closing in and provided the men with a grim warning of the dangers facing the polar party, who were scheduled to be making their return at around this time the following year.

After returning to Hut Point on 24 March, the group waited patiently for the sea to freeze over. But they had to wait until 11 April, with the days shortening, before they could set out for Cape Evans. It was a risk because the sea had not fully frozen and some in the party were understandably concerned. But they arrived safely to a warm welcome from comrades they had not seen for almost three months.

They were an unkempt bunch, unshaven and dirty after ten weeks in tents out on the Barrier. Ponting, the photographer, wanted to catch a picture of Crean, but he had already clipped off his bushy black growth – thus robbing history of the sight of the Irishman with a full-set beard!

After a brief stopover the group returned to Hut Point to pick up Wilson and six others who had stayed behind. Scott, who led the group of eight back to Hut Point, took two of his talismen – Crean and Lashly – and was much impressed with their contributions. He wrote:

'I am greatly struck with the advantages of experience in Crean and Lashly for all work about the camps.'[13]

Crean had time before the season closed in to show that he was apparently impervious to the cold. He was sharing a tent with Bowers, Hooper and Nelson and during the night temperatures had fallen fast to –38 °F (–39 °C) or 70° of frost. Crean somehow managed to slip head first, half out of the tent and let in a freezing cold stream of air which disturbed the others. Crean, however, slept through the experience and a bemused Bowers was moved to observe:

'It takes a lot to worry Captain Scott's coxswain.'[14]

The bulk of the group returned to Cape Evans on 21 April, tired after three months of hard, cold labour but relieved that the depot-laying work was now finished. But there was no disguising the disappointment felt throughout the group. What was supposed to be a fairly straightforward affair had fallen far short of expectations and delivered a major blow to Scott's painstaking preparations for the Pole. Only one of the eight ponies had survived the journey and it had taken thirteen men over one month to drag supplies to 79° 28½' south, about 140 miles from Hut Point.

In contrast, Amundsen and his dogs had carried considerably more supplies another 120 miles further south. Amundsen was equipped for faster travel, nearer the Pole and now better prepared.

While Scott had no idea of Amundsen's progress, he was concerned at the threat posed by the Norwegian party. To compound his anxiety, the loss of the vital ponies would hamper his efforts to transport large caches of food and supplies across the Barrier. As he surveyed the pony losses and helped to pull Bowers and Cherry-Garrard from the ice floe,

Scott was heard to remark: 'This is the end of the Pole'.

On 23 April, two days after most of the men were reunited at Cape Evans, the sun disappeared for four months and they settled down for another winter of blackened isolation. And to contemplate the challenges ahead.

8
Hopes and plans

Cape Evans was a happier home base than *Discovery*, possibly because the individuals rubbed along together better and possibly because the routine was less rigid. For example, there were more scientists from civilian life on *Terra Nova* than on *Discovery*, which had been dominated by Royal Navy personnel and subject to the stricter naval codes of discipline. The civilians had neutralised the effect of the stiff naval routines.

To his credit, Scott worked hard to ensure that the men were not idle and devised a number of tasks and events which, generally speaking, kept people busy. While there were inevitably differences between individuals, the diaries and letters of the 25 men who lived at Cape Evans rarely display any deep sense of personal dislike among a diverse group of people who were, after all, literally living on top of one another for months on end. There were people who did not get along with others and their diaries show certain resentments, hardly surprising in the circumstances. There was also criticism of Scott's methods and decisions. However, these differences never boiled over, perhaps because somehow individuals found a little space away from each other, even in the cramped confines of the 50 ft x 25 ft (15.2 m x 7.6 m) hut perched on a frozen outcrop in the blackness of an Antarctic winter.

With 25 people inside, the hut was inevitably crowded but comparatively cosy, even if the permanent pall of pipe and cigarette smoke would be frowned upon today. Comparisons with the *Discovery* routine, particularly the eating habits, were strong.

Breakfast began with lashings of hot porridge, freshly baked bread and generous helpings of butter and steaming mugs of cocoa. Occasionally fish might be served if someone had managed to catch something in the traps, although fishing was a thoroughly uncomfortable experience in the Antarctic winter.

Lunch, a more modest affair, was usually bread and cheese, washed down with ample supplies of cocoa. On odd occasions the cook, Thomas Clissold, would serve up tinned sardines or even lamb's tongues. Supper was the most substantial meal, starting with tinned soup and followed on six days a week by seal meat and tinned fruit. Clissold would vary things a little by serving fried seal liver or seal steak and kidney pie. The highlight of the culinary week was undoubtedly Sunday when Clissold prepared best New Zealand lamb which had been brought down especially on *Terra Nova*, courtesy of the generous New Zealanders.

Midwinter's Day, the surrogate Christmas Day for Antarctic explorers, was celebrated in lavish style. Gran said it was a day of 'champagne and celebration' and the tables were decorated with flags and bunting. Bowers and the seamen made a Christmas tree from ski sticks and penguin feathers and decorated it with candles and bunting. Drink flowed throughout the day with unusual freedom and the small party needed no second invitation to relieve the winter boredom. Gran remembered that he was forced to climb over 50 bottles of Heidsieck 1904 champagne stacked up in the crew's quarters.

Ponting recalled that the meal was 'food for the gods' and years later members were able to recall the exact menu. A seal soup was followed by roast sirloin of beef, Yorkshire pudding, horseradish sauce, Brussels sprouts and potatoes. Afterwards a huge plum pudding was carried in head-high to the table, accompanied by joyous shouts from the expectant diners. Those with room to spare could feast on a selection of mince pies, raspberry jellies, walnut toffee, butter bonbons and other delicacies. It was all rounded off with fine liqueurs and rum punch which were served long into the evening while the gramophone played a tinny, nostalgic reminder of home.

Away from the feasting, one important duty was to ensure that the remaining ten ponies were properly treated and in fit shape to carry out their planned task of shifting tons of essential supplies across the Barrier to the foot of the Beardmore Glacier. Trusted people like Crean were asked to assume responsibility for individual ponies and take them for regular exercise throughout the winter.

Where possible, the men also took as much exercise as the conditions would allow and regular games of football were played on the ice in bone-chilling temperatures of −30 °F (−34 °C) and with winds howling to 40 mph. Scott also recorded that the best players were Atkinson, Hooper, Taff Evans and Tom Crean.

There were other diversions apart from eating and smoking. The gramophone, donated by HMV, was popular and the small collection of records was played over and over again in the winter evenings. Ideally the men might have enjoyed a little more musical variety from the pianola. Unfortunately, the repertoire of the musicians was limited and these lost their popularity as winter advanced!

Chess, draughts, backgammon and dominoes were also played and individuals could always retire to their bunks to read and reread the small library which had been provided. Tastes varied, with a few popular cheap novels contrasting with the works of Kipling or Dickens. Oates was famed for burying his nose in Napier's *History of the Peninsula War* and, of course, there were the obligatory volumes of recent polar books for those who needed to stir their imagination about the hostile climate outside their door.

Church services were held on Sundays, with hymns sung. Crean, as a Catholic, was excused, just as he had been on *Discovery* and would say his prayers alone. There were occasional games of moonlight football and the *South Polar Times*, which first appeared on *Discovery*, was revived under the editorship of Cherry-Garrard. A few inveterate gamblers played poker but with money virtually useless in Antarctica, the currency was cigarettes.

One of the regular features which Scott introduced to help keep people busy was a series of three evening lectures a week delivered by individuals on a wide range of subjects. Ponting was a particular favourite with his talks and lantern shows on his lengthy travels around the world to countries like Burma, India and Japan. Bowers talked about polar clothing and Wilson lectured on the Antarctic's birds. Oates, predictably, ventured forth on horse management, the physicist Charles Wright tried to hold everyone's attention with The Constitution of Matter and geologist Frank Debenham lectured on the classification of rocks which, he admitted to his diary, was a 'very dry subject'.

The highlight of the lecture season came on 8 May when Scott outlined his plans for the forthcoming polar journey which provided the first clear indication that the explorers faced a very tight and potentially hazardous schedule. He estimated that the party would be gone for a total of 144 days and would not return to Hut Point until about 27 March.

Scott could not afford to start earlier because of the weakness of the ponies who, as the depot-laying journey had demonstrated, were not suited for travel across the ice and highly vulnerable to the low temperatures of the Antarctic spring. Just as worrying to some was that the scheduled date of return was dangerously late in the season when temperatures would plunge.

It was certainly too late to catch the ship, *Terra Nova*, which would have to leave the South by about 10 March to avoid being frozen in like *Discovery*. This, in turn, meant that the men on the polar party faced a second winter in the Antarctic, an unhappy prospect for some as they were only just starting their first sojourn.

The men who would lead the assault on the Pole faced a daunting itinerary. It consisted of five months of sledging, first about 400 miles (640 km) across the Barrier, then a 120-mile climb of 10,000 ft (3,000 m) up the Beardmore Glacier and finally around 350 miles across the uncharted Polar Plateau.

After reaching the Pole they would retrace their steps across the Plateau, down the Beardmore and across the Barrier at a time when, as experience had shown, the weather conditions would be deteriorating badly. From the start, it was a high-risk exercise with precious little margin for error.

It was a round trip of about 1,800 miles (2,896 km), the longest polar journey ever attempted. The men would have to walk every mile, each one responsible for dragging up to 200 lb (90 kg) across the ice. More worrying than anything else was the knowledge that the party would have to spend 84 days – almost three months – on the hostile Polar Plateau itself, 10,000 ft above sea level and exposed to its fearsomely low temperatures.

The intention was to take groups of men in parties of three or four, dropping off support parties en route. It was still not clear whether Scott would lead a three- or four-man party on the final assault to the Pole and at this stage, no one knew who would be in the final party. Indeed, it is not clear from his writings at the time that Scott had entirely made up his mind about the men he would take to the Pole. Although he had many months to weigh up the merits of his men, he apparently did not choose his polar party until long after the expedition was under way.

Significantly, Scott again dismissed the idea of using dogs for the main assault and insisted that a combination of ponies and good old-fashioned man-hauling would be used to get to the Pole. His faith in the motor tractors had vanished during the winter.

Gran, who fully understood why Amundsen would employ dogs, was sceptical. He already felt distinctly uncomfortable as the sole Norwegian at Cape Evans but his reservations about the planned polar journey were purely practical. He wrote:

> 'I personally doubt whether the dogs are as useless as he [Scott] says. I wonder whether there isn't an element of complacency in his attitude when we compare Amundsen's plan with his 100 dogs?'[1]

In the meantime, preparations were under way for a short but highly risky trip in the depths of the dark Antarctic winter to collect the eggs of the Emperor penguin from the rookery at Cape Crozier for embryonic research. The idea was Wilson's, and Scott, who did not like confrontation, readily agreed to allow him to take along Bowers and Cherry-Garrard, even though he was concerned about the enormous risks of the venture. It was a horrendous trip which would later prompt Cherry-Garrard to call his classic book on the expedition *The Worst Journey in the World*.

The purpose of the jaunt was primarily scientific, although Scott also hoped that the three men would test out key equipment and food supplies for the more important polar journey in the spring. What he did not appear to appreciate was that the terrible journey would expose three important members of the expedition team, who were likely to be included in the polar party, to the most appalling travelling conditions and serious risks from which they were very lucky to survive.

The hazardous and unnecessary journey reflected the essential conflict between exploration and scientific study which characterised Scott's last expedition and contrasted starkly with the single purpose of Amundsen's expedition. While Scott had two aims, Amundsen was able to be single-minded.

A more decisive leader would have vetoed the winter journey in 1911, perhaps saving it for the following season when the Pole had been reached. It is inconceivable that

Amundsen would have risked key personnel on the Cape Crozier journey ahead of his attempt on the Pole.

The three-man group, pulling a 757-lb (343-kg) sledge, managed only a few miles of slog each day in the pitch darkness and almost unimaginable weather conditions. There were constant winds of around 60 mph and temperatures frequently sank to –50 °F (–45 °C). At one stage the thermometer plunged to an astonishing –77.5 °F (–61 °C). In such intense cold, their breath and bodily sweat froze and in one highly graphic recollection Cherry-Garrard said the three men in the sleeping bags shook with cold until they felt their backs would break. He said 'madness or death may give relief' and added that they thought of death 'as a friend'.

They survived their horrible 36-day ordeal but the penguin eggs proved to be of little scientific value. The three, who were photographed by Ponting immediately after returning from their ordeal, had the haunted, shattered look of men who had stared a terrible death in the face. Gran perhaps summing up the feelings of many at Cape Evans, said that without doubt the three men were in 'bad shape' and added:

> 'Wilson is so thin it's almost frightening to see; the sight of him brought to mind a starving, dying wretch during a famine. He was all skin and bone.'[2]

However, the men had only been out for 36 days, a quarter of the time the polar party faced and their poor condition aroused concern among the men at Cape Evans who were shortly to embark on their own hazardous trek. The fond hope was that the weather, at least, would not be as bad.

While they had been away, Crean's experience of the Antarctic had been summoned once again to help surgeon Atkinson, who had gone out with Gran to read the thermometer in temperatures that had sunk to –28 °F (–33 °C) and with the wind howling at up to 45 mph. Gran returned unscathed but to illustrate the severity of the conditions, reported that it had taken an hour to travel no more than 200 or 300 yards (274 m). But Atkinson was still missing.

Crean, Taff Evans and Keohane were sent out with lanterns but returned empty-handed. By now concern for Atkinson had grown and Scott ordered a major search. Crean, Evans, Keohane and Dimitri took a light sledge, a sleeping bag and a flask of brandy out into the freezing, dark Antarctic night.

Atkinson was eventually found with a badly frostbitten hand, having been wandering around aimlessly for five hours. It was another grim warning of the ever-present dangers and Scott said 'we must have no more of these very unnecessary escapades'. He had overlooked the Cape Crozier trip.

Scott was equally busy putting together his plans for the march to the Pole and he had been much impressed with the contribution so far from his three stalwarts in the ranks, Crean, Evans and Lashly. He wrote:

> 'Crean is perfectly happy, ready to do anything and go anywhere, the harder the work, the better. Evans and Crean are great friends. Lashly is his old self in every respect, hard-working to the limit, quiet, abstemious and determined. You see altogether I have a good set of people with me, and it will go hard if we don't achieve something.'[3]

The sun returned on 26 August after four months and preparations for the spring season and the march to the Pole began to accelerate as the gloom slowly lifted. But, as before, there were more mishaps which, although not fundamental to the success or failure of the expedition, merely reinforced the belief that it was an unlucky venture. The superstitious among the men would have been worried.

First Teddy Evans took Gran and Forde on a short spring trip to dig out Corner Camp, less than 50 miles from Cape Evans, where the polar party would turn due south and head for the Pole. The trio, pulling over 600 lb (270 kg) ran into severe weather, with temperatures dropping sharply to −73.3 °F (−58.5 °C) or 105° of frost. Only weeks after the Cape Crozier ordeal, the spring temperatures had caught them out and Forde was badly frostbitten on the hands. Forde, who came from Cork, never fully recovered and was invalided home on *Terra Nova* in 1912 while the others headed towards the Pole. A little later the Australian geologist, Debenham, suffered a bad knee injury whilst playing in a football match on the ice outside the hut at Cape Evans. Ponting had wanted to record an ice-match on film and Debenham's injury caused an irritating three-week delay in taking a geological party to the western mountains. In another film-related escapade, the cook, Clissold, had fallen heavily and was concussed while posing on the ice for Ponting.

Along the Barrier at the Bay of Whales, Amundsen, too, was getting impatient. Despite outward signs of confidence, he was worried about losing the race to the British party. On 8 September, while Evans was struggling against the elements on the Corner Camp journey, Amundsen's eight-man party and teams of dogs had set out for the Pole. But it was far too early in the season, with temperatures on the Barrier sinking to close to −70 °F (−56 °C) and even the hardy dogs suffered badly. It was a rare mistake by Amundsen and after only a few days he bowed to the inevitable and returned to his base camp, Framheim, a chastened man.

Scott, meantime, was putting the finishing touches to his preparations. The years of meticulous planning, tedious fund-raising and idly sitting out the bleak Antarctic winters were finally over. The last great overland journey on earth was about to begin.

9
The last great land journey

Tom Crean had an unusual role to play in the days before the historic polar journey began. Ponting was anxious to capture at first hand the experience of polar travelling on moving film and the ever-willing Crean was recruited for a starring role. He joined Scott, Wilson and Taff Evans in a man-hauling harness to demonstrate the method of travelling to be used for the next five months in the assault on the Pole.

Despite his long legs, Crean had a short, stabbing stride and the characteristic gait was clearly evident on Ponting's cine film as he pulled the lightly-laden sledge alongside his friend Evans and behind Scott and Wilson in the mock exercise.

However, Ponting's film is a marvellous record of the Heroic Age of polar exploration, which has never been surpassed. Although it could never catch the true horror of the fateful journey, the little film has left an indelible memory. He spent several hours photographing the four men, shooting a total of 700 ft (213 m) of film. He recorded the men pulling a sledge, erecting a tent and cooking in what was a faithful reconstruction of the daily routine on the ice. Wilson wrote about the filming in his diary:

> '. . . there is no humbug about them at all; they are all straightforward photos of what we do every day on trek, only they can't possibly be taken under those conditions.'[1]

In another filming session shortly afterwards, Ponting poignantly captured revealing close-ups of four men inside a tiny cramped tent, cheerfully removing their foot-gear and joking and smiling as they prepared a hot meal. The four men in this footage were Scott, Wilson, Bowers and Taff Evans – all destined to die a few months later.

Soon after, the real thing was under way. In spite of Scott's meticulous planning and attention to detail, the enterprise was unnecessarily complicated and occasionally muddled. Transport, the key to the enterprise, was typically convoluted and did not make the difficult task of covering the near 1,800 miles to the Pole and back any easier.

Scott used sixteen men with four entirely different methods of travel – motor tractors, dog teams, ponies and man-hauling – which added to the complexity of preparations and co-ordination of the parties. But they were all travelling at different speeds, which contrasted starkly with the simple form of travel – a small experienced party all using ski and dog teams – adopted by Amundsen.

The first steps on the British trek to the Pole were taken at 10.30 a.m. on 24 October 1911, when the two remaining motor tractors spluttered into life. Lashly drove one and Day, the mechanic, the other, while the steward Hooper lent a hand. In charge was Teddy Evans, ostensibly the expedition's Number Two but in reality now replaced by Wilson as Scott's deputy and confidante. Scott had turned against Evans during the winter, labelling him 'a duffer' who was not fit to be second-in-command. Given that he had also lost faith in the motor tractors, there was a certain symbolism in the decision to pair the two together.

Lashly recalled that two tractors pulled 6,290 lb (2,850 kg) – almost 3 tons – of stores, pony food and petrol in six sledges which, it was hoped, would save the struggling ponies for the longer march to the foot of the Beardmore. The aim was to depot the supplies about 200 miles (320 km) to the south at 80½°, or about 60 miles (96 km) further on from One Ton Depot.

However the tractors, like the ponies on the depot-laying trip, were a grave disappointment and fell far short of expectations. They spluttered and crawled along, covering only 3 miles in the first three hours and providing a clear indication that they would not be as valuable as hoped. After numerous irritating breakdowns, they finally came to a standstill a week later on 1 November. They had covered a paltry 51 miles (82 km) in seven days and the large amount of equipment on board was taken off and depoted in the snow.

Evans packed 740 lb (335 kg) of supplies and equipment onto a sledge and the four men climbed into the man-hauling harness. It was a highly significant moment for the expedition as it made the unhappy transition from machinery to men and Lashly recorded:

'Now comes the man-hauling part of the show.'[2]

On the same day, 1 November 1911, the main twelve-man party paraded out of Cape Evans to an enthusiastic send-off from the remaining men who waved flags and cheered. Ponting ensured that he captured the moment as the polar party trudged off into the distance, turning occasionally to wave a last farewell.

The party was Scott, Wilson, Bowers, Oates, Atkinson, Cherry-Garrard, Wright, Taff Evans, Keohane and Tom Crean. Each man led one of the ten surviving ponies, while Meares and Dimitri followed with 23 dogs. Crean was blessed with one of the relatively stronger ponies and Scott was able to report:

'Bones ambled off gently with Crean and I led Snippets in his wake.'[3]

The start of the great venture was marked by a strange event which, at the time, seemed innocuous. Scott was preoccupied with his complex plans and completely forgot to bring the Union Jack which Queen Alexandra, the Queen Mother, had given to him to plant at the Pole. The irony was that he sent

Gran to fetch it and thus history records that a Norwegian carried the British flag on its first steps towards the Pole.

On the eve of departure, Scott had written:

> 'The future is in the lap of the gods; I can think of nothing left undone to deserve success.'[4]

Elsewhere on the Barrier, Amundsen was already almost 200 miles (320 km) further south, travelling at up to 25 miles a day. The hand-picked five-man Norwegian party – Amundsen, Olav Bjaaland, Helmer Hanssen, Sverre Hassel and Oscar Wisting – had set out almost two weeks earlier on 19 October with 52 dogs and the race was as good as over.

For Scott's party, the weather was not good and the travelling surface poor because light snowfalls made the going soft and sticky. It was particularly tough going for the ponies who were each hauling almost 700 lb (320 kg) of supplies on sledges. Both men and ponies frequently sank deep into the snow as they marched off and it was clear from the start that a mighty struggle lay ahead.

However, in those early hopeful days, with the party at its strongest, the men somehow found time for the odd slice of light-hearted mischief to offset the heavy work and occasional setback. Teddy Evans, who had an energetic sense of humour, poked gentle fun at the animal-loving Crean, who was still mourning the loss of one of the dead ponies. Evans' diary for 4 November recorded the occasion:

> 'Marched up to Blossom cairn where we tied a piece of black bunting to pull Crean's leg – mourning for his pony.'[5]

But there was little scope for developing the humour as the travelling conditions worsened and the language of Scott's diary provides ample evidence of the difficult conditions. On 10 November Scott recorded a 'horrid march' and two days later he said the marches were 'uniformly horrid' with concern growing about the fitness of the ponies. On 13 November he reported 'another horrid march' and said the ponies were being 'tried hard by the surface'.

In contrast, the dog teams of Meares and Dimitri were covering the same distances in a third of the time and were not reporting the same hunger and tiredness. The dogs, if anything, were greatly under-worked while the ponies found it very difficult to cope.

On 21 November the main party caught up with Evans and the former motor tractor team, which had man-hauled their supplies to a large new depot almost 60 miles (96 km) south of One Ton, called Mount Hooper after the young steward. For the first time the entire polar party was brought together on the Barrier. But, ominously, some early signs of weakness among the men were appearing and Scott reported that Evans' team – who had already dragged their heavy sledge for almost three weeks – were 'very hungry'.

With the motor tractors left forlornly behind in the snow, the party was now drawing on only three forms of transport – dog teams, ponies and man-hauling. However, they were still all moving at different speeds, which meant that they began and ended each day at different times and added another task to Scott's daily organisation. Scott himself admitted it represented a 'somewhat disorganised fleet'. By 21 November, the polar party had travelled only 192 miles (309 km) in the 21 days since they left Cape Evans – an average of a little over 9 miles a day – and was still close to 700 miles (1,126 km) from the Pole.

On the same day Amundsen had already climbed the unexplored Axel Heiberg Glacier and reached the Polar Plateau. On that day alone his party had travelled 17 miles (27 km) and climbed 5,000 ft (1,520 m), pulling almost one ton of supplies up the hazardous glacier. Amundsen was only about 300 miles (480 km) from the Pole. However, the reward for many of the dogs was a bullet in the brain. On 21 November Amundsen ruthlessly culled the pack, reducing it from 42 to eighteen and depoting their carcasses to feed the survivors on the way home.

Three days later the first of Scott's ponies was shot and the travelling parties were rearranged. Hooper and the mechanic Day were sent back to Cape Evans and for the first time the party split into three groups of four, plus Meares and Dimitri with the dogs. Crean was by now comfortable sharing a tent with his friend Taff Evans, plus Bowers and Oates.

The weather deteriorated badly, a blizzard confining the frustrated party to their tents for four days within sight of Beardmore Glacier and close to the towering mountains which point up the Polar Plateau. These were precious days lost, days which at the end of the journey would prove costly. Four days in a period of five months may not seem very much, but on polar journeys it might be the difference between life and death. Each day lost meant that the men would be tramping back to Cape Evans later and later in the season, when the vicious autumn weather would be closing in. Each day meant a further erosion of the safety margin.

As the party approached the end of the 400-mile (640-km) Barrier stage and the bottom of the Beardmore, they began to kill off the weakening ponies. Crean's animal, 'Bones', was among the final five to be despatched on 9 December at what became known as Shambles Camp.

The entire party, except Meares and Dimitri with the dogs, was now man-hauling and there remained nearly 450 miles (720 km) to go. Because of the time lost by the blizzard, the expedition was already behind schedule and eating into the rations which were meant to be consumed a little later on the Beardmore and the Plateau.

The heavy work meant the men were often hungry because they were not getting enough food to compensate for their arduous and continuous labours. The mainstay of the diet was pemmican, a not-very-palatable concentrated dried meat paste, which was mixed with melted snow and broken biscuits to make a thick porridge-like dish the men called 'hoosh'. There were also biscuits and butter to nibble and the men drank tea and cocoa, laced with sugar. All water for tea or cocoa had to be generated by melting snow in the primus stove so it is likely that the men were also very thirsty from their heavy labour.

The late start to the journey and the hold-ups caused by the bad weather posed considerable difficulties for the men even before they embarked on the toughest part of the trip, the 120-mile (190-km) climb up the treacherous Beardmore Glacier. At least one writer – David Thomson in his 1977 work, *Scott's Men* – said it would have been no disgrace if Scott had turned back at the foot of the Beardmore.

Many of the party were quietly relieved that they were no longer leading the ponies and positively warmed to the idea of man-hauling. Wilson, though admitting to feeling very tired due to the marching, wrote:

> 'Thank God the horses are now all done with and we begin the heavier work ourselves.'[6]

The work became even harder as the party approached the Beardmore because the immense pressure of the floating Ice Barrier thrusts against the mountainous land and causes massive disturbances on the surface. Shackleton, who had been there three years earlier, called it the 'Gateway'.

Even in the cold, windy conditions, sweat poured off their bodies as each group jerked and pulled 600 lb (270 kg) sledges. Cherry-Garrard recorded that on one day it required six hours of draining exertion to cover one painful hard-won mile. Evans' team hauled and strained for an exhausting fifteen hours on 9 December and he arrived at Shambles Camp 'dead cooked'. Scott said the work was 'extraordinarily fatiguing'.

It was ten years to the day that Crean had signed up for the *Discovery* expedition and became a polar explorer.

But doubts were emerging about the fitness of the men as the heavy work of man-hauling in terrible conditions began to take its daily toll. Wilson reported that Wright was 'getting played out' and that Lashly, who had already man-hauled almost 400 miles (640 km) was 'not so fit'. It was, Scott wrote, a 'very serious business if the men are going to crock up'.

It was doubly worrying because they were only now beginning the most arduous part of their journey, the 120-mile (190-km) climb up the daunting Beardmore which rises over 10,000 ft between two mountain ranges and up to the Polar Plateau. The uphill pulling, with each man now hauling at least 170 lb (77 kg), would be the most exacting they had so far experienced. On the Beardmore, there was also the ever-present fear of plunging through any number of life-threatening crevasses which are scattered across the broken, tortured terrain.

The parties were again rearranged leaving Crean with Bowers, Cherry-Garrard and Keohane. But Scott's real concerns were elsewhere and it is also clear that the gulf between Scott and his deputy, Teddy Evans, was widening. When Evans was admonished for not keeping up, he had to forcibly point out that he and Lashly had been man-hauling for five weeks longer than everyone else. It was a fair point, but it intensified the growing rift between the two men.

On 11 December they deposited a large cache of supplies – including a bottle of medicinal brandy – for the returning parties and called it 'Lower Glacier Depot'. Meares and Dimitri turned round and headed for Cape Evans carrying a note from Scott to his wife, Kathleen, which gave a fairly pessimistic view of prospects. Scott, although barely six weeks into his journey, wrote that 'things are not so rosy as they might be, but we keep our spirits up and say the luck must turn'.

Progress for the three four-man groups was painfully slow, with only 4 miles covered on 13 December and the strain was beginning to tell, even on the toughest of men. Lashly, who was never one to complain and regarded as one of the party's strong men, reported 'very heavy going' and Teddy Evans said they were 'panting and sweating' as they frequently sank into soft snow, often eighteen inches deep. Scott gloomily reported a 'most damnably dismal day' and Wilson said it was 'killing work' when the sledge hung up in the soft, sticky snow. Crean's tent-mate, Bowers, said it was 'the most back-breaking work' he had ever encountered.

Crean and Keohane followed behind Cherry-Garrard and Bowers in the harness and it was Bowers who would provide a chilling account of how strenuously the four men were labouring up the Beardmore. His description of man-hauling, clearly written from bitter experience, has rarely been bettered. He wrote:

> 'It was all we could do to keep the sledge moving for short spells of a few hundred yards, the whole concern sinking so deeply into the soft snow as to form a snowplough. The starting was worse than pulling as it required from ten to fifteen desperate jerks on the harness to move the sledge at all. The sledges sank in over twelve inches and all the gear, as well as the thwartship pieces, were acting as brakes. I have never pulled so hard, or so nearly crushed my inside into my backbone by the everlasting jerking with all my strength on the canvas band round my unfortunate tummy.'[7]

Bowers also gave an interesting insight into the character and strength of purpose which helped the men overcome the daily ordeal of pulling the heavy loads in frightful conditions and build the essential camaraderie between themselves. He told his mother in a letter:

> 'One gets down to the bedrock with everybody, sledging under trying conditions. The character of a man comes out and you see things that were never expected. You get to know each other inside out and respect some more and, unfortunately, some less.'

Despite the heavy going, they hauled a relatively good 10 miles on 14 December, although Scott began the day with another gloomy observation, which may have strengthened the belief among some later observers that he should have turned back at this point. He recorded:

> 'We are just starting our march with no very hopeful outlook.'[8]

On 14 December 1911, hundreds of miles away, Amundsen and his four companions had reached the South Pole. At 3 p.m. the small cavalcade of men and dogs came to an abrupt halt on the polar plain and the sledge-meters were checked. Amundsen's casual, almost matter-of-fact recollection was:

> 'The goal was reached, the journey ended.'[9]

Amundsen insisted that all five men should plant the Norwegian flag together as a measure of his gratitude to his companions. He wrote:

> 'This was the only way in which I could show my gratitude to my comrades in this desolate spot. Five weather-beaten, frostbitten fists they were that grasped the pole, raising the waving flag in the air, and planted it as the first at the geographical South Pole.'[10]

Crean marked the historic day by breaking into an 18-inch wide crevasse as he pitched the tent. The area was a mass of treacherous, frequently unseen crevasses and Keohane remarked that it was impossible to move 5 yards from the tent in safety. The fissure ran barely a foot from the tent door and as if to emphasise the Irishman's narrow escape, Cherry-Garrard threw an empty oil can into the gaping abyss. 'It echoed for a terribly long time,' he remembered. Having come so close to death, Crean would remember the historic day for a different reason.

While the Norwegians were enjoying their moment of triumph, the thoughts of Scott's party were increasingly dwelling on the delicate question of who would be going to the Pole. The intention was to drop off one four-man team near the top of the Beardmore and the 'last supporting party' of four somewhere on the Polar Plateau. Wilson, for example, speculated about being in the last eight but was doubtful about making the final four.

On 20 December Scott made his initial choice and sent back his first supporting group, Atkinson, Wright, Cherry-Garrard and Keohane. It was a bitter disappointment, particularly to the Canadian Wright who had been an energetic and enthusiastic member of the man-hauling party, though he was undoubtedly very tired. He confided to his diary that he was 'too wild to write more tonight. Scott a fool'. Keohane was more philosophical but admitted: 'Sorry to part with old Crean.'[11]

Scott said he 'dreaded the necessity' of choosing and explained to Cherry-Garrard that the seamen, with their specialist knowledge, would be needed for the journey. Wilson, now closer than ever to Scott, also told Cherry-Garrard that it was a toss-up between him and Oates for the last eight. Cherry-Garrard, who was also upset at being told he was leaving, recorded in his diary:

> 'There is a mournful air tonight – those turning back and those going on.'[12]

A new cache of stores was built, the Upper Glacier Depot, and the men prepared to turn for home. The returning party generously gave away any spare gear they would not need for the homeward run and anything which might be valuable to the remaining men. Cherry-Garrard gave Crean half of his scarf and left some tobacco for both Scott and Oates. Then, after a slightly emotional farewell, the four turned around and went back down the Beardmore.

It was 584 miles (940 km) back to Cape Evans and almost 300 miles (480 km) to the Pole.

The two parties, now approaching the Polar Plateau, were feeling more hopeful. Scott's team was Wilson, Oates and Taff Evans and the other four were Teddy Evans, Bowers, Lashly and Tom Crean. They were pulling 190 lb (86 kg) per man, which included twelve weeks' rations and Scott wrote:

'We are struggling on, considering all things against the odds. The weather is a constant anxiety, otherwise arrangements are working exactly as planned. Here we are practically on the summit and up to date in provision line. We ought to get through.'[13]

It was still not clear who would be in the final party that would make the historic march to the Pole. The first clear indication of Scott's plans emerged unknown to anyone else on 22 December when Scott started a new notebook for his diary. On the flyleaf he wrote simply:

'Ages: Self 43, Wilson 39, Evans (PO) 37, Oates 32, Bowers 28. Average 36.'[14]

However, the flyleaf entry in Scott's journal was apparently not shown to his seven comrades who remained blissfully unaware of their leader's decision. Instead, they were each able to while away the endless hours labouring in the man-hauling harnesses, silently wondering whether they would be chosen for the final march to the South Pole and lasting fame.

Christmas Day brought a terrifying reminder of the hazards of polar travel as the men heaved and strained their way up the final miles of the crevasse-strewn Beardmore. Lashly, who was pulling alongside Crean, suddenly plunged through the ice, yanking Crean and Bowers off their feet with the effect of the unexpected jolt. He was left hanging by his sledging harness, spinning helplessly over a 50-ft drop which he said was a 'ghastly sight'. A couple of days earlier his rope attachment had looked a little worn and by good fortune had been replaced.

Crean's harness had jammed under the 12-ft (3.6-m) sledge which was lying half across an 8-ft (2.5-m) bridge of ice. But he was temporarily immobilised and had to be freed by Bowers and Teddy Evans before they could begin rescuing Lashly.

They crawled gingerly towards the edge of the precipice but could not see Lashly because of a large overhanging piece of ice which blocked their view. All that was visible was the rope and they feared that he had gone. The men called down the gaping chasm and Lashly was able to reassure his comrades that, while badly shaken, he was still very much alive. He recalled:

> 'I was all right, it is true, but I did not care to be dangling in the air on a piece of rope, especially when I looked round and saw what kind of place it was. It seemed about 50 feet deep and 8 feet wide and 120 feet long. This information I had ample time to gain while dangling there. I could measure the width with my ski sticks, as I had them on my wrists.'[15]

An alpine rope was quickly found and a bowline made for Lashly to step into before hauling him out. It was his forty-fourth birthday and Crean cheerfully wished him 'many happy returns of the day' as he was pulled to his feet. Lashly's reply, said Evans, was 'unprintable'. Lashly's diary innocently records that he 'thanked him politely'.

After composing themselves, the eight men gathered for Christmas dinner, an improvised affair huddled together in two small green tents pitched 9,000 ft (2,740 m) up the Beardmore Glacier in temperatures of –7 °F (–22 °C). In defiance of the isolation, the bone-chilling cold and all-round discomfiture, the men enjoyed a splendid four-course dinner. Mankind's enduring adaptability was never better displayed.

First course was a full whack of pemmican with slices of horse meat flavoured with onion and curry powder and thickened with biscuit, followed by an arrowroot, cocoa and biscuit hoosh. A plum pudding was then produced and the feast was rounded off with a mixture of caramels and ginger, plus generous mugs of cocoa. Lashly said he 'could not hardly move' afterwards.

The warmth of the hearty meal flowed through their tired, cold bodies and for a brief period, the toil and hazards of dragging their heavy sledges in sub-zero temperatures was forgotten. The men were able to indulge in the more diverting pleasure of chatting with comrades on a full stomach and the moment struck a chord with Teddy Evans, who remembered the scene years later in his book, *South With Scott*:

> 'But we had such yarns of home, such plans were made for next Christmas, and after all we got down our fur sleeping bags and for a change we were quite warm owing to the full amount of food which we so sorely needed.'[16]

Normal business resumed in the morning, although the men were understandably a little slower off the mark after their feast. Pulling remained very hard and the rivalry between Scott and Evans intensified.

At the same time, the fatigue was readily apparent, particularly for Teddy Evans and Lashly who had now man-hauled for over 700 miles (1,125 km) across the Barrier and up the Beardmore. Along with Crean, the four were repeatedly lagging behind Scott's party, partly because their sledge runners were not as good but largely because Evans and Lashly were close to exhaustion. Evans, perhaps pointing the finger at Wilson, a doctor, said that 'a man trained to watch over men's health . . . would have seen something amiss'.

On New Year's Eve, Scott took the astonishing decision to ask Evans, Bowers, Lashly and Crean to abandon their skis, although his own party kept theirs. Scott did not explain his motives but with hindsight it is clear that Scott was narrowing his choice of the men he would take to the Pole. Scott also decided to establish Three Degree Depot and reduce the size of the sledges from 12 ft to 10 ft to ease the pulling weight, a minor event which was to have significant consequences.

Crean, Lashly and Taff Evans were deployed for many hours in the open air cutting down the sledges in the sub-zero temperatures of the Polar Plateau while the other five sat in the warmth of their tent discussing future prospects and drinking tea. But bad luck, which had dogged the party from the outset, struck again. Evans cut his hand very badly while working on one sledge. Stupidly, he did not report the accident to the doctor, Wilson, or to Scott, probably because he knew that the injury would force him out of the final party.

Taff Evans, a simple man, had banked on going to the Pole as a means of achieving fame, some money and perhaps even as a means of leaving the navy. His ambition was to retire from the navy and open a pub and the Pole was the key to fulfilling his ambition. However, the wound to his hand did not heal properly and, as events showed, was to become a factor in the big Welshman's subsequent breakdown on the awful journey back from the Pole.

The new year, 1912, began in typical fashion, the eight men pulling and straining for ten hours in temperatures which sank to −14°F. Scott said prospects seemed brighter but reported that Teddy Evans' team was 'not in very high spirits'. He had made up his mind.

The bombshell was dropped on 3 January when Scott announced that he was taking a party of five men, not four, to the Pole. Crean, Lashly and Teddy Evans were to return home and Bowers would be added to the party of Scott, Wilson, Oates and Taff Evans for the final march of about 150 miles (240 km) to the Pole.

Crean, who had stood loyally behind Scott for the best part of ten years, was devastated. What offended him most was that Scott could not bear to face him, man-to-man, and explain the reasons why he was not going to the Pole.

There are two slightly different versions of how Crean learnt his fate, though Gran is the source for both stories, which he wrote down after discussions with Crean.

When Scott entered the smoke-filled tent with news of his polar plans, Crean, a pipe-smoker all his life, was coughing. Scott saw an opportunity to avoid confronting the loyal Irishman with the uncomfortable truth and had unexpectedly found a suitable excuse to avoid facing him.

In his book, *Kampen om Sydpolen*, Gran said that Scott greeted the Irishman's cough with the comment:

'You've got a bad cold, Crean.'[17]

But Crean, who was no fool, immediately saw Scott's true meaning and was not prepared to let the disingenuous 'excuse' pass meekly into history. He retorted:

'I understand a half-sung song, sir.'[18]

However, in the English translation of his diaries, Gran recounted the tale after chatting with Crean back at Cape Evans and wrote down the following exchanges. After sticking his head through the tent door, Scott said:

'You've got a nasty cough, Crean, you must be careful with a cold like that!'[19]

Crean's response in this version was more straightforward and the Irishman replied:

'You think I can't take a hint, sir!'[20]

There is very little difference between the two versions of events, although there is almost half a century between when they were written by the Norwegian. Gran's book, *Kampen om Sydpolen* was not published until 1961, almost 50 years after the event, whereas the entry in his diary was written on 28 May 1912, less than five months after the episode and followed a chat with Crean at Cape Evans. However, Gran's diary was unequivocal about what he clearly saw as Scott's real motives. Gran's own interpretation was:

'Crean's "cough" was an excuse for Scott, but Crean understood his Captain and saw through him.'[21]

Crean was ordered out of the tent as Scott asked Teddy Evans if he could 'spare' Bowers from his team. Evans, by now very tired after the exertions of so long in the harness and deeply disappointed at being excluded from the polar party, was in no position to argue. His writings dismiss the disappointment, almost as though he was half-expecting it. In *South With Scott* he wrote:

'Briefly then it was a disappointment, but not too great to bear.'[22]

Perhaps more accurately, Bowers observed that Evans was 'frightfully cut up' and had expected to be in the final group. In a symbolic moment of surrender, Evans gave Bowers a small silk flag which his wife had given him to fly at the Pole. Scott, perhaps uneasy at his own decision, barely discussed the move in his diary. He simply recorded:

> 'Last night I decided to reorganise and this morning told off Teddy Evans, Lashly and Crean to return. They are disappointed, but take it well.'[23]

It was an astonishing decision. The entire enterprise had been founded on groups of four, notably the food and fuel which was carefully measured and broken into units of four. The little tent would be even more cramped and cooking for five on the howling Polar Plateau would take much longer, slowing the party's progress at the very time when they needed to travel fast. Ponting's revealing film footage of the men at Cape Evans camping and cooking showed how difficult it was for a party of four fit men squeezed into a small tent. A fifth man would inevitably pose extra and unwanted difficulties and discomfiture.

At the same time, Crean, Lashly and Evans would have to do the work of four men and spend valuable time at the homeward depots separating each unit of food and fuel to ensure that one quarter was left behind for the men on the way back from the Pole.

Equally the decision to send back three men was a huge risk for the returning party, particularly as only Evans was capable of navigation. The bleak featureless Plateau and the Barrier are little different to being afloat at sea and sound navigation was essential. The risk of having only one navigator, when accidents were commonplace, was immense.

Scott's motives, which have been the subject of intense

debate since 1912, are difficult to fathom. The decision to take an extra man, Bowers, only days after ordering him to depot his skis, is bizarre. In addition, closer inspection of the team's physical fitness would have revealed Taff Evans' worsening hand injury and the growing weakness of Oates. Some historians believe that Scott panicked and simply wanted more pulling power for the final march.

The eight men rose early, at about 5.45 a.m., on 4 January 1912, but the reorganisation of supplies and sledges took somewhat longer than expected and they were late getting away. Eventually the two parties started out together, still heading due south. After what must have been a tense, silent few miles in the harness, the little caravan came to an abrupt halt at around 10 a.m. They were at latitude 87° 34', about 146 geographic miles (268 km) from the Pole.

It was an emotional moment for Crean, the final grim realisation that, despite the prodigious efforts of the past two months, he was not going to the Pole. He was perhaps no more than ten to fifteen days of good marching away from the prize and the honour of being the first Irishman to stand at the Pole.

It was too much for the muscular Kerryman. On the barren Polar Plateau, in freezing, flesh-numbing temperatures of –17 °F (–27 °C), Crean openly broke down and cried, leaving his bitter tears of disappointment on the endless white snow plain. Scott recorded the sorrowful moment in his diary:

'Poor old Crean wept and even Lashly was affected.'[24]

Many years later, Crean told members of his family that his tears were both for himself and for Scott, who he realised had taken a huge risk in adding an extra man to the polar party. With his experience of ice travel, it may well have struck Crean that Scott's decision smacked of desperation.

They all shook hands and said goodbye for the last time. Crean probably gave an especially warm clasp to his old messmate and long time friend, Taff Evans. Oates, who was the most affected of the polar party, gave Teddy Evans a letter for his beloved mother and his considerate last words were to console the three returning men over their disappointment of not going to the Pole.

Bowers handed over some letters and was almost dismissive of the severe difficulties the three men faced on the long journey home, writing that they had a 'featherweight sledge' and ought to 'run down the distance easily'. Lashly said the group felt the parting 'very much' but wished the men 'every success and safe return'. Scott gave Evans a letter for his wife, Kathleen, which he said was 'a last note from a hopeful position'.

As the moment of parting approached, the silence of the Polar Plateau was broken with 'three huge cheers' from Crean, Lashly and Evans as they watched their five comrades trudge slowly off towards the bleak, white horizon. It was the last appreciation they would hear.

The trio then stood, watching in silence as their comrades moved slowly away into the distance and only shook themselves into action when the biting cold of the Plateau's sub-zero temperatures began to take a grip. The Polar Plateau is no place to linger and for Crean, Lashly and Evans it was now time to turn round and begin their melancholy walk northwards to Cape Evans. The forlorn group frequently stopped in their tracks and looked back to the south to see the dark figures of Scott, Wilson, Bowers, Oates and Taff Evans silhouetted against the endless white backdrop.

Slowly the five figures began to disappear towards the horizon. The polar party grew smaller and smaller, until they were just a distant little black speck on the vast white expanse. Suddenly they were gone, melting into the whiteness.

It was the last time anyone would see the five men alive.

10
A race for life

Crean, Lashly and Evans faced a desperate march as the last supporting party began the homeward journey on 4 January 1912, a gruelling 750-statute-mile (1,206 km) journey which was to develop into a race of a different kind to the one they had endured with Scott – a race for life. From the start, the odds were stacked against the three men.

Scott had admitted before the separation on the Polar Plateau that Evans and Lashly were 'stale', the two men being badly weakened by over two months of energy-sapping man-hauling across the Barrier and up the Beardmore. In particular, Scott should have been more sensitive to the fact there were very serious risks involved with a three-man party, with only one navigator, pulling a sledge for hundreds of miles in sub-zero temperatures as the season began to close in. The fraught, winter journey to Cape Crozier under Wilson six months earlier was full testament to the risks facing a three-man team.

Also, the recent experience of all British polar expeditions suggested that, at best, the return journey would be a close run thing. Scott's 'furthest south' on the *Discovery* expedition in 1902–3 was a typically narrow escape for a three-man team and Shackleton's own 'furthest south', when he came to within 97 miles of the Pole in 1909, only averted complete disaster by the slimmest of margins.

An injury to any one of the men, such as breaking a leg by a fall through a crevasse, would probably have fatal consequences for the other two. Nor did the men have the benefit of a sledgemeter to measure their daily distances and steer dead ahead, a huge impediment for men with a critical need to find their food supply depots. If the trio could not pick up their depots, they would die of starvation.

Clearly an accident to Evans as navigator would be disastrous and would leave Crean and Lashly reliant on the precious few cairns of snow which were dotted across the snowy landscape. It would be foolish to rely on these few markers to pick a way across the ice to safety, especially in a blizzard when all landmarks were blotted out. Crossing the Barrier might be a little easier because more depots had been laid. But the Barrier was as flat and featureless as an ocean and without adequate navigation they would be highly vulnerable to missing the depot flags.

Finally, Evans was already in the early stages of scurvy.

The perilous journey was divided into three distinct phases – 230 miles (370 km) across the 10,000-ft high Plateau, 120 miles (190 km) down the crevasse-strewn Beardmore and then about 400 miles (640 km) across the desolate Barrier. Each stage, said Evans with classic understatement, had its own 'special excitements, dangers and peculiarities'.

Evans was aware of the dangers, particularly the risks of a three-man party covering such long distances across the frozen wastes at that time of the season when the weather can wreak havoc. Unlike Scott, he was prepared to share his fears with his comrades. To his credit Evans was able to admit freely that they were all in the same mess and that survival was dependent on a combined effort. In his words:

> 'Reluctant as I was to confess it to myself, I soon realised that the ceding of one man from my party had been too great a sacrifice, but there was no denying it and I was eventually compelled to explain the situation to Lashly

and Crean and lay bare the naked truth. No man was ever better served than I was by these two.'[1]

The scale of their task was abundantly clear on the very first day that the three trekked northwards. The men marched for nine hours in radiantly fine weather on a surface that Evans said was 'all that could be desired'.

But even with the environment in their favour, it was not enough. Evans quickly realised that nine hours was not enough if the men were to remain on full rations for the prolonged walk home and before long they were in the harness for ten hours and sometimes even thirteen hours a day. He concluded that they had to cover an average of 17 miles (27 km) a day for the first 230 miles across the Plateau. It was a demanding schedule for men who had already covered so many weary miles.

As a first step, Evans decided to 'steal' some time by secretly advancing his watch an hour each morning and putting it back to normal at the end of the day in the hope of fooling Crean and Lashly into spending more time marching. However, both Crean and Lashly later admitted that they were perfectly well aware of Evans' ruse but, equally, they were aware of the urgency and never let on. Playing the game was in everyone's interest and Evans confirmed the seriousness of their plight when he conceded that the march was now a 'fight for life'.[2]

The men, who were hauling around 400 lb (180 kg) on the sledge, made solid progress immediately after turning for home, despite an early blizzard and the rarefied air which at around 10,000 ft (3 km) above sea level made breathing a little difficult. However, they were particularly cheered after picking up their 'depoted' skis on 6 January when they covered a welcome distance of 19 miles (30 km) in one day.

Crean was initially in the lead, but paid a heavy penalty by developing an attack of snowblindness. Evans, who was prone to snowblindness, said the crippling ailment was as though 'the eyes were on fire' and he improvised a treatment of bandaging them with a poultice made of old tea leaves.

They marched on in eerie silence, each man alone with his thoughts. The only noise was the grating sound of their skis scraping across the top layer of snow and the occasional muffled curse from one of their companions in the harness. They spoke little. It may be that, after months of close confinement with each other, they had simply run out of things to talk about. Temperatures were frequently −20 °F (−29 °C) and Evans recalled that the wind blew directly into their faces, slashing their cheeks 'with the constant jab of frozen needle points'.

Inevitably the men lost their way in the bad weather and broken terrain at the point where the Plateau gives way to the descent of the Beardmore. By 13 January, Evans calculated they were miles off course, situated high above the Shackleton Ice Falls and gazing down on the Beardmore Glacier 2,000 ft below. He was concerned that it might take three days to make the long detour round the Ice Falls to get onto the Beardmore.

In their plight, with food supplies critical, delay was out of the question. The men could not afford to lose time on their marches and so Evans decided to take drastic action.

He proposed a desperate do-or-die solution. They would climb aboard the sledge and glissade down the Ice Falls, regardless of the dangers and the unknown fate which waited them at the bottom.

The men were taking their lives in their hands with what seemed a cavalier and reckless plan. If one of the party suffered a serious injury in the haphazard enterprise it would probably spell the end for all three. But the alternative of 'wasting' three days on a detour round the Ice Falls with dwindling food stocks was even worse. Evans, true to form, discussed their precarious prospects with Crean and Lashly.

Evans later told members of his family that Lashly bowed to rank, accepting the apparently crazy scheme and Evans' authority with the casual, almost dismissive remark: 'You're the officer.' But Crean was not afraid to question authority and he openly clashed with Evans. He protested:

'Captain Scott would never do a damn fool thing like that.'

Evans was prepared to listen but had clearly made up his mind. He retorted:

'Well, Captain Scott is not here – so get on board!'[3]

Evans, writing later, confirmed that the discussion with Crean and Lashly was 'very short-lived' and they promptly began the perilous descent into catastrophe or safety.

They packed their skis on the sledge, attached spiked crampons to their finnesko snow boots and guided the sledge through the maze of hummocks and crevasses. Quickly the men climbed on board and kicked off, sending the sledge racing down the slippery slopes of blue ice. They had attached themselves to the runaway sledge by their harness in the faint hope that they would be saved if it went into a crevasse.

Crevasses, described as 'gaping gargantuan trenches' up to 200 ft (60 m) wide, were all around and Evans later wrote:

'We encountered fall after fall, bruises, cuts and abrasions were sustained, but we vied with one another in bringing all our grit and patience to bear; scarcely a complaint was heard, although one or other of us would be driven almost sick with pain as the sledge cannoned into this or that man's heel with a thud and made the victim clench his teeth to avoid crying out.'[4]

Suddenly the men came across a very steep blue ice slope and the sledge began to accelerate even faster down the slippery hill like a toboggan, with the three terrified men lying face-down and clinging onto the straps which held their precious gear in place. The sledge, which had no means of braking, raced to a frightening speed of about 60 mph as it plunged helter-skelter into the unknown. At one point it seemed that it had literally taken off as it shot straight across a yawning crevasse with the men hanging on for dear life. Evans cast a quick glance at Crean who raised his eyebrows as if to say 'What next!'

Seconds later, the sledge crashed into an ice ridge, capsized and rolled over and over, dragging the bewildered men along in its wake until it finally came to a shuddering standstill. One of Evans' ski sticks was wrenched from the sledge and plunged down a blue-black chasm which had nearly swallowed them whole. Then silence.

Crean hauled himself to his feet and discovered that his windproof trousers were torn to ribbons and Evans said the big Irishman was left 'standing there in a pair of Wolsey drawers and fur boots'. But they were all alive and thankfully, no bones were broken.

Taking their lives in their hands, the three men had glissaded down about 2,000 ft onto the Beardmore Glacier and saved three precious days of marching and food. None of them was entirely sure precisely how far they had come and no one was going back to check the distance. They knew how lucky they had been and Evans admitted:

'How we ever escaped entirely uninjured is beyond me to explain.'[5]

Years later Evans remembered the terrifying descent and wrote:

'It makes me sweat, even now, when I think of it. I've run a good many risks in my life, but none compares with that tobogganing over the Ice Falls.'[6]

But the gamble had paid off and the men were now embarked on the descent of the Beardmore. They reached the Mount Darwin Depot on 14 January, replenished their food supplies and on 16 January managed somewhere between 18 and 20 miles (32 km) in a very good day's march.

Although the weather had improved, the travelling was slow and heavy going, while the absence of a sledgemeter meant they were having difficulties steering directly. They marched across a maze of crevasses and pressure ridges, which they occasionally overcame by slinging the sledge across gaping chasms and making a bridge. The heavy work and constant fear of crashing down a crevasse was beginning to take its toll on the weary men and Lashly's diary on 17 January said:

> 'We have today experienced what we none of us ever wants to be our lot again. I cannot describe the maze we got into and hairbreadth escapes we have had to pass through today. This day we shall remember for the rest of our lives. Don't want many days like this.'[7]

On the same day, Scott reached the South Pole only to find that Amundsen and his Norwegian companions had beaten them by a month.

The three men of the last supporting party had little choice but to plough on through the labyrinth of passageways and crevasses, hoping the weather would not break and that the deadly broken ground would give way to smoother travelling. They were, however, coming closer together, increasingly aware that they depended upon each other for survival. Bonds were forming between the three men which would remain for the rest of their lives. Evans said Crean and Lashly had 'hearts of lions' and as fresh difficulties presented themselves, 'the more valiantly did my companions set themselves to work'.[8]

Evans fondly remembered Crean as 'a raw-boned Irishman with the most comically serious face'. More pertinently, he also described Crean as 'imperturbable' and with the greatest dangers still ahead of them, the Irishman's mental strength would be as valuable as his physical power. Crean himself tried to keep up their spirits with the occasional tune and in his diary Lashly remembered one night when '. . . old Tom is giving us a song while he is covering up the tent with snow'.

Evans developed a severe bout of snowblindness and soon after they ran into a major problem with vast and dangerous crevasses blocking their route. The men remembered 'stupendous gulfs' and Lashly later said it would have been possible to drop St Paul's Cathedral down some of the yawning icy canyons.

One vast chasm meant another desperate and dangerous decision. Going back or around it was out of the question because their food was running out and they could not spare the time. Reaching the next depot was vital, so they elected to struggle across one gaping hole via a connecting bridge of hard snow. But no one knew whether the bridge would take the weight. It was another huge gamble by three desperate men and Crean said afterwards:

'We went along the crossbar to the H of Hell.'[9]

Lashly went across first but was so concerned about the 'bridge' collapsing that he dared not walk upright. He sat astride it, moving gingerly across while Crean and Evans played him out on the end of an alpine rope. The snow bridge was an inverted 'V' so that the 400-lb (180-kg) sledge had to be balanced on its apex and guided across, inch by inch with Crean and Evans each holding one side to prevent it toppling into the inky depths below. Evans recalled:

> 'Neither of us spoke, except for the launching signal but each looked steadfastly into the other's eyes – nor did we two look down. As in other cases of peril, the tense quiet of the moment left its mark on the memories of our party for ever.'[10]

After a while, Crean and Evans had joined Lashly on a small slope on the other side and they began to pull up the 400-lb sledge. The strenuous exertion with the sledge was a timely reminder that the men were getting weaker and even this effort stretched them to the limits of their endurance.

They were on the point of physical exhaustion and badly needed rest and a hot drink. But, in the broken maze of crevasse fields, there was simply not enough room to pitch the tent safely. Evans would later remember looking into the 'hollow-eyed and gaunt' faces of his two exhausted comrades as they gasped for air and contemplated their next move.

Evans, once again, defied convention and took a big risk by setting off on his own to find a pathway out of the tangled mess of crevasses and ice ridges. Crean and Lashly tried to dissuade him, knowing that a fall through a crevasse would be fatal or that, simply, he could get lost in the maze. But in reality, there was little alternative.

It was another desperate act by desperate men and Evans felt a huge responsibility for the two men who sat and watched as he disappeared behind the ice ridges in search of a route out of the maze. In *South With Scott*, he declared;

> 'I felt a tremendous love for those two men that day. They had trusted me so implicitly and believed in my ability to win through.'[11]

To his everlasting relief, Evans soon discovered that they were virtually at the end of the broken, crevasse-ridden ice fields and that ahead lay a smoother journey. They were close to the Mid Glacier Depot, well over halfway down the Beardmore and edging nearer to the Barrier where travelling would be far easier and depots easier to locate.

A mood of optimism swept over the small weary party at the thought that they had survived the worst part of their journey and they marched on to the next depot. But Evans had paid a terrible price for his mission to find a way out of the crevasses and was struck by a most severe attack of snowblind-ness, which lasted for almost four days.

Late on 21 January, the tired but relieved men stumbled into the Lower Glacier Depot and a day later they caught the first sight of the Barrier, bringing uninhibited whoops of joy from the embattled trio. Lashly recalled:

> 'Crean let go one huge yell enough to frighten the ponies out of their graves of snow . . .'[12]

But the relief at entering the most straightforward part of their journey was shattered by a grim discovery. Evans, who had man-hauled for about 1,100 miles (1,770 km), was now displaying clear signs of scurvy.

Evans had reported stiffness at the back of the knees and 'looseness of the bowels' and a few days later Lashly, who had spent the same time man-hauling, came over 'giddy and faint' while they were pitching the tent. Crean, too, began to suffer with a touch of diarrhoea and the constant interruptions were slowing their progress. It was still approximately 400 miles (640 km) to Cape Evans and the men were getting no fitter.

The men had been out on the ice for almost three months, existing on a diet very low in the vitamins which provide the necessary safeguards against scurvy, notably vitamin C. With all the classic signs of scurvy emerging, Lashly, who had assumed the role of doctor, stopped Evans' pemmican. In addition, he prescribed a mixture of opium pills and chalk. His legs had become swollen, bruised-looking and olive-green in colour, while his teeth were now loose and gums ulcerated. The diarrhoea continued and then, disturbingly, Evans began to haemorrhage. He later recalled:

> 'Crean and Lashly were dreadfully concerned on my behalf and how they nursed me and helped me along no words of mine can properly describe. What men they were.'[13]

On 25 January 1912, as the men were beginning the haul across the flat, featureless Barrier, Amundsen arrived back at his Framheim base and casually asked if the coffee was on the stove. The journey to the Pole and back, some 1,860 miles (3,000 km), had taken 99 days.

By 30 January Evans and Lashly had been out in the icy wilderness for over 100 days and the normally buoyant Evans was getting uncharacteristically gloomy and pessimistic, at a time when keeping up morale was never more important if the men retained any chance of pulling through. He wrote that the disappointment of not being included in the polar party had 'not helped me much' and he believed that the prospects of getting back to safety were diminishing every day. Four days later he broke down.

Lashly, who was increasingly worried about Evans, wrote on 3 February:

> 'This morning we were forced to put Mr Evans on his ski and strap him on, as he could not lift his legs. They are rapidly getting worse, things are looking very serious on his part.'[14]

But Lashly was also suffering. Apart from the physical exhaustion, he also reported that he was 'a bit depressed'[15] as they struggled to the depot at Mount Hooper. The deterioration of Evans was bad enough, but Crean would have been alarmed to learn Lashly, a calm and redoubtable figure throughout his Polar career, was also struggling. Crean thought very highly of his fellow seaman and once said that 'whatever he did was first class'. Now, in the face of their growing ordeal, a run-down and dejected Lashly was unthinkable.

It was 180 miles (290 km) to the safety of Hut Point and they were now straining their eyes for the first sight of land, probably the peaks of either Mount Erebus or Mount Discovery, which would signal that they were close to safety. Or at least it would offer hope.

Crean, though, remained indomitable and nowhere in the diaries of Evans or Lashly is there any indication that the Irishman showed any sign of weakening, either physically or mentally. Or, more importantly, that he had succumbed to the effects of scurvy, even though his diet for the past three months was precisely the same as Evans and Lashly.

He was also optimistically on the lookout for Scott's party, who he assumed, with five fit men in the harness, would be travelling faster than the slow-moving and weakening trio. He continually looked back over his shoulder in hopeful anticipation of catching a glimpse of an approaching black speck on the distant horizon. However, the little speck never materialised.

But Crean and Lashly had more pressing problems. By now Evans was going rapidly downhill, passing a great deal of blood and prompting Lashly to report that he had to 'do nearly everything for him'. He plodded on wearily on his skis, unable to help with the pulling.

The two seamen were desperately worried at the consequences of Evans breaking down, which meant them having to do the work of three men in the man-hauling harness. It also meant weakening men hauling extra weight. Another fear was the loss of Evans' navigational ability before they reached some easily recognisable landmark which would guide them home.

It was clear that the strength of Crean and Lashly was also ebbing away, partly because they were not eating enough to compensate for the draining daily rigours of dragging the sledge. For the two tired, hungry men the extra burden of carrying their sickening lieutenant was something they dreaded. However, there was no question of abandoning Evans and Lashly grimly summed up the worsening position on 7 February:

> 'No better luck with our patient, he gets along without a murmur. He is determined to go to the last, which he knows is not far off, as it is difficult for him to stand . . . but shall have to drag him on the sledge when he can't go any further.'[16]

Their ordeal eased a little when they reached One Ton Depot on 9 February and enjoyed a feed of oatmeal, a welcome change of diet from endless mugfuls of pemmican. They took nine days' food from the depot and set out for Hut Point, over 140 gruelling miles (190 km) away across the flat Barrier landscape. It would be touch-and-go, with Evans a passenger and two tired men doing the back-breaking pulling of three.

The only encouraging feature of the slog was that both Crean and Lashly were showing no major signs of scurvy, which was remarkable after so long without an intake of vitamin C from fresh meat and fruit. But the fatigue of man-hauling was beginning to tell and something had to be done to cut down the weight. On 11 February they 'depoted' all the gear they could manage without in the hope of making the pulling a little easier.

Two days later their worst fears materialised when Evans could not stand and they had to strap him on the sledge, a passenger in every sense of the word. They were about 100 miles (160 km) from the safety of Hut Point and slowly but surely losing the race for life.

Evans was deteriorating fast and one morning he suddenly fainted. They thought he was dead and Crean openly wept. Crean, Evans recalled, was very upset at his condition and he wrote:

> 'His hot tears fell on my face and as I came to I gave him a weak kind of laugh.'[17]

Crean and Lashly had each covered 1,500 miles (2,400 km) in three and a half months with 44-year-old Lashly man-hauling without a break for almost the entire trek. On a cosmetic level, the three men had not washed, shaved, cleaned their teeth or cut their hair for about 15 weeks.

However, such thoughts were easily dismissed as they began to realise that they were fighting a losing battle. Once again, they dropped off any remaining items of surplus gear, leaving them with the barest essentials for survival – a tent, sleeping bags, cooker and what little food and oil that remained. Even the skis were left behind in the snow. They had little left to abandon but their lives.

The weary marches, dragging the heavy sledge and the dying Evans, became a desperate race against time and the elements, with food running out and temperatures steadily dropping as the season began to close in.

But they were still managing an astonishing 10 miles a day at about 1 mile per arduous hour, wearily and silently plodding through the snow for over ten hours with their minds fixed solely on pitching the tent and getting some hot food inside themselves. Evans would later recall Crean and Lashly's 'wild and roaming eyes as they gasped with exhaustion at the end of the day'.[18]

But, despite the intense daily effort and the endurance of Crean and Lashly, they were not travelling fast enough and all three were keenly aware that, barring a miracle, they faced certain death. A tortuous march of ten hours a day was the limit of their capacity, but not enough to bring them to safety.

Evans knew the position was hopeless and courageously asked his companions to leave him behind in the snow and save themselves. Crean and Lashly flatly rejected the suggestion. Evans would later recall that it was the only occasion in his long and distinguished naval career that an order of his was openly disobeyed.

They were 83 miles (134 km) from Hut Point and Crean and Lashly now feared that Evans was close to death. Lashly said they were now almost too afraid to sleep at night. Just as disturbing, the food position was now critical and on 16 February they took the drastic decision to cut their ration by half, the last thing that ravenously hungry men needed.

The small, bedraggled party was now about 40 miles (65 km) from Hut Point, but only four days' food remained and in their weakening state, that would hardly be enough. Pulling the sledge and Evans for 10 miles (16 km) a day was now beyond the two exhausted men but cutting the ration might buy them a precious extra day or two travelling. However, reducing the food would make the already weakened men even weaker. It was a terrible risk, either way.

Their faltering hopes were briefly raised when suddenly and unexpectedly they ran across one of the motor tractors, which had been abandoned in the snow on the outward journey months earlier. They quickly searched for any bits of food which may have also been left behind and were pleased when they uncovered a few stale biscuits. Every scrap was welcome in their condition.

They were now fairly close to Corner Camp, the point where the Polar parties turn away from the base camp area and head due south to the Pole. It was about 35 miles (56 km) from Hut Point – tantalisingly close to food and warmth.

But both Crean and Lashly could barely muster the strength to carry on dragging their dying companion, exhausted by the draining marches of the past months. Temperatures were dropping as the season closed in and snow was falling incessantly as they camped. Time was running out and Lashly forlornly recorded:

'I don't think we have got the go in us we had, but we must try and push on.'[19]

They camped for the night on 17 February, hoping for a miracle, or even more remotely, that the dog teams might happen to pass by. It was a forlorn hope.

On the same day, some 400 miles (640 km) away to the South and near the foot of the Beardmore Glacier, Crean's friend Taff Evans collapsed and died, the first of Scott's party to perish on the return from the Pole.

Crean and Lashly rose wearily from their sleeping bags on the morning of 18 February 1912. It was cold, their 'breakfast' left the men still hungry and they knew the fight was as good as over. The mathematics were brutally simple. In their weak condition, it would take four or five days, or even longer, to travel the 35 miles (56 km) to the safety of Hut Point, even if they could summon the strength to make the journey. But all that remained was enough food for three meals, sufficient perhaps for one and a half or two days. Their reserves of strength had been drained.

As they lifted the stricken Evans onto the sledge, once again he collapsed. Both men thought he was dead. Crean was again moved to tears and only jolted from his sorrowful mourning by a sharp rebuke from Lashly, which had the desired effect. In his diary, Lashly recorded the tense scene:

> 'Crean was very upset and almost cried, but I told him it was no good to create a scene but put up a bold front and try to assist.'[20]

They poured the last remaining drop of brandy into Evans in an attempt to revive the critically ill man and tenderly placed him back on the sledge to make him as comfortable as possible. They knew that, for Evans at least, it was probably to be the last march. But they had no intention of leaving him behind.

Crean and Lashly began to drag and pull the sledge and Evans movingly described the grim scene as they took their increasingly weary steps in the snow:

> 'I could see them from the sledge by raising my head – how slowly their legs seemed to move, wearily but nobly they fought on . . . Their strength was spent, and great though their hearts were, they now had to give up. In vain they tried to move the sledge with my wasted weight upon it – it was hopeless.'[21]

In biting wind and sub-zero temperatures, the two exhausted men stopped in their tracks, unable to move any further. They had courageously carried their colleague 100 miles (160 km) across some of the most hostile terrain on earth. But their strength had all but ebbed away and their struggle was virtually at an end.

With heavy hearts, they pitched the tent and carried their dying comrade inside. Evans himself thought the end was near and recalled being dragged by 'two hungry exhausted and hollow-eyed companions to a deserted camp on the Great Ice Barrier under the shadow of Mount Erebus'.[22] He remembered them placing him on Crean's sleeping bag and recorded:

> 'I thought I was being put into my grave.'[23]

Outside Crean and Lashly held a brief two-man council of war. Evans overheard what he described as 'low notes of sadness, but with a certain thread of determination running through what they said'.[24]

It was clear that the men were spent, unable to drag Evans any further and with food supplies down to virtually nothing. Leaving Evans alone would be signing the lieutenant's death warrant, even if it meant saving their own lives. Nor could they expect any relief, either from the dogs or man-hauling teams.

In the grim circumstances, there was only one option. One of the men would remain behind with Evans and the other should proceed on foot to Hut Point, 35 miles (56 km) away where he might expect to find help. It was another desperate act by two desperate men and, as before, there was no reasonable alternative.

Crean now took the bravest decision of his life and volunteered to make the solo walk to Hut Point, leaving Lashly to nurse Evans. He had taken a similarly brave decision a year earlier when, as the only experienced member of the party, he went single-handedly to find help for Bowers and Cherry-Garrard adrift on the ice floes with the ponies. But then he was fit, rested and fully fed. Today, as he contemplated his epic march, Crean was bitterly cold, thirsty, starving hungry and physically drained after months of walking and man-hauling for over 1,500 miles (2,420 km).

Even a man like Crean, who was always confident in his own ability, must have doubted his chances of survival.

Lashly recalled the conversation when Crean offered to make the hazardous attempt to reach Hut Point and recorded in his own words:

> 'I offered to do the journey and Crean remain behind, but Tom said he would much rather that I stayed with the invalid and look after him, so I thought it best I should remain . . .'[25]

They stuffed Crean's pockets with the only food they could find, which was three biscuits and two sticks of chocolate. Lashly tried to make a drink for him but the Irishman could not carry it.

Crean ducked his head inside the tent to say goodbye to Evans who somehow summoned the strength to thank him weakly for what he was doing. Crean then stepped out into the snow, with Lashly holding open the little round tent door flap to allow Evans to see him depart. Evans remembered the scene:

> 'He strode out nobly and finely – I wondered if I should ever see him again.'[26]

Lashly propped up the frail Evans to watch Crean begin the lonely march for survival. His large dark silhouette was the only visible object in the vast white wilderness. Years later he remembered the Irishman 'staggering forward in a stooping posture in knee-deep snow, his arms folded across his face as a shield against the blizzard'.

It was 10 a.m. on Sunday 18 February 1912, and the march began with some good luck. The weather brightened and the travelling surface was fairly good, though the soft snow was a problem.

Remarkably, Crean trudged 16 miles across the ice before he even stopped for a break. Then he halted for barely five minutes to eat his meagre provisions, devouring two of the three biscuits and two sticks of chocolate. He placed one biscuit back in his pocket – for emergencies!

The travelling was hazardous, particularly as Crean did not have the skis which he had dumped miles back on the Barrier to save weight. He frequently sank up his thighs in the soft snow and there was the ever-present fear of crashing through a crevasse, from which there would be no rescue. He had no tent to shelter from the weather, no means of navigation and no hot food. Any accident, such as breaking a leg in a fall, would be fatal.

Shortly after Crean departed, Lashly made the 1-mile trip to Corner Camp in search of some scraps of food for himself and Evans. He found some butter, cheese and a little treacle. He also found a disturbing note from Day, the motor mechanic, which warned of 'a lot of very bad crevasses' between Corner Camp and the Sea – the very direction in which Crean was heading. Significantly, Lashly never told Evans about Day's note on the grounds that he had enough to worry about.

Soon Crean's long legs had carried him past Safety Camp, which sits about 2 miles (3.2 km) from the very edge of the Barrier and only 6 or 7 miles (11 km) from Hut Point. Shortly after midnight on Monday he finally reached the Barrier's edge, though the weather was breaking up and Crean, by now desperately tired, was feeling the cold terribly. In his tiredness, he frequently slipped on the glassy ice, occasionally and painfully tumbling on his back, yet he had no choice but to soldier on.

In desperation he started to move around Cape Armitage towards Hut Point, but the sea ice had not frozen sufficiently and he felt the slush coming through his finnesko snow boots. Even though he was on the edge of exhaustion, he could not risk taking the shortest route crossing weak ice. He avoided Cape Armitage and went round to the side of Observation Hill, which looks down on the Hut Point Peninsula and the familiar site of the old *Discovery* hut.

But there was disappointment waiting for him after he had clawed his weary frame up to the top of the hill. Although he could dimly pick out the hut below, there was no sign of activity, no people moving about and no dog tracks. The lack of dogs was a particular disappointment, since they offered the fastest means of travelling back onto the Barrier to rescue Evans and Lashly.

Many people would have wilted at the prospect that there was no help at Hut Point because this would have meant trudging another 14 or 15 miles to Cape Evans without food or shelter where he could be certain of finding help. After coming so far, the disappointment must have been acute. But Crean, composed and imperturbable, simply sat down on an ice ridge and finished his last biscuit with a bit of ice. 'I was very dry,' he remembered.[27]

The weather, which had so far been mercifully kind on the march, was now closing in. Wind was blowing up the drifting snow and visibility was deteriorating fast. A blizzard could be seen approaching in the distance and even at the point of sanctuary, the brutal Antarctic weather was prepared to have the final word. Crean knew he could not defeat a blizzard.

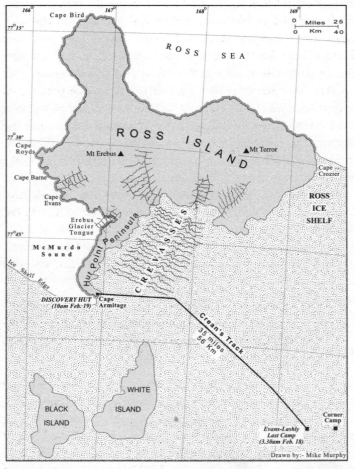

Tom Crean's epic solo walk of 35 miles from near Corner Camp to Hut Point to save the life of Teddy Evans in 1912.

He somehow scrambled down the hill as the wind picked up and made his way slowly towards the hut, casting worried glances back towards the weather which threatened to engulf him. Then, to his utter relief, Crean suddenly saw the dogs and sledges in the distance out on the sea-ice.

The sight invigorated him and he somehow found enough strength to reach the hut. Crean finally stumbled into the hut and fell to his knees, almost delirious with hunger and exhaustion, and numbed with cold. Inside he found the Russian dog driver, Dimitri, and Atkinson, luckily the one doctor within 400 miles (640 km) of Hut Point.

He blurted out the alarming news about his two companions on the Barrier and collapsed on the floor. As soon as he was revived, Crean asked if he could go back out onto the Barrier with the party of rescuers for Evans and Lashly who were stuck in their tent 35 miles away.[28] Atkinson, sensibly, refused.

It was 3.30 a.m. on Monday 19 February 1912, and Tom Crean's remarkable 35-mile solo journey, which had lasted nearly eighteen hours, was over.

According to his own account of the remarkable walk, Atkinson immediately gave Crean hot food and a drink. Crean recalled:

> **'He gave me a tot first and then a feed of porridge – but I couldn't keep it down; that's the first time in my life that it ever happened and it was the brandy that did it.'[29]**

Within 30 minutes of reaching the safety of the Hut, the blizzard which had threatened to overwhelm Crean on the way in, suddenly struck the area with full ferocity, raging throughout the day and into the next night. Had the blizzard come down half an hour earlier, Crean would certainly have perished on the Barrier's edge and no one would have known about the plight of Evans and Lashly huddled in their small green tent 35 miles away. Cherry-Garrard, who witnessed the savage brutality of the blizzard, said 'no power on earth could have saved him'.[30]

Crean's epic journey had taken him to the very brink, though once again his own account of proceedings is overwhelmingly modest and can scarcely do justice to the terrible ordeal.

Crean did not write his own account of the remarkable journey and very few of his recollections in letters have survived the passage of time. But, thankfully, he gave an oral version of events to Cherry-Garrard which, in turn, Cherry translated into his own words and included in *The Worst Journey in the World.*

The story of the eighteen-hour march is told in almost matter-of-fact language as though describing a quiet stroll in the countryside on a sunny afternoon. It conveys little of the dangers he faced from hunger, blizzards or crevasses, or his own appalling physical state and the freezing cold. Nor does it give any insight into his personal feelings at the exhaustion, starvation and ever-present hazards. Or, finally, the elation and relief he must have felt at pulling through against truly impossible odds and seeing the faces of his comrades, Lashly and Evans.

Crean's version, written by Cherry-Garrard for *The Worst Journey in the World,* simply says:

> 'He started at 10 on Sunday morning and "the surface was good, very good indeed," and he went about sixteen miles before he stopped. Good clear weather. He had three biscuits and two sticks of chocolate. He stopped about five minutes, sitting on the snow and ate two biscuits and the chocolate, and put one biscuit back in his pocket. He was quite warm and not sleepy.
>
> He carried on just about the same and passed Safety Camp on his right some five hours later, and thinks it was about 12.30 on Monday morning that he reached

the edge of the Barrier, tired, getting cold in the back and the weather coming on thick.

It was bright behind him but it was coming over the Bluff, and White Island was obscured though he could still see Cape Armitage and Castle Rock. He slipped a lot on the sea-ice, having several falls on to his back and it was getting thicker all the time.

At the Barrier edge there was light wind, now it was blowing a strong wind, drifting and snowing. He made for the Gap and could not get up at first. To avoid taking a lot out of himself he started to go round Cape Armitage; but soon felt slush coming through his finnesko (he had no crampons) and made back for the Gap.

He climbed Observation Hill to avoid the slippery ice. When he got to the top it was still clear enough to see vaguely the outline of Hut Point, but he could see no sledges nor dogs. He sat down under the lee of Observation Hill, and finished his biscuit with a bit of ice; "I was very dry." [He] slid down the side of Observation Hill and thought at this time there was open water below, for he had no goggles on the march and his eyes were strained.

But on getting near the ice-foot he found it was polished sea-ice and made his way round to the hut under the ice-foot. When he got close he saw the dogs and sledges on the sea-ice, and it was now blowing very hard with drift. He walked in and found the Doctor and Dimitri inside.'[31]

A brief glimpse of Crean's personal feelings are contained in two letters which he wrote in the Antarctic after his rescue mission. The first, dated 26 February 1912, was composed only seven days after he had staggered into Hut Point. It was written to a friend while he was recovering from the trek and the date he gives for his arrival was the day he went back to Cape Evans after completing his round trip of 1,500 miles to within 150 miles of the Pole. It says:

> **'I returned on the 24th from sledging after being 4 months away. It was very trying indeed. If any one has earned fame, it is your own County Kerry man.**
>
> **There were three of us returning after being 140 miles from the Pole. Lieut. Evans was taken bad and we had to drag him 90 miles on the sledge. Then we had to go over to our hut and we were in a bad way regarding food, and our patient got very bad.**
>
> **So it fell to my lot to do the 30 miles for help, and only a couple of biscuits and a stick of chocolate to do it. Well, sir, I was very weak when I reached the hut.**
>
> **It's a fine record for us, but I don't know how things will turn out until the Captain returns.'**[32]

A year later, on 18 January 1913, Crean again remembered his heroics with disarming modesty and in a further letter he wrote:

> **'Comm. Evans is in charge of the whole show now. And he told me he would never forget me, or the other man. There is no doubt about it but we saved his life. You might tell Catherine my long legs did the trick for him. But I must say I was pretty well done for when I finished.'**[33]

The grim state of Crean and the news about Evans and Lashly alarmed Atkinson, particularly when the blizzard grew in intensity and temperatures plunged. But, frustratingly, he could not move until the weather eased off.

He waited a day and a half until late in the afternoon of 20 February when he set off with two dog teams to scamper the 35 miles to the little tent on the Barrier.

Lashly had wisely torn up an old piece of coating and attached it to a long piece of bamboo so that the recovery party would not miss seeing the tiny green tent on the vast Barrier landscape. Evans confessed that he was 'at his last gasp'. They were down to their last paraffin-stained biscuits and, as Evans put it, '. . . when everything looked blackest'. He added:

'If Crean had not got through, it was all up with us.'[34]

But the stillness and silence of the Barrier was suddenly shattered by the howling and yelping of Atkinson's dogs, who galloped right up to the tent door. One animal, who may have grasped the gravity of the situation, stuck its head through the little tent flap and licked the face and hands of the stricken Evans. To hide his emotion, Evans grabbed its ears and sank his face deep into the hairy mane of the grey Siberian dog. The two men, Evans recalled, were 'both dreadfully affected' by the rescue.

Atkinson immediately gave Evans and Lashly fresh vegetables, fruit and seal meat and began preparing them for the return to Hut Point. The men were placed on the sledges and the dogs charged off, covering the 35 miles in little more than three hours – a fraction of the eighteen hours it had taken Crean to stumble and scramble the same distance.

At Hut Point Evans and Lashly were reunited with the beaming and hugely relieved figure of Crean. Sadly, we do not know what Evans said to the Irishman who had just saved his life.

What none of them could quite explain was how Crean and Lashly had managed to survive the dreadful journey without succumbing to scurvy like Evans. All three had covered the same distance, eaten the same food and endured the same appalling weather and stress over the near four-month trip. Although Crean and Lashly were undoubtedly very weak, they had somehow managed to avoid the debilitating effects of scurvy.

Even today, doctors remain uncertain about why one person can be struck down by scurvy while another escapes. It is a complex subject involving the different rates at which bodies retain residual elements of vitamin C and the stress which the body is suffering at the time. In a normal environment the lack of vitamin C would bring on scurvy in a period of four to six months. But doctors would expect the ailment to be greatly accelerated in the hostile Antarctic climate when men were experiencing extremely hard work like man-hauling a heavy sledge over soft, sticky snow and feeling undernourished because of lack of food.

But doctors are convinced about one thing: people who smoke regularly are more likely to be affected by scurvy. Crean, however, defied even this piece of medical knowledge – he smoked a pipe almost every day of his life!

11
A tragedy foretold

The harrowing sight of the last supporting party – Crean, Lashly and Evans – aroused the first serious concern for the safety of Scott's polar team. The men at Cape Evans and Hut Point quickly realised that Scott's team might be in trouble, suffering the same effects of scurvy, hunger and exhaustion which had reduced Crean, Lashly and Evans to wrecks. Scott by now had travelled further than the three men and was still out on the Barrier with the temperatures sinking fast and the winter season closing in.

However, Crean, Lashly and Evans had returned with a generally optimistic assessment of the polar party's prospects of reaching the South Pole and returning safely. Crean had kept a constant watch on the horizon, expecting to be caught up by the five men on their way back to Cape Evans.

But, unknown to the outside world, the tragedy started to unfold almost from the moment Scott left Crean, Lashly and Evans on the bleak Polar Plateau straining their eyes for a final glimpse of their doomed colleagues. Although they moved off in hopeful mood, it took Scott less than 24 hours to appreciate the added difficulties of taking the fifth man, Bowers, when the entire operation had been built around four-man teams. On 5 January, the day after leaving the final supporting party, he wrote:

'Cooking for five takes a seriously longer time than cooking for four; perhaps half an hour on the whole day. It is an item I had not considered when reorganising.'[1]

The travelling surface was abominable, a clogging, cloying soft snow covering the frozen wave-like undulations of the 'sastrugi', which grew to several feet in height and made dragging the sledge immensely hard. It meant they were moving ever slower in ever falling temperatures. On 7 January they covered only 5 miles in four hours in temperatures of –23 °F (–30 °C). Scott also discovered Evans' badly cut hand and Bowers, a short man whose little legs sunk deep into the snow, was having a torrid time without his skis which had been depoted miles back on the Plateau. On 14 January he made the first reference to the run-down condition of Oates who, said Scott, was 'feeling the cold and fatigue more than rest of us'.

Scott, though tired from the heavy hauling, was confident of reaching his goal and on 15 January he wrote:

'. . . it ought to be a certain thing now, and the only appalling possibility the sight of the Norwegian flag forestalling ours.'[2]

A day later on Tuesday 16 January, the keen-eyed Bowers spotted a small black speck on the otherwise unblemished white horizon, which spelt the end of their dreams. Initially they thought it might be some piled up snow, but soon it became grimly apparent that this was a man-made object. They pulled on and eventually came across a black flag tied to a sledge bearer, surrounded by clear traces of dog tracks in the snow. 'The worst has happened,' Scott wrote.

The next day they marched on to the Pole in temperatures down to –22 °F (–30 °C) and Scott mournfully recorded:

'THE POLE. Yes, but under very different circumstances from those expected.'[3]

Oates, who took the defeat better than the others, said the dejected men were 'not a happy party' that night and Scott memorably summed up the enormous sense of disappointment after hauling and pulling for almost 900 wearisome miles (1,450 km) in dreadful conditions:

> 'Great God! This is an awful place and terrible enough to have laboured to it without the reward of priority.'[4]

The following day they came across a tent erected by Amundsen which contained a record of the Norwegian's achievement, a personal letter to Scott and a few items of surplus equipment such as a sextant and some socks. Amundsen, to safeguard news of his great achievement against accident on the return journey, had also asked Scott to deliver a letter to King Haakon VII of Norway. It was humiliating for Scott. His colleague, Raymond Priestley, would later write that Amundsen's letter transformed Scott from 'explorer to postman'.

After putting up their 'poor slighted Union Jack' and taking a few poignant photographs, the men turned for home. It was, like the last supporting party, going to be a desperate race against time and Scott was well aware of the hazards ahead. As they began the journey, he wrote:

> 'Well, we have turned our back now on the goal of our ambition and must face our 800 [geographical] miles of solid dragging – and goodbye to most of the daydreams.'[5]

The return journey began fairly late on 18 January, helped by the ground cloth from their tent which they rigged up as a makeshift sail to catch the strong wind blowing into their backs. But it was getting perceptibly colder, with the temperature down to −30 °F (−34 °C) by 23 January and Scott reporting that Evans was 'a good deal run down'.

Food, too, was causing a problem and on 29 January Scott conceded that the men were not eating enough to satisfy the demands of their continuous heavy labour. In short, they were hungry and getting hungrier as they pulled with increasing effort to cover the distances between supply depots. It is also likely that they were very thirsty.

A day later the men's worrying physical problems began to emerge, first Wilson straining a tendon in his leg and then Evans began to lose two fingernails because of severe frostbite. Scott was worried about both Evans' physical and mental condition and wrote:

'His hands are really bad, and to my surprise he shows signs of losing heart over it.'[6]

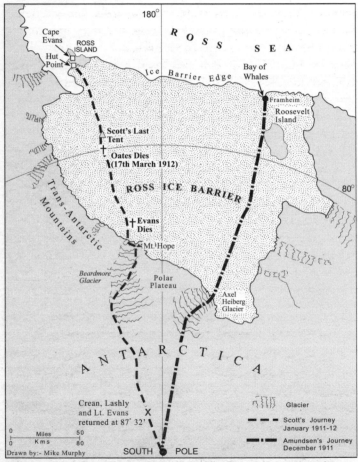

The route to the pole: Amundsen and Scott's tracks on their historic 1,800-mile journeys in 1911–2.

On 3 February the indefatigable Bowers stopped writing his diary and on 4 February Evans fell into a shallow crevasse. Scott commented that his long-time comrade was becoming 'rather dull and incapable'. The next day Scott recorded that Evans was 'a good deal crocked up' with frostbitten and suppurating fingers and a 'very bad' nose. On 7 February he noted that Evans was 'going steadily downhill'.

Evans had taken the Norwegian victory very badly, perhaps because it dealt such a severe blow to his ambitions of leaving the navy as a famous explorer and even making some money from his adventures. His demoralisation may also have stemmed from the fact that, psychologically, he was the least equipped to cope with defeat. Wilson suggested in his diary that his failure to cope was because he had never been sick before. Oates wondered how he would manage the remaining 500 miles (800 km) to base camp.

Wilson, the doctor in the party, believed that Evans' deteriorating health came from concussion sustained when he fell into the crevasse. More likely is the fact that Evans, like the others, was suffering from a serious loss of vitamin C and was in the initial stages of scurvy. A side-effect of scurvy is that the blood vessels became very fragile and it is probable that the fall triggered some form of brain haemorrhage. By 14 February Evans had virtually ceased to function as a full member of the team and on 16 January Scott grimly revealed:

> 'Evans has nearly broken down in brain, we think. He is absolutely changed from his normal self-reliant self.'[7]

The next day, 17 February, Petty Officer Edgar Evans died. It was 'a very terrible day' according to Scott. Shocked and alarmed at the loss of the party's strongest man, the four survivors pressed on down the last leg of the Beardmore and arrived at Shambles Camp where they feasted on depoted pony meat. For once the hungry men were full.

New life came with a full stomach but as they prepared for the 400-mile (640-km) slog across the Barrier, a new hurdle emerged as the travelling surface became almost impossible. On 19 February they exhausted themselves all day to cover only 4.6 miles on a surface which was likened to desert sand. Although the loss of the big Welshman provided them with a welcome dose of extra rations, Scott conceded that the party was missing the enormous strength of a fit, vigorous Evans.

As they plodded defiantly onto the Barrier, the men struck another insurmountable hurdle when they discovered a shortage of oil at the depots. The leather washers had perished in the cold and oil had evaporated, leaving the men facing the unhappy prospect of eating cold food and having little spare fuel to melt snow for drinking water. Temperatures were now plummeting and on 28 February the usually calm, influential Wilson ceased keeping his diary.

The men were over 300 miles (480 km) from safety and March began with temperatures sinking to –41.5 °F (–41 °C), or 73.5° of frost. With the rate of progress now slowed to one mile an hour, the men were obliged to march for at least ten hours per day to reach their supply depots.

The next blow came on 2 March when Oates uncovered his feet to show severe frostbite. The pulling had become extremely hard and by now the tired, cold and hungry men were spending one and a half hours each morning simply putting on their footgear, which further slowed them down. It was becoming clear that they were not moving quickly enough and on 5 March Scott wrote:

> 'God help us, we can't keep up this pulling, that is certain. Amongst ourselves we are unendingly cheerful, but what each man feels in his heart I can only guess.'[8]

On 7 March, Amundsen's ship *Fram* sailed quietly into Hobart, capital of Tasmania, with news that he had reached the South Pole. Amundsen's triumph was in stark contrast to the defeat staring in the face of Scott and his companions.

Over the next few days Oates' condition deteriorated and he was unable to get into the man-hauling harness, a humiliating moment for the once proud cavalry officer. On 10 March Scott reported 'things steadily downhill' and said that Oates 'must know that he can never get through'. Oates asked Wilson if he had any chance of pulling through and Wilson lied when he said he did not know.

By now the exhausted men were only capable of covering 6 miles a day and Scott did a dismal and disheartening sum. In his diary he calculated:

> 'We have seven days' food and should be about 55 miles from One Ton Camp tonight, 6 x 7 = 42, leaving us thirteen miles short of our distance, even if things get no worse.'[9]

It was a forlorn hope as the winter season approached, with temperatures plunging to –43 °F (–42 °C) at midday on 14 March. Scott insisted that they could not afford to reduce the rations to give them extra marching time.

They were now roughly at the spot where, according to his original plans, Scott had intended to place One Ton Depot. But to save the ponies from more hardship on the depot-laying journey a year earlier, he had placed One Ton about 30 miles further north. Had they reached One Ton, the men might have stood some slim chance of survival. They were in very poor condition but the massive depot contained sufficient quantities of food and fuel which might have given them time to recuperate and regain some strength. The major difficulty would have been the weather, which was deteriorating fast and would have made the 140-mile (225-km) journey to Hut Point perilous and probably impossible.

It is hardly surprising that at this point Scott became confused and mixed up his dates. He was therefore not sure whether it was Friday 16 March or Saturday 17 March when he recorded the ultimate tragedy for Oates.

Oates, bravely, asked to be left behind in his bag, but the three men refused to leave him. In the morning he woke up to the sound of a howling blizzard and, according to Scott, said:

'I am just going outside and may be some time.' As he slowly and painfully crawled through the tent flap, the temperature outside in the raging blizzard was −40 °F (−40 °C).

17 March 1912 was the thirty-second birthday of Lawrence Edward Grace Oates.

Scott depoted some surplus gear to lighten their load and set out to make One Ton, some 25–30 miles (40–48 km) away. A stiff wind was blowing and the temperature was down to −35 °F (−37 °C) on 18 March and −40 °F (−40 °C) the next day. Scott's feet were now in a terrible state and he grimly conceded that 'amputation is the least I can hope for'.

Scott, Wilson and Bowers stumbled forward by about 4½ miles and on 19 March came to within 11 miles (18 km) of One Ton Depot where they were laid up by another severe blizzard. The men had two days' food and the fuel had run out, so they were even deprived of the small comfort of a hot drink. The blizzard pummelled their little green tent for the rest of the week and the end probably came on 29 March 1912, exactly 149 days after they had started out from Cape Evans. Scott made his last and most famous entry into his diary on 29 March:

> 'Every day we have been ready to start for our depot eleven miles away, but outside the door of the tent it remains a scene of whirling drift. I do not think we can hope for any better things now. We shall stick it out to the end, but we are getting weaker, of course, and the end cannot be far.
>
> It seems a pity, but I do not think I can write more.
>
> R. Scott.

Last entry.

> For God's sake look after our people.'[10]

Robert Falcon Scott was 43, Edward Adrian Wilson, 39, and Henry Robertson Bowers, 28.

12
Fatal choice

Captain Scott made a fundamental error in his polar plans when he declined to include Tom Crean in the final party which went to the South Pole. Although it is a grisly exercise to dissect events after all these years, there is nevertheless a compelling case for declaring that the Irishman should have gone to the Pole and that his powerful presence might have made the vital difference on the fateful return journey. For Scott and his companions it could have been the difference between life and death.

Scott, it must be said, made two basic mistakes in selecting his final party to reach the Pole. First, he chose the men at the wrong time and second he chose the wrong men.

There is little evidence to show that Scott had picked his final team when the party first marched onto the Barrier in November 1911, at the start of the long journey. At his disposal, including himself, he had some 25 men, although this can be reduced to under twenty after allowing for injuries, alternative scientific work and the need for some like Ponting to return home on *Terra Nova*.

He started the trek with sixteen men, although arguably the best ice traveller, the Norwegian ski expert Gran, was left behind and consigned to a minor geological expedition. In addition, he failed to understand the strength and suitability of the dog teams and chose to employ them in a subsidiary role.

It seems a bizarre decision all these decades later, but Scott did not pick his men for the key stage of the journey until the journey was already half done. He had the months of idleness at Cape Evans beforehand to weigh up their strengths and weaknesses, and choose the men who were best suited for the lengthy trip.

With careful handling on the initial stages of the journey across the Barrier and up the Beardmore, he could have sheltered the final party from too much laborious man-hauling work. This would have ensured that the key personnel would be fresher and fitter to make the dash to the Pole and back. Instead the men all pulled and worked as hard as each other, so were almost equally as tired before the final lap.

In contrast, he did precisely that with the ponies, who in any event, were doomed to execution at the foot of the Beardmore. He decided that the ponies were to carry relatively light loads on approximately 150 miles of the 400-mile trek across the Barrier, although the unexpected shortage of feed did mean that they were eventually pushed a lot harder.

Scott's assault on the Pole was organised like a relay race, except that the men on the final stages were also used as pace-makers and were already severely tired when they were asked to sprint the final lap.

The first clear indication of the polar team make-up did not emerge in his otherwise frank diaries until 22 December, seven weeks after starting out and by then more than 7,000 ft (2,140 m) up the Beardmore. On that date he wrote the names of five men – Scott, Wilson, Oates, Bowers and Taff Evans – in the flyleaf of his notebook.

But by this stage, his options had been severely reduced. The underutilised dog teams under Meares and Dimitri, who had been travelling well, had gone back and so had Day and Hooper. This left twelve and on 21 December he sent another four men back – Atkinson, Wright, Keohane and Cherry-Garrard.

Over 60 years later in 1974, Gran would claim that Scott should have taken the strong young Canadian physicist

Wright, who was also trained in navigation, to the Pole.[1] Gran's view was that Taff Evans should have been jettisoned from the team. Wright himself said he was 'quite certain' that he and Cherry were 'in better shape than at least one who was chosen to go on'.[2] This was presumably a reference to either Taff Evans or Oates.

Scott was down to the last eight men at the top of the Beardmore and it is apparent that his deputy Teddy Evans was not destined to go to the Pole, partly for personal reasons and partly because he was on the point of exhaustion. He was also in the early stages of scurvy. Realistically this left seven. But Lashly, an otherwise wholly suitable candidate for the final party, had already been man-hauling alongside Evans for well over 500 miles (800 km) when Scott wrote the five names into his notebook.

Lashly, a powerful man, had been drained by the extra effort, though in different circumstances he would have been an ideal choice for the final party. Cherry-Garrard always insisted that Scott should have taken Lashly on the final lap, but this ignores the obvious weakness of the seaman after strenuous man-hauling hundreds of miles more than his companions.

To all intents and purposes Teddy Evans and Lashly were no longer fit enough for the task. This left six possible choices – Scott, Wilson, Oates, Bowers, Taff Evans and Tom Crean.

Scott had given little away about his final selection and even Wilson said he fully expected to return with the last supporting party. Scott, he said, was 'going to take the strongest fellows, perhaps three seamen'. The seamen in question were Taff Evans, Lashly and Tom Crean. But Lashly was already exhausted beyond redemption and Taff Evans was in decline, though it appears likely that Scott did not fully appreciate how badly the Welshman had deteriorated.

Scott himself was always destined to go for the obvious reason that he was the leader. But he also earned his place on merit. He was immensely strong and capable, despite being the oldest of the eight men.

Wilson was taken largely for personal reasons. He was by now Scott's closest confidante, had borne his share of the work far better than expected and his overall performance made a strong case for inclusion. He was also a doctor, which might prove helpful. But he did not expect to be in the final team.

Taff Evans was Scott's personal favourite, a man he had stood by during the worst excesses of his drinking and was always destined to be in the final party. Evans had been loyal and had proved a stalwart on many hazardous sledge journeys in the past. Scott also nursed the patronising notion that the 'ranks' should be represented at the Pole. Evans represented what Scott saw as the embodiment of the finest qualities of the ordinary British seaman. But Evans was beginning to fail by the time the party reached the top of the Beardmore, partly because of the serious cut to his hand and partly because as the largest of the party, he was probably not getting enough food. Scott chose to overlook this or simply did not spot it. Wilson had privately suggested to others that Evans was not ideally suited for the final lap but, weakly, appears to have refrained from giving Scott his blunt assessment.

There was also a sentimental touch to the choice of Oates, the cavalry captain. Scott wanted to reward Oates for getting the dilapidated ponies to the foot of the Beardmore and was also taken with the equally patronising belief that the army should be represented at the Pole. But Oates was already feeling the severe cold and limping because of the effects of a severe leg wound sustained in the Boer War which had made one leg slightly shorter than the other. It is also likely that he was in the early stages of scurvy. One of the early symptoms is that old scar tissue begins to weaken. Oates himself was undoubtedly surprised to be included in the final party and his friend, Atkinson, confided after the disaster than he had not wanted to go on. Scott was either not told about Oates' condition or let sentimentality affect his judgement, much the same as he had done with Evans.

Bowers, on the other hand, had emerged as a giant. His strength and organisational ability were astonishing and he developed an outstanding case for inclusion. Also, he could navigate, which was vital on the featureless landscapes of the Plateau and Barrier. Bowers virtually picked himself.

The shortage of trained navigators was another important issue. Only three of the final eight – Scott, Bowers and Teddy Evans – could navigate. But since Scott had warmed to Bowers, it meant that there was no alternative to Evans leading the last supporting party back down the Beardmore and finding a path across the Barrier. Teddy Evans' exclusion from the final party could be justified on that point alone.

Then there was Tom Crean, whose case for inclusion in the final party has been poorly considered by historians. Crean was among the toughest of all the men at Cape Evans and, more by luck than judgement, had emerged at the top of the Beardmore Glacier physically fitter than most. Indeed, Crean may well have been the strongest of all the eight men who stood on the Polar Plateau as Scott prepared his final selections.

Crean had been saved from much of the heavy labour of man-hauling because he walked the 400 miles (640 km) across the Barrier leading his pony, Bones, which was in the final batch of animals to be shot. His man-hauling, the most arduous back-breaking work of all, did not start until the Beardmore. It meant, for example, that he had man-hauled at least 350 miles (560 km) fewer than Lashly or Teddy Evans. More important, he did not have a nagging problem like Oates' weeping war wound or Evans' severely cut hand.

While the diaries and writings of the men on the Polar Plateau were already beginning to pick up indications of weakness here and there among the individuals, there is not a single reference to Crean showing any signs of deterioration.

Atkinson and Wilson, the two doctors, had a revealing conversation near the top of the Beardmore about the physical and mental fitness of the three seamen. Atkinson's choice was Lashly and Wilson readily agreed.[3] But, as has been demonstrated, Lashly was already seriously drained and would have been a liability. Atkinson then said he would take Crean, although Wilson did not altogether agree. But, significantly, neither Atkinson nor Wilson proposed taking Taff Evans – Scott's first choice.

Scott greatly complicated matters when, at the last moment, he decided to take an extra man to the Pole. The decision to raise the final party to five was a mistake, given that the entire expedition had been planned around units of four. But by then, halfway across the plateau and 150 miles from the Pole, Scott was probably worried about the pulling power of the weakening men. He felt the need for more strength on the final lap. He appears to have been aware of the collective weakness, but not all the individual deficiencies.

With hindsight, it is arguable that Scott should have made his final selection of the polar party at Cape Evans in October 1911, well before the cavalcade set out. The four – or even five – men could then have undertaken the lightest possible work over the Barrier and up the Beardmore, pacing themselves and leaving them fresher and fitter for the final dash.

In the circumstances, the best equipped four-man team to start from Cape Evans would have been Scott, Bowers, Lashly and Tom Crean. For back-up reserve strength he could have nominated Taff Evans and Wright.

But, on the freezing Polar Plateau, after weeks of strenuous man-hauling and niggling little injuries, the options open to Scott were strictly limited. In terms of health and strength, Scott and Bowers were fine, Wilson a marginal case and Taff Evans and Oates in decline. Teddy Evans and Lashly were too run-down even to be considered.

Crean, by contrast, was noticeably fitter than Taff Evans, Oates, Lashly and Teddy Evans, and more naturally stronger than Wilson.

Cherry-Garrard, some years after the tragedy, wrote that if Scott had stuck to his original four-man party the men would have survived every misfortune. Cherry's suggestion was a final team of Scott, Wilson, Bowers and Lashly, though Lashly was obviously in no fit state for the journey when the final choice was being taken after the haul up the Beardmore.

The final party, chosen from the eight men left on the Plateau, should have been Scott, Bowers, Wilson and Tom Crean. If Scott had wanted the extra pulling power of a fifth man, the choice would probably fall between Lashly and Taff Evans, though neither was in ideal condition.

Under both scenarios, Tom Crean should have gone to the South Pole and those who doubt his qualifications need only read about his remarkable contribution to the last supporting party. Crean was a colossus and even after an exhausting journey of 1,500 miles (2,420 km), still had the strength and resourcefulness to walk 35 miles (56 km) alone across appalling terrain, without food and shelter, to save Teddy Evans' life. The irony is that the day before his remarkable solo march, his friend Taff Evans died at the foot of the Beardmore and the Polar party had begun to disintegrate.

Crean's endurance and immense strength of character was to prove the difference between life and death for Teddy Evans. While it is generally accepted that Scott's final party were doomed to die, it is difficult to ignore the argument that the big Irishman might possibly have made the crucial difference. His outstanding performance on the last supporting party demonstrates that he would not have cracked coming down the Beardmore as Taff Evans did. Indeed, Scott noticed the loss of Evans' pulling power with the sledge immediately after his death and Crean's extra strength at this stage would have been critically important in covering vital mileage before the terrible weather engulfed the party just short of One Ton Depot.

It has been calculated that the Polar party would have reached One Ton Depot if the men had managed to travel a paltry 280 yards further each day between 4 January, when the last supporting party turned back, and when they camped for the last time on 19 March. Once there the men could have rebuilt their strength, weather permitting, for the final slog to

Hut Point, 140 miles (225 km) away. A slim hope, but hope nonetheless.

The case against Crean is that, if he had gone with Scott, he would have needed to cover about 300 miles (480 km) more than he did with Evans and Lashly on the last supporting party. Scurvy, in this case, may certainly have struck. Nor was there any realistic chance of survival, even if the party had reached One Ton Depot. A trip of 140 miles (225 km) to the safety of Hut Point in temperatures down to –40 °F (–40 °C) as the season closed in would have been a massive test for fit, well-fed men.

But what cannot be denied is that Tom Crean was the difference between life and death for Teddy Evans.

13
A grim search

The mood at Cape Evans and Hut Point in the early months of 1912 was initially optimistic. The first returning party – Atkinson, Cherry-Garrard, Wright and Keohane – had averaged over 14 miles a day on the way to the safety of One Ton Depot and there was a general belief that Scott would probably reach the Pole. Although everyone knew it would be a close-run thing because of the late start, the party was confidently expected to make it back to base.

However, Crean's dramatic return to Hut Point was a bolt from the blue which shook everyone from their complacency. His heroics in saving the life of Evans could not disguise the realisation that Scott, too, was probably in trouble out on the Barrier with the season closing in. The appalling state of Evans and the sight of hard men like Crean and Lashly on the brink of collapse had shattered any illusions that the Pole had been lightly won. Crean's arrival was the harbinger of doom.

Despite his punishing ordeal, Crean made an astonishing recovery, travelling with a dog team to Cape Evans on 23 February – only four days after he had staggered into Hut Point delirious with hunger and fatigue after his eighteen-hour walk across the ice. He was carrying vital news about the polar party from Atkinson, the doctor, who was now the most senior able-bodied man at base camp.

Atkinson had elected to remain at Hut Point with the sick man, Evans, and suggested that either Wright or Cherry-Garrard should take a dog team south to meet Scott's party on the return from the Pole. However, Wright was needed for other scientific work and with no other fit men available, Cherry-Garrard was placed in charge of the mission.

Cherry-Garrard was hopelessly ill-suited for the crucial task. He had never driven dogs before so he took along the Russian, Dimitri. But neither could navigate and Cherry's glasses, which he needed to combat serious short-sightedness, were a serious impediment to polar travelling because they frequently became misted.

Although Scott was relying heavily on the dogs to come out to meet him on the Barrier, he had contributed to his own downfall with a series of muddled and contradictory orders for the dog drivers. His specific order was that the dogs were not to be risked because they would be needed for other field trips. This was interpreted as meaning that the dogs were not to be taken too far south to meet the in-coming party, so Atkinson was not proposing an outright rescue mission for the polar party. Atkinson, acting on earlier orders from Scott, insisted that the polar party was 'not in any way dependent' on the dogs.

Cherry-Garrard, with deep misgivings, set out on 25 February and reached One Ton, some 150 miles (240 km) away from Cape Evans, late on 3 March. There was no sign of Scott. Cherry-Garrard, inexperienced and unused to command, was unsure what to do. In addition, the weather was so bad that it was impossible to see anything at a distance, which meant that he might easily miss Scott in the swirling snow if he travelled further south.

More important, there was a lack of dog food for a long journey. Nor was Cherry-Garrard equipped to improvise by exploiting the dogs Norwegian-style. He possessed the typical British mawkishness towards dogs and could not stomach the notion of copying Amundsen's brutally efficient method of killing dogs to feed the others as they travelled. And, of course, at the back of his mind was Scott's order not to risk the dogs.

He waited until 10 March and with no sign of Scott, departed back to Cape Evans with temperatures down to −33 °F (−36 °C) or 65° of frost. There was, he wrote some years later, 'little anxiety' for the polar party.

On the same day, about 70 miles (112 km) to the south, Scott's party were struggling to Mount Hooper Depot and Oates was on the verge of collapsing.

Cherry-Garrard, sadly, never forgave himself for not driving south and felt great responsibility for the death of his friends. However, he was not equipped for such a journey and there was no guarantee he would have spotted the party in the awful swirling weather on the Barrier. It is quite possible that the names of Cherry-Garrard and Dimitri would have been added to the casualty list if he had driven south, though it was no consolation for the sensitive, emotional Cherry-Garrard who brooded over the tragedy until his own death in 1959.

It was readily apparent that Cherry-Garrard and Dimitri had been weakened by their brief, three-week journey onto the Barrier in search of Scott. But Cherry and Dimitri had been fit, rested and well fed before they started. By contrast, the polar party was now seriously undernourished and had endured a terrible four and a half months' slog over more than 1,600 miles across the worst terrain in the world in rapidly falling temperatures.

The men at Cape Evans kept a constant lookout on the horizon to the south, half-hoping to see a flare in the distance from Hut Point which would signal that the polar party had finally come in. On 17 March, the day that Oates committed suicide, Cherry-Garrard calculated that Scott's return would be five weeks after the arrival of Crean at Hut Point, namely 26 March. He wrote:

'We feel anxious now, but I do not think there is need for alarm until then, and they might get in well after that and be all right.'[1]

By 25 March, the day before Cherry-Garrard expected the party's arrival, concern was beginning to mount among the men at Cape Evans. Gran's diary read:

'We have begun to worry a little about the fate of the polar party. No one says anything but you can see it in most of their faces. When the watchman comes down from Vane Hill each night to report, everything comes to a standstill in the hut and every eye is fixed on him.'[2]

Atkinson and Keohane went on a short man-hauling excursion to Corner Camp but were hampered by the poor weather which was by then engulfing Scott further to the south. On 30 March, the day after the polar party is likely to have perished, Atkinson said he was 'morally certain' that they were dead. Slowly, but with greater certainty, the grim reality began to sink in and each man began to come to terms with the loss.

Despite the tragedy, the men had little option but to buckle down and prepare for a second Antarctic winter. The *Terra Nova* had already left for New Zealand, taking the seriously ill Teddy Evans and others who for various reasons wanted to serve only one year in the South. Evans, still on the brink of death, had to be carried on a sledge to the waiting ship at the beginning of March. He was placed in a bunk and was unable to move until the *Terra Nova* reached New Zealand on 2 April.

Two others – the new cook Archer and the ex-*Discovery* seaman Thomas Williamson – had joined the shore party, which now numbered fifteen. Atkinson, now installed as leader of the expedition, reorganised things and placed Crean in charge of all the sledging stores and equipment. This was an important role because it was clear that at least two very substantial journeys would have to be undertaken in the

Antarctic spring and summer of 1912 and Crean's extensive experience on the ice would be invaluable.

Crean's heroic march and the 750-mile haul with the final supporting party had earned the Irishman even greater respect among his colleagues and his was undoubtedly a voice to be heard in any discussion about future plans. Few, if any, of the men at Cape Evans could match Crean's experience of ice travel.

Many years later, Gran would fondly recall the Irishman's substantial presence and stature at that time in the hut at Cape Evans. Crean clearly left a big impression on the Norwegian and in an interview in 1973 he said:

> '. . . [Crean was] a man who wouldn't have cared if he'd got to the Pole and God Almighty was standing there, or the Devil. He called himself the "Wild Man from Borneo" and he was.'[3]

Crean was also a popular member of the party and Wright described him as 'very good natured'. Debenham remembered that his 'quips and brogue kept the mess-deck part of the hut merry' and added:

> 'In the winter it was once more Crean who was the mainstay for cheerfulness in the now depleted mess deck part of the hut . . .'[4]

The first priority for the men at Cape Evans in the winter of 1912 was to locate Lt Campbell's six-man northern party which was long overdue, and unknown to anyone, was still stranded in the Cape Adare region. A rescue party, it was assumed, would be needed in September or October.

The second priority was the sorrowful task of searching for the bodies of their dead companions in the Polar party, although some felt this would be largely a waste of time. It was felt that the men had probably fallen down a crevasse on the descent of the treacherous Beardmore and were lost forever. However, the men felt a duty to try to locate the bodies, if only to establish that the men had indeed reached the Pole.

Atkinson, although a naval officer, was far less rigid and secretive than Scott in his approach and one innovation was that he openly discussed the spring travel plans with the entire wintering party. There was a lengthy discussion about the two options – either to look for Campbell or hunt for the bodies of the polar party. After an open discussion, they elected to search first for the polar party. To paraphrase Cherry-Garrard's assessment, they would be leaving live men to search for dead men.

The sun soon disappeared and the winter routine began, though the weather was noticeably worse than the previous year. Temperatures were frequently recorded as low as –50 °F (–45 °C) and winds were logged at up to 89 mph. One blizzard raged unbroken for eight days and the hut literally shook under the strain of the constant onslaught.

Conditions inside the hut were far more comfortable than in the previous winter. The fifteen men occupied the space reserved for 25 and they endured none of the food shortages which had characterised the polar journeys. But it was an altogether more low-key and subdued atmosphere than the previous year. In the grim circumstances, there was little to look forward to. They passed a fairly comfortable winter, peppered with the regular business of scientific readings, lectures, eating, and making preparations for the coming southern journey.

The men took as much outdoor exercise as the violent weather allowed and inside the hut, they played endless games of cards, draughts and bagatelle. Crean managed to win a billiards tournament in May, a game which Gran said was the 'very best medicine against low spirits'. The midwinter celebration was held on 22 June in the now customary fashion of any wintering group in the ice, with a lavish meal, elaborate party games and the obligatory mock Christmas tree.

A month later Crean celebrated his thirty-fifth birthday by shaving off his beard and discovering that there was to be an important change to the diet for the coming sledging season.

A rare picture of Crean taken soon after the ordeal of saving Evans' life on the Barrier, February 1912. (SPRI)

Crean (bearded, 3rd left) tucks into mid-winter feast at Cape Evans, June 1912, shortly before setting out to find the bodies of Scott, Wilson and Bowers. (SPRI)

Heroes. A rare photograph of Tom Crean (right) and Bill Lashly. The picture of the two Albert Medal winners was taken on board Terra Nova *the day the expedition returned to Cardiff on 14 June 1913. Crean's signature can be seen near the bottom of the photograph. (Trevor R. Cornford Antarctic Collection).*

The search party. Crean (1st right, arms folded) pictured on board Terra Nova *with members of the search party that had found the bodies of Scott, Wilson and Bowers in November 1912. Back row, left to right: Keohane, Williamson and Hooper. Centre left to right: Gran, Lashly and Crean. Front row left to right: Cherry-Garrard, Atkinson and Nelson.*

A hero honoured. Tom Crean (centre holding paper) leaves Buckingham Palace in 1913 with colleagues from Scott's last expedition after collecting their Polar Medals from King George V. Crean is holding the citation for his Albert Medal awarded for saving the life of Lt Evans.

Crean proudly displays his Polar Medals. (Crean family)

The Endurance *party prepares to set sail for Antarctica on the eve of the First World War, 1914. Crean stands 2nd from left, 2nd row, hand on rail, wearing flat cap. Also pictured are Shackleton (2nd row centre, white pullover), Wild (behind, next right) and Worsley (white pullover next to Wild). (SPRI)*

Polar Veterans. Crean (right) went South three times in fifteen years and here poses on board Endurance *in 1915 with Alf Cheetham, who sailed on four Polar expeditions. (SPRI)*

Alone. Endurance *stuck in the ice – 28 men stranded in one million square miles of the frozen Weddell Sea. (SPRI)*

Crean loved animals and Frank Hurley caught the gentle giant with an arm-ful of wriggling puppies on Endurance, 1915. *(SPRI)*

Hauling the boats. The cast-aways, who were drifting on an ice floe, made a futile attempt to drag their boats to open sea. The picture shows that the strain was enormous and they were forced to abandon their attempt. (SPRI)

After Evans' dreadful scurvy on the final supporting party and the likelihood that the polar team had succumbed to the same ailment, Atkinson now ordered the men to eat an onion every day. Gran remembered:

> 'I think this is a good idea, not only as a prophylactic against scurvy but also a foodstuff. At any rate, the men will get the impression that they're not just on a slimming course. At the moment the whole hut smells of onions.'[5]

The sun returned in late August and preparations for the southern journey gathered pace, with food and equipment being arranged and packed onto the sledges and the men getting a little more exercise as the weather improved. In mid-October they began to take horse fodder out to Corner Camp, near to where Crean had started his brave solo march to save Evans. *Terra Nova* had brought down seven mules from the British army in India, which Scott had ordered as insurance for a second assault on the Pole if his first attempt failed. The mules would now be needed for a different reason.

On 29 October 1912 the eleven men of the search party left Cape Evans, headed southwards on their mission to establish the harsh truth of Scott's last expedition.

As before, Crean led a draught animal, a mule called Rani. He was joined by Wright, Gran, Nelson, Hooper, Williamson, Keohane and Lashly. The dog teams led by Atkinson, Cherry-Garrard and Dimitri followed on 2 November. The aim was to travel at night when the surfaces were firmer, making 12 miles (19 km) a day to One Ton Depot.

It is impossible to know what was going through the minds of men like Crean and Lashly who, only months earlier, had battled against the most cruel and vicious weather and travelling surfaces to cross the formidable featureless landscape of the Barrier. The men would not have been human if they did not fear the Barrier and vividly recall to themselves how close they had come to perishing along with the men whose bodies they were now trying to find in the bleak, forbidding wilderness.

One insight into their thinking is contained in diaries kept by Debenham, the geologist, who had evidently spoken about the hazards of the Barrier to Crean and others during the long winter nights. He was discussing the prospect of a second winter in the Antarctic and wrote:

> 'One thing is very marked – a universal dread of the Barrier. When such "hard nuts" as Crean and Lashly say they would give anything not to travel on the Barrier again it shows it has a pretty bad effect.'[6]

Fortunately, it was an uneventful journey. Although the weather was cold and temperatures dipped below −20 °F (−29 °C), the two parties made solid progress and reached One Ton Depot at midnight on 11 November. Even at this very late stage, some even held onto the dim hope that they might escape reality and find the men alive. Gran later recalled:

> 'Our hearts beat a little faster as we drew near, for in spite of everything there was a tiny possibility that the Polar party had reached the place after the dogs had left. But no: we found the depot quite untouched.'[7]

They rose the next day, 12 November, and pressed on a further 11 or 12 miles (18–19 km) south of One Ton. Towards the end of their march, Crean was among the first to notice what looked like an old cairn of snow with a black flagstaff pointing out, lying about half a mile off to the right of their course. Keohane thought it was a broken bamboo from one of last year's camps. Wright, on skis, veered off towards the object. It was the tip of a tent. They had found the polar party.

Inside the small green tent they saw three bodies – Scott in the middle flanked by Wilson and Bowers. Wilson, on Scott's left, had his hands folded neatly over his chest. The flap to Scott's sleeping bag was open and his arm was thrown across his old friend Wilson. Everything was neat and tidy. Beside his head lay a bag of tea and some tobacco and under his shoulder they found a little wallet containing his three notebooks. Alongside the bodies were their final letters.

The cold had turned Scott's skin yellow and glassy and Gran said there were 'masses of marks of frostbite'. It was a 'horrid sight,' he added. 'It was clear he had had a very hard last minutes. His skin was yellow, frostbites all over.'[8]

The search party was deeply affected by the scene and Williamson admitted:

'I shed a few tears and I know the others did the same.'[9]

Atkinson asked each man to go into the tent one by one to see the bodies and make sure that there would be no dispute over the details of their sad discovery. Williamson remembered 'a most ghastly sight' and Gran was so upset that he had to leave the tent.

Crean, who had wept when bidding farewell to Scott ten months earlier, was again in tears. Although he had been very disappointed at not being selected for the polar party, the Irishman could not disguise the powerful sense of loss which he felt for the man whom he had loyally served for over ten years. In a letter written some time afterwards, he expressed his feelings:

'I must say I have lost a good friend.'[10]

Crean entered the tent and saw the bodies. Once again, the tears welled up inside and the big Irishman leant over and gently kissed Scott's forehead.[11] Some years later Crean remembered the mournful scene and wrote to an acquaintance:

'I was one of the search party to look for their last resting place and was first of the search party to see it some fourteen miles from One Ton Camp on November 15th 1912 [*sic*]. I noticed what appeared to be a tent because of the flagstaff about 400 yards

on my right. When I entered I found Wilson and Bowers were tied up in their bags, but poor Scott was not, proving that he had died last and been able to fasten up the bags of the others. They had all died as proper English gentlemen, although they were given the necessary medicine with which to take their own lives if they so desired.'[12]

While Crean was obviously distressed, he composed himself and graciously went across to Gran to break the historic news that his fellow Norwegians under Amundsen had been the first men to reach the South Pole. It was an enormously generous and noble gesture by the Irishman and many years later Gran still remembered the touching scene in the snow. In his own words, Gran recalled:

'Tom Crean came over to me and said, "Sir, permit me to congratulate you. Dr Atkinson has just found Scott's diary, where it is written that our people found the Norwegian flag when they came to the South Pole." I grasped the outstretched hand, shook it and gazed into his tearful eyes. Then I too was overwhelmed with emotion.'[13]

Atkinson read the diaries from cover to cover and then called the men together and passed on details of the tragedy, notably the loss of Evans and Oates. He read aloud Scott's 'Message to the Public,' which concluded with the now famous words:

'Had we lived, I should have had a tale to tell of the hardihood, endurance and courage of my companions which would have stirred the hearts of every Englishman. These rough notes and our dead bodies must tell the tale . . .'[14]

The men collected their watches, notebooks and other valuables and collapsed the bamboo tent pole over their fallen comrades. A massive 12 ft (3.6 m) cairn of snow was built over the bodies and topped off with a cross made from Gran's skis. Each member of the party signed a note recording the five deaths, which ended with the words: 'The Lord gave and Lord taketh away . . .'

The eleven sorrowful men then stood bareheaded on the bone-chilling Barrier and said their own silent personal farewells, forgetting for a brief moment the biting cold. It was, said Gran, 'a truly solemn moment'.

The next day they set out to find the body of Oates. All they discovered was his sleeping bag, a theodolite and a finnesko snow boot which had been slit down the side to accommodate his badly swollen and frostbitten foot. Another large cairn was built and a note attached to a cross which recorded the death of a 'very gallant gentleman'.

Crean had a special memory of Oates, with whom he had shared a tent in the first five weeks of the journey from Cape Evans. In 1918, six years after Oates' death, he fondly recalled him in a letter to an acquaintance:

'I will never forget him the Gentleman he lived and a hero he died.'[15]

Oates, too, was fond of Crean and shortly before the fateful expedition set out from Cape Evans in October, 1911, he had written to his mother that Crean and another unnamed man were 'splendid chaps and great friends of mine'.

The eleven disconsolate men finally returned to where they had found the three bodies and set up camp near the cairn. It was a sombre gathering and Keohane said:

'We had no sleep last night thinking of our dead comrades laying in the snow grave a hundred yards away.'[16]

It was bitterly cold and the wind whipped up the snow as the men began the journey back to Cape Evans. Gran travelled with Scott's skis, a symbolic gesture which ensured that they, at least, completed the 1,800-mile (3,000-km) trip to the South Pole and back. The quicker-moving dog teams returned to Cape Evans on

25 November to discover that Campbell's northern party had survived being stranded for a winter and were safely back at base. It was the first cheering news they had received for many months and their survival helped lift spirits generally.

Three weeks later the *Terra Nova* sailed from Lyttelton to pick up the 21 souls now camped together at Cape Evans. On board was Teddy Evans, now Commander Evans, who had made a full recovery from scurvy and in typical fashion, was raring to go. The little ship, a very welcome sight, sailed back into McMurdo Sound on 18 January 1913, to the noise of hearty cheers from the joyful men on the land. Evans shouted a cheerful greeting through a megaphone to the men gathered on the shore and was surprised at the silence which quickly descended on the little group. No one was quite sure what to say, or how to break the news. Campbell, now the most senior officer at Cape Evans, paused and yelled back:

> 'The Southern Party reached the Pole on January 18 last year, but were all lost on the return journey – we have their records.'[17]

Evans said it was a moment of 'hush and overwhelming sorrow'. *Terra Nova's* stewards hurriedly took down the banners and bunting and stored away the champagne and cigars which had been assembled to welcome the conquering heroes. A renewed sense of gloom soon descended.

All the men of the wintering party were anxious to get away from Antarctica, especially those with two years of isolated service under their belts. But there was one final solemn duty to perform before leaving Cape Evans.

It had been decided to erect a large wooden cross to commemorate their dead companions. Frank Davies, the ship's carpenter, set about the task of making a cross from jarrah, a hard wood from Western Australia, which would be able to withstand Antarctica's harsh and corrosive climate. Two days later on 20 January Crean trudged off with seven others towards Hut Point for the last time.

The men – Crean, Atkinson, Wright, Lashly, Debenham, Keohane, Davies and Cherry-Garrard – headed for Observation Hill, a 700-ft (215-m) volcanic cone overlooking the old *Discovery* camp at Hut Point and one of the most prominent and welcome sights to greet weary men returning from the Barrier. Crean knew Observation Hill better than anyone else. Ten months earlier he had somehow summoned the strength to scramble around the hill in the final stages of his walk to save the life of Teddy Evans.

The journey out to Hut Point was the last significant piece of man-hauling undertaken on Scott's last expedition and right to the end, the hostile Antarctic environment was determined to remind the explorers of its supremacy.

As they approached Hut Point, the wind struck up and Crean was nearly lost. He crashed through the slushy ice and no sooner had he been hauled out than the Irishman plunged back into the freezing waters for a second time. Fortunately, Crean was in his sledging harness and his worried comrades managed to pull him out before the weight of his thick polar clothing dragged him under. Some dry clothes were found at the hut and in customary phlegmatic style, Crean seemed unmoved by the experience. His temperament was firmly intact despite the ordeals of the past year and Cherry-Garrard recalled:

> 'You would not think Crean had had such a pair of duckings to hear him talking so merrily tonight . . .'[18]

The solemn duty of erecting the huge cross, which had been cut into several pieces for transportation, involved heavy hauling of the blocks of wood up the steep Observation Hill. Finally, by about 5 p.m. in the afternoon, the blocks were bolted together and the cross, measuring almost 12 ft and weighing close to 300 lb (136 kg) was erected.

For a brief moment the men punctured the tranquillity around Hut Point Peninsula with three rousing cheers for their dead comrades. As the silent stillness returned to the hilltop, the men cast a final glance upwards at the cross towering over them, which carries the names of the five men and the fitting inscription from Tennyson's *Ulysses*:

> '*To strive; to seek,*
> *To find,*
> *And not to yield.*'

14
A hero honoured

Crean was back on board the familiar *Terra Nova* as the small ship eased its way out of McMurdo Sound on 23 January 1913. The British Antarctic Expedition, soon to be known as Scott's Last Expedition, was nearly over.

While they had been away, the world had lost Florence Nightingale and Leo Tolstoy, and the passenger vessel, *Titanic*, had struck an iceberg on her maiden voyage and sunk with the loss of 1,600 people.

After a fairly reasonable trip across the usually treacherous Southern Ocean, *Terra Nova* sighted New Zealand on 9 February, the first glimpse of trees and vegetation since they pulled out of Port Chalmers well over two years earlier. The next day the ship slipped quietly into the harbour at Oamaru on New Zealand's South Island and the dependable Crean went ashore with Atkinson and Lt Pennell to provide the world with the first news of the tragedy.

Scott had an exclusive contract with the Central News Agency in London for information about the expedition and the men were ordered not to answer questions as they made their way to the cable office. A message would be sent to the Agency in London, who would then flash the news around the world.

The men returned to *Terra Nova*, dutifully dodging questions from inquisitive New Zealanders, who were surprised at the earlier than expected return of the ship. It was no easy task considering the huge interest in the expedition and Crean told Cherry-Garrard that they had been chased, 'but they got nothing out of us'.[1]

Terra Nova sailed away from Oamaru as the men unpacked their shore clothing and prepared to greet civilisation face to face. It was an uncomfortable preparation. Beards were shaved off, hair was cut, feet were crammed into tight-fitting boots and the men struggled into unfamiliar clothes that seemed as though they were last worn a lifetime away.

At dawn on 12 February, *Terra Nova* crept into Lyttelton, the White Ensign flying at half-mast. Small silent crowds had gathered on the quayside as the ship moved slowly towards her berth and the first visitors came on board carrying newspapers with big bold headlines screaming: 'CAPTAIN SCOTT DEAD'.

It was the first time the men appreciated the scale of the disaster and the effect it had on ordinary people. Understandably, the men had totally underestimated the impact the tragedy had made on the general public and Cherry-Garrard explained:

> '. . . we had been too long away and the whole thing was so personal to us, and our perceptions had been blunted: we never realised. We landed to find the Empire – almost the civilised world – in mourning. It was as though they had lost great friends.'[2]

Two days later on 14 February, King George V attended a memorial service at St Paul's Cathedral in London and an estimated crowd of 10,000 mourners stood quietly outside in the damp chilly winter air to pay their own personal respects.

Terra Nova returned to England as plans were being made to commemorate the dead and to look after the surviving relatives. The Lord Mayor of London launched a special fund which raised £74,000 (today: £6,150,000), almost double what the expedition itself had cost. Scott's widow, Kathleen, was granted £8,500 (today: £700,000) and a £300 annual pension (today: over £25,000). In contrast, Lois Evans, mother of three small children and widow of Taff Evans, was given £1,250 (today: £100,000) and a pension of £48 a year (today: £4,000). Even in death the British class system prevailed.

Terra Nova made its way back to Cardiff where, according to Teddy Evans, 'the real friends of the expedition' could be found. Kathleen Scott and her three-year-old son, Peter, came aboard on 14 June and there was a poignant moment for Tom Crean as he met the youngster.

The child grew up to become the naturalist and painter Sir Peter Scott and 70 years later he was still able to recall that distant day at Cardiff Docks. The highlight of the day, he remembered, was when the big muscular Crean took the awestruck little boy up to the crow's nest of *Terra Nova* for a panoramic view of proceedings below.[3] It left a permanent impression on the youngster.

Crean, too, showed that he had remembered the day and 22 years later in 1935 he wrote to Peter Scott, passing on some appreciative comments about his father and politely requesting a photograph of the young man. Scott thanked the Irishman for his kind comments and sent Crean a signed reproduction of a self-portrait of himself.[4]

Crean never forgot Scott, despite the obvious disappointment he felt at being excluded from the final polar party. While he might be excused for harbouring a sense of bitterness about the rejection, Crean never bore a grudge. Almost 60 years after Crean's own death, his two daughters recalled that they had never heard their father speak a bad word against Scott and they remembered him talking only in fond terms of his dead leader.

Scott's widow, Kathleen, also knew Crean and appears to have liked him. As early as August 1912, months before she knew that her husband had perished on the Barrier, Kathleen had been touch with Francis Drake, the expedition's secretary and paymaster. It had been decided – probably at the instigation of Teddy Evans – that Crean and Lashly should each be awarded a 'bonus' of £100 (today: £8,000) after saving Evans' life. Kathleen was wholly supportive of the plan and she told Drake in a letter dated 10 August 1912:

> 'I am so very pleased that you have thought of Crean and Lashly [Evans' rescuers]. They are both magnificent fellows. Both are old *Discovery* men and Crean has been with my husband in all his ships ever since. I know him well and in a personal letter to me . . . my husband says Crean is profoundly happy and ready to do anything and go anywhere.

> 'We shall all be very grateful to you if you have them suitably rewarded for indeed they are fine fellows and both of them very quiet and modest.'[5]

The surviving members of the party congregated at the expedition's offices in London's Victoria Street on 26 July 1913, and marched the short distance to Buckingham Palace. The men were presented to King George and Prince Louis Battenberg and were decorated with their Antarctic medals. It was a proud moment, though inevitably touched with great sadness at the loss of their five colleagues.

Kathleen Scott stood alongside Mrs Wilson and Lois Evans. Bowers' mother, Emily, collected her son's medal and clasp and Mrs Caroline Oates, the devastated mother of the tragic hero, specifically asked Teddy Evans to collect the honours on behalf of her dead son. Each man was awarded the King's Medal and the Polar Medal from the Royal Geographical Society.

Crean was awarded a silver clasp to go with his earlier Polar Medal. But there was a very special separate ceremony for Crean and Lashly, who were awarded the Albert Medal, the highest recognition for gallantry, for saving the life of Teddy Evans.

The Albert Medal, first issued in 1866 in memory of Queen Victoria's husband, was a rare honour, awarded on very few occasions. Only 568 were issued in its 105-year history, the medal being withdrawn in 1971 and replaced by the George Cross.

The citation gave only a brief summary of the last supporting party's ordeal and concluded with an almost casual description of Crean's heroics on the solo walk across the Barrier to fetch help for the stricken Evans. It read:

> 'After a march of eighteen hours in soft snow Crean made his way to the hut, arriving completely exhausted. Fortunately, Surgeon Edward L. Atkinson RN was at the hut with two dog teams and the dog attendant. His party, on the 20th of February, effected the rescue of Lashly and Lieutenant Evans, who but for the gallant conduct throughout of his two companions would undoubtedly have lost his life.'[6]

Ponting, the photographer, was somewhat more fulsome in his praise and said Crean's march had been 'one of the finest feats in an adventure that is an epic of splendid episodes'.

There was also praise for Crean from polar experts who, perhaps more than most, appreciated the full scale of his achievements. Louis Bernacchi, who had been with Crean on *Discovery*, said the Irishman made 'one of the greatest polar marches alone' and Dr Hugh Mill, a close associate of many famous characters during the Heroic Age and a later biographer of Shackleton, was equally struck by his deeds. While Crean was sitting out the Antarctic winter at Cape Evans in May 1912, Mill had written about the Evans rescue in the *Geographic Journal*:

> 'This is certainly one of the smartest pieces of work ever done in the Polar regions.'[7]

Teddy Evans, who was later to have a distinguished naval career and become Lord Mountevans, never forgot those who had saved his life and he perpetuated their memory by 'affectionately' dedicating his book on the expedition, *South With Scott*, to Crean and Lashly. A little earlier, at a gathering of the Royal Geographical Society at London's Albert Hall on 21 May 1913, Evans addressed the members and reserved a special appreciation for Crean and Lashly. Remembering their monumental struggle and life-saving feat, he concluded:

'No tribute could be too great.'[8]

There was another personal tribute and heartfelt thanks from Evans' parents who, after learning about the Crean–Lashly rescue and the death of the five-man Polar party, were fully aware of just how close they were to losing their son to the Antarctic. Mere words are often inadequate to express the gratitude which any parent feels when someone saves the life of their child and the Evans were brief and to the point. Frank Evans and his wife, Eliza, each sent Crean and Lashly a signed photograph of themselves with a simple inscription which needed no further elaboration to convey the sincerity of the message. Eliza's inscription to Tom Crean reads:

'In grateful remembrance of a mother for the saving of the life of Commander ERGR Evans, RN by Lashly and Crean in the Antarctic, in 1912.'

Crean also arrived back to civilisation to receive a warm letter from Oriana Wilson, wife of Dr Wilson, thanking the Irishman for his role in the party which eventually found her husband's body alongside Scott and Bowers on the Barrier. Mrs Wilson, writing from Christchurch, New Zealand, only two weeks after learning about her husband's tragic death, told Crean:

'I shall always be grateful to you all, that you persevered in looking for the tent. For as a result of your search I have had the comfort and help of receiving the last words Dr Wilson wrote to me, and I am more thankful to you all than I can say.

You were also one of the last to see him alive and I know from his letters how much he thought of you.

His friends shall be my friends and I shall always take an interest in your future. If it is ever within my power to do anything for you and yours at any time, I hope you will tell me.'[9]

After the medals ceremony at Buckingham Palace, the men walked back to nearby Caxton Hall for a farewell drink and the final partings. In the slightly austere central London setting, Scott's Last Expedition was quietly disbanded.

Crean, meanwhile, had been promoted to the rank of Chief Petty Officer in recognition of his extraordinary exploits in the Antarctic, his promotion dating back to 9 September 1910, when the *Terra Nova* had been ploughing her way across the oceans to New Zealand. It was a welcome gesture and meant a useful bonus from almost three years of back-pay.

However, there was one final piece of irony before the expedition drew to a close in the summer of 1913. According to Crean's official military record, the Irishman was listed as having died in the Antarctic on 17 February 1912, the day before he set out on his remarkable march to save Evans. The irony is that 17 February was the day that Crean's friend, Edgar 'Taff' Evans died at the foot of the Beardmore Glacier.

15
The ice beckons

Crean, now 36 and a veteran of two famous voyages of exploration to Antarctica, formally returned to the Royal Navy on 6 October 1913 and was assigned to the familiar barracks at Chatham.[1] He had been away from the navy for three and a half years.

For the second time in nine years, Crean now faced the job of reintegrating himself into the routine of naval life, a difficult task after the adventurous and high-profile years in the Antarctic. He had spent six of the previous eleven years on journeys to the south. Chatham, with its stiff formality and navy drill, must have seemed unutterably dull compared with life on the edge on the Barrier.

It was probably the unappetising prospect of a return to the pedestrian naval routine which at this point prompted Crean to take a momentous decision. After precisely twenty years in the Royal Navy, Crean now prepared to make his exit.

At the age of 36, he knew his formal naval career was approaching an end and it appears that the obvious alternative of a life in the merchant service held little attraction. Instead, his thoughts were of returning to his Irish homeland and settling down.

Shortly after returning from Scott's last expedition in the summer of 1913, Crean returned to his native Kerry and bought a public house in his home town of Anascaul. The old pub, with its decrepit thatched roof, was run down and hardly a thriving concern. As an investment it was a dubious prospect. But Crean, looking beyond his time in the naval ranks, wanted the pub premises primarily for its liquor licence. He was planning ahead.

It seems likely that Crean's ambition of retiring from the navy and opening a pub had been fostered during his time in the South. Taff Evans had been planning a similar move. It is thought that Evans, who had the responsibility of three small children, had set his sights on returning to his native south Wales where he would open a pub and perhaps enjoy something of a local celebrity status. He had also acquired first-hand experience of the pub trade. His wife, Lois, was the daughter of a pub landlord in Rhosili at the tip of the Gower Peninsula, near Swansea.

It is reasonable to assume that Evans helped influence Crean's decision to enter the pub trade, particularly as the pair had ample time to talk over their dwindling longer-term prospects in the navy during the many long days and nights together at Cape Evans.

But, unknown to Crean, momentous plans were being put together which would delay the Irishman's proposed smooth passage into the licensed trade. While Crean was weighing up his investment in the old thatched pub at Anascaul and settling back into naval routine, events elsewhere were beckoning him back to Antarctica.

A new expedition, the most ambitious ever contemplated, was being planned by his old *Discovery* colleague, the now famous Sir Ernest Shackleton. Although he did not know it at the time, Shackleton's bold plan would take Crean back to the South for the most remarkable story of all in the Heroic Age of polar exploration.

Shackleton in 1913 was a man without a mission. Amundsen had reached the South Pole and the lasting glory of the era had gone to Scott for the heroic and tragic failure of his last expedition. Shackleton's own achievement – the 'furthest south' of 1909, when he struggled to within 97 miles of the Pole – was largely forgotten by the general public which was now consumed with the Scott tragedy. But the lure of the South was too great for Shackleton to ignore and in response, he came up with the ultimate challenge, what he called the 'last great journey on earth'.

Shackleton's hugely ambitious plan, which began to take shape in mid-1913, was to walk 1,800 miles (3,000 km) across the Antarctic Continent from coast to coast. It was a task which no one had accomplished before and was a massive undertaking, even for someone with the imagination and flamboyance of Shackleton.

It involved taking a ship's party through the frozen and largely unknown Weddell Sea and landing a small group of specially selected men on the opposite side to Scott's base in the Ross Sea. The men would first march about 900 miles (1,500 km) across unexplored wilderness to the South Pole. They would then travel the same route taken by Scott, across the Polar Plateau, down the Beardmore Glacier and finally over the Barrier to Cape Evans in the McMurdo Sound – another 900 miles. The key to the bold plan was that the men at Scott's old base would lay down a supply line of food and fuel depots on the Barrier and up the Beardmore for Shackleton's party to pick up after leaving the Pole.

By the autumn of 1913, Shackleton was sounding out his many acquaintances for the princely sum of £50,000 (today: £4,000,000) to finance the expedition. He hoped to find a single backer to sponsor the journey in return for the now customary newspaper and publishing rights, scientific collections and the single honour of having the expedition named after him, or her. Helped by the additional promise of £10,000 (today: £800,000) from the Chancellor of the Exchequer, David Lloyd George, he broke the first official news of the expedition in a letter to *The Times* on 29 December. With typical flourish, he called it the Imperial Trans-Antarctic Expedition.

Initially Shackleton planned to take only one ship, dropping off men and supplies on the Weddell Sea side of the continent. The ship would then circumnavigate the frozen land mass to Cape Evans at McMurdo Sound and drop off the depot-laying party. But he later amended the plans and opted to take one ship into the Weddell and despatch another, the *Aurora*, to Cape Evans.

Shackleton decided to take six men on the epic journey. Mindful of Amundsen's almost leisurely stroll to the South Pole, he planned to take about 120 Alaskan and Siberian dogs, who would pull the heavy loads and save the men from the dreadful ordeal of man-hauling.

Early indications were that Shackleton proposed leading the march and would take along Frank Wild as his deputy. Wild, who virtually devoted his life to serving Shackleton, had already been on three expeditions to the South. He had been on *Discovery* with Scott in 1901–4, *Nimrod* with Shackleton in 1907–9 and with the Australian Douglas Mawson in Antarctica around the time of Scott's last expedition. He was by now a toughened polar veteran, hard as nails and thoroughly reliable.

Shackleton had also selected Bernard Day, the mechanic who had struggled in vain to get Scott's two motorised tractors to cross the Barrier with tons of supplies in 1911. Two others initially chosen for the journey were Aeneas Mackintosh and George Marston, both old *Nimrod* hands.

The unnamed sixth was to be 'one of two men who have had experience with me and Scott', Shackleton recorded.[2] This obviously fits the description of Crean but it is not clear whether he could not name him at the time because of his naval commitments or indeed that he had someone else in mind. In the event only Wild, Marston and Crean would go with Shackleton, while Mackintosh went with the depot-laying team in the Ross Sea party.

Shackleton knew Crean well from *Discovery* and had heard even more about the Irishman's powerful presence from Teddy Evans, who had become a regular acquaintance of Shackleton after his return from the South in 1913. Few knew more about Crean's strength and reliability than Evans who was alive only because of those very qualities. Crean's rescue was full testament to his endurance and courage and Shackleton could not fail but to be impressed with the story Evans told.

In addition, Shackleton knew that Crean was trustworthy and no sycophantic yes-man. Crean had a particularly forthright manner and was not afraid to speak his mind. Although this may have been less easy to accommodate within the strict regime of the navy, on the unforgiving polar landscape there was no room for half-truths and idle flattery. Shackleton, who came from the merchant navy, was far less of a disciplinarian than the strict Royal Navy types of the late Victorian era which characterised Scott's men and did not see the need to surround himself with servile characters. Also, he was fond of Crean.

For Crean the opportunity to venture South again was too much to turn down. There was one potential difficulty, however, which was the intense rivalry between Scott and Shackleton and their respective supporters. This antagonism had begun when Shackleton was sent home from *Discovery* in 1903 after the near disaster on the 'furthest south' journey. A dislike had grown up between the men and it erupted again in 1907 in a dispute over whether Shackleton could use Cape Evans as the base for his *Nimrod* expedition. Scott claimed priority over the area and Shackleton was eventually forced to winter there because he could not find a suitable alternative. Scott was furious and the rivalry intensified in 1911 and 1912 in the Antarctic as Scott became almost obsessive about beating Shackleton's best distance to the Pole.

But Tom Crean wanted no part of the simmering feud. He held both in high regard and in his simple, straightforward reasoning, the dispute was none of his business. Crean was loyal to his chosen leader. But equally he was always his own man.

Shackleton opened an office at 4 New Burlington Street in central London and invited volunteers to sign up. He was swamped with 5,000 applications to join the expedition, mostly from wholly unsuitable characters. The deluge of applications was put into three large drawers cheerfully labelled '*Mad*', '*Hopeless*' and '*Possible*'.

One particularly hopeful application came from 'three sporty girls' who promised to wear male clothing if 'our feminine garb is inconvenient'. Shackleton's biographers, Margery and James Fisher, said it was the only time in his life that he refused a challenge.

There is the apocryphal story that Shackleton opened the floodgates of applications by placing an extraordinary advertisement in newspapers which reportedly read:

> 'Men wanted for Hazardous Journey. Small wages, bitter cold, long months of complete darkness, constant danger, safe return doubtful. Honour and recognition in case of success.'

Apocryphal or not, the 'advertisement' is a reasonable summary of Polar exploration at the time and gives some indication of the types of people needed to undertake such journeys. Shackleton, in particular, was a shrewd judge of character and knew the type of men he wanted for his 'Hazardous Journey'. Tom Crean was one of those men, a true stalwart whose polar record was now second to none.

The precise circumstances of Crean's appointment to the Imperial Trans-Antarctic Expedition are unknown. Scott's biographer, Elspeth Huxley, claimed that Crean had bought himself out of the navy in 1912, which was erroneous on two counts. First, he spent the whole of 1912 out of touch with civilisation in Antarctica and, second, his service record shows that he had an unbroken career in the navy, apart from secondment to three polar expeditions.

Crean officially joined Shackleton's expedition as second officer on 25 May 1914, at a salary of £166 a year, the equivalent of £13,800 at today's values.[3] The formal contract signed away all Crean's rights to publish articles or books, hold onto scientific material or even speak about the expedition to a third party without first gaining Shackleton's permission. It was a strict agreement designed to give Shackleton full control of the profits from sales of literary and artistic works which, in turn, would help finance the expedition itself. But Crean did not care too much since he did not keep diaries on any of his three expeditions and was not a prolific letter writer.

Shackleton had by now made his final selection of the six-man party for the historic crossing of the Continent. It was to be Shackleton, Wild, Macklin, Hurley, Marston and Tom Crean. In contrast to Scott's secrecy over the final polar party and poorly considered last-minute choices, Shackleton was prepared to name his men before setting out, thus avoiding any disputes and disappointments when the expedition was under way.

Shackleton was a supreme optimist, which he demonstrated by proposing to cover the 1,800 miles (3,000 km) across the largely unknown Continent in only 100 days – a staggering performance for someone who was no expert at driving dogs. Amundsen had taken 99 days to cover much the same distance to and from the South Pole, but Amundsen and his companions were experts and experienced at both ski and dogs.

Wild was to be Shackleton's deputy on the expedition and another *Discovery* veteran, Alf Cheetham, was third officer. Captain of the ship was Frank Worsley, a tough Anglo-New Zealander widely known as 'Skipper', who joined up in strange circumstances. He claimed to have dreamt one night that Burlington Street in central London was blocked with ice and he was navigating a ship along the thoroughfare. Next morning he went along to Burlington Street and found the offices of the Imperial Trans-Antarctic Expedition and he was signed up after meeting Shackleton for only a few minutes.

In another bizarre episode, Shackleton decided to take a young medical student, Leonard Hussey, because 'I thought you looked funny'. Also on board was Frank Hurley, an adventurous photographer from Australia who had previously been to Antarctica with Mawson. The rest of the *Endurance* team included a crew of officers and hardened seamen, plus a mixture of doctors, biologists, geologists and other scientists. Shackleton, to one and all, was known as 'The Boss'.

Shackleton had already found his two ships. He bought the 350-ton Norwegian polar vessel, *Polaris*, and renamed her *Endurance*. She was destined for the main chunk of the expedition, crossing the largely unmapped Weddell Sea and dropping the trans-continental party somewhere on the Antarctic coast near Vahsel Bay. He had arranged with the Australian, Mawson, to take over the specialist polar ship, *Aurora*, for the Ross Sea party at Cape Evans. The Ross Sea party was to be led by Mackintosh and included Wild's brother, Ernest, the Antarctic veteran, Ernest Joyce, and a blend of scientists, engineers and even a padre, Rev Arnold Spencer-Smith who would go as photographer.

As ever, Shackleton's biggest problem was raising money. The Government had agreed to advance £10,000, which left about £40,000 (today: £3,300,000) to be raised from a variety of wealthy private donors. Typical of the supporters were the industrialist, Dudley Docker, who gave £10,000 and Janet Stancomb-Wills, the rich adopted daughter of a tobacco millionaire. The biggest contribution came from Sir James Caird, a jute manufacturer and philanthropist from Dundee, who generously gave Shackleton £24,000 (today: over £1,900,000), almost single-handedly ensuring that the expedition would go ahead.

The *Endurance*, specially built in Norway as an ice ship, was brought to London in June and berthed at Millwall Docks, Isle of Dogs. Work began to load the mountain of stores and equipment, including a wooden hut which would serve as a base camp on the Weddell Sea side of the Continent.

There was a constant trickle of curious visitors, eager to catch a glimpse of the explorers. On 16 July, the Dowager Queen Alexandra came on board, as she had done on the eve of the departure of both *Discovery* and *Terra Nova*. She later gave Shackleton a bible, with her handwritten message inscribed on the flyleaf. Worsley said the royal party stayed for an hour, taking their own photographs and showing 'a huge interest in everything'.

Crean, as second officer, was introduced to the glittering array of guests, who included Princess Victoria and the Dowager Empress Marie Feodorovna of Russia, and the formidable Lord 'Jackie' Fisher, Admiral of the Fleet. One of the party's doctors, Alexander Macklin, would later recall a humorous moment when the tall, burly Irishman was being introduced to the refined, well-heeled dignitaries. Macklin remembered a lady in Queen Alexandra's entourage:

'. . . laying a small delicate finger on Crean's massive chest opposite [a] white ribbon, asked "And what might that be for?" Tom replied, "That is the Polar Medal." "O," said the lady, "I thought it was for innocence."

One had to be familiar with Tom's hard bitten dial to really appreciate this piece of irony.'[4]

But in the midst of the preparations, the shadow of the coming war was growing by the day. The heir to the Austrian throne, Archduke Ferdinand, had been assassinated at Sarajevo on 28 June and the relentless countdown to the Great War had begun.

On 1 August, *Endurance* moved out of her berth at Millwall Docks and into the Thames; there was little of the celebrations which had seen *Discovery* and *Terra Nova* away from English shores. Attention was focused on the worsening diplomatic situation and the growing prospect of war with Germany. This time there was a small crowd and a solitary piper to wish the men *bon voyage*. In deference to Shackleton, Crean and the other Irishmen onboard, the Scottish piper thoughtfully played 'The Wearing o' the Green'.

The low-key send-off was no surprise given the deteriorating political climate, which was getting worse by the day. The world was moving inexorably towards war and on 1 August the final pieces of the macabre jigsaw were moved into place as Germany declared war on Russia. It drew Britain closer to the brink and many people felt that the expedition would have to be abandoned.

However, the ship sailed down the Thames to Margate on the north Kent coast where Shackleton called the entire party together and said each man was free to leave and join the war effort if he chose. Several men accepted the offer and immediately left to enlist. He then telegraphed the Admiralty offering to place the ship and its provisions at the military's disposal. Within an hour, the First Lord, Winston Churchill, had telegraphed a laconic one-word reply:

'Proceed.'[5]

On 4 August, *Endurance* sailed round the southern coast of England to Eastbourne where Shackleton disembarked and hurried to London to meet the King. Events were moving apace and Britain had now moved one step from war by giving the Germans an ultimatum to respect the neutrality of Belgium. Despite the mounting crisis, King George V saw Shackleton for 25 minutes, gave him a Union Jack and urged him to go South. At 11 p.m. on 4 August the ultimatum expired and the First World War had started.

Endurance went first to Plymouth and then sailed for Buenos Aires in Argentina on 8 August as the first shots of war were being fired in Europe. It was a largely uneventful trip under the leadership of the easy-going Worsley, although Crean was on hand to save the life of one fortunate sailor as the *Endurance* crossed the Equator in mid-September.

In the exuberant celebrations of 'crossing the line,' several seamen became very drunk and one tried to throw himself overboard. Crean rushed forward, grabbed the man's leg and saved him from certain death.

Shackleton remained behind in England, finalising his money-raising plans. He was still deeply concerned about the wisdom of disappearing off to Antarctica while the country was plunging into war but on 25 September he finally sailed from Liverpool and eventually caught up with *Endurance* in Buenos Aires in mid-October. There he weeded out the more unruly and drunken seamen, took on a few more willing hands and prepared to depart a world which, in itself, was on the brink of unimagined horror and sweeping change.

On 25 October the small British community in Buenos Aires gathered on the quayside to bid farewell to *Endurance* as she set forth for the island of South Georgia, the most southerly point in the British Empire. There was concern that the ship, despite its peaceful intentions, might be vulnerable to attack from one of the many German warships gathering ominously in the South Atlantic for what would later materialise into the Battle of the Falklands on 8 December. Shackleton, fortuitously, decided to abandon his original plan to visit the Falklands and instead headed for the island of South Georgia.

Endurance sailed peacefully southwards, the only diversion being the discovery of a stowaway on the third day out of Buenos Aires. This turned out to be a nineteen-year-old Welsh seaman, Percy Blackborrow, who was given a full-scale dressing-down by Shackleton. With a twinkle in his eye, he finally told the terrified lad that stowaways were the first to be eaten if things got tough on polar expeditions and the party ran out of food. Blackborrow's unusual recruitment brought the *Endurance* party to 28.

Endurance put into Grytviken, the Norwegian whaling station on South Georgia, in early November and stayed for a month, as the party made final preparations and took on the last supplies of coal. During this time, Shackleton spent many hours talking to the seasoned Norwegian whalers, who were in the middle of their hunting season and knew more than anyone on earth about ice conditions in the Weddell Sea.

South Georgia had been a centre for adventurous and entrepreneurial seamen for well over a century. Captain Cook had made the first landing in January 1775 and named the island after King George III. But his published account two years later, which gave the first reports of South Georgia's teeming wildlife, brought a huge influx of seal-hunters from Britain and America. By the turn of the twentieth century, after over 100 years of plunder, the seals had been hunted to near-extinction and new booty was sought. Norwegian whalers arrived and in 1904 established a base at Grytviken, South Georgia's most attractive natural harbour. Grytviken, which means 'Pot Cove', was named after the sealers' trypots found on the site.

However, what the whalers had to say was not very encouraging. The ice in the Weddell Sea, they divulged, was further north than any of the seamen could remember and they urged caution before allowing the ship to enter the hazardous, mostly uncharted waters.

But Shackleton was impatient to get under way. The expedition could wait no longer and on 5 December 1914, *Endurance* quietly severed links with the civilised world and pulled out of Grytviken on the first leg of the 1,000-mile (1,600-km) journey to the coast of Antarctica. The world would be a different place when they returned.

Departure was another subdued affair with none of the fanfare which saw off *Discovery* or *Terra Nova* from the New Zealand staging post of Lyttelton. There was no flag-waving, no bands to play stirring patriotic tunes and no thronging, cheering crowds to bid the party of 28 men a warm farewell. Shackleton remembered:

> 'I gave the order to heave anchor at 8.45 a.m. on December 5th and the clanking of the windlass broke for us the last link with civilisation. The morning was dull and overcast, but hearts aboard *Endurance* were light.'[6]

The mail ship, carrying the last letters from home, steamed into Grytviken two hours after *Endurance* had disappeared across the southern horizon.

Tom Crean's memory of home was still carried in the scapular he wore around his neck.

16
Trapped

E	*ndurance*, heavily laden with coal and equipment in the tradition of all polar vessels, pushed slowly across the Southern Ocean towards the Weddell Sea. But, as if to warn of the dangers ahead, three days out of South Georgia the ship ran into heavy pack ice at latitude 57°. This was farther to the north than anyone had expected and confirmed the fears of the experienced Norwegian whalers on the island.

It was just the first of many brushes which *Endurance* would soon encounter with the ice. The advice from the Norwegians to wait until the southern summer was more advanced must have weighed heavily on the minds of Shackleton and his senior lieutenants.

There followed several days as *Endurance* picked her way through the belt of ice, which Shackleton graphically described as a 'gigantic and interminable jigsaw-puzzle'. The worry, however, was that the ice stretched unbroken as far as the eye could see and Vahsel Bay, the ship's intended destination, was still nearly 1,000 miles (1,600 km) away to the south. To reach it, *Endurance* would have to sail in a semi-circle around the daunting pack of ice, heading first eastwards and then turning south, deep into the Weddell Sea.

The Weddell Sea, named after the nineteenth-century Scottish naval captain, James Weddell, was a largely unexplored area as the *Endurance* pressed south in late 1914. Weddell had sailed into the region in 1823 and named it after King George VI. It was not until 1900 that it was finally given Weddell's name, by which time its heavy pack ice had gained a fearsome reputation among seafarers. Even today ships rarely penetrate the waters.

By 1914, the sea had been only partially mapped by another Scottish explorer, William Speirs Bruce. It was Bruce who a decade earlier had crossed the sea and discovered Coats Land on the Antarctic continent, which he named after his industrialist backers. Ominously enough, Bruce was lucky to escape disaster when his ship, *Scotia*, came close to being crushed by the ice in the seas that were now *Endurance*'s intended destination.

Progress was painfully slow. *Endurance*, dodging and weaving, took twenty days to cover just 480 miles (770 km), or about one mile an hour southwards. Spirits were lifted by a typical celebration of Christmas, which included the now-traditional indulgence of a massive feast and a hearty sing-song. Hussey enlivened proceedings with an impromptu session on his banjo and there was a big demand for Irish jigs.

By early January the ship had passed 70° south and appeared to have cleared the worst of the pack by judiciously picking her way through the ice belt. Open water lay ahead and *Endurance* began to make good progress, eventually sighting the snow-shrouded peaks of far-off Coats Land. On 12 January they passed the land mapped by Bruce and ran close to new territory on their left which Shackleton named Caird Coast in honour of his prime benefactor, Sir James Caird, another Scottish industrialist to have part of the continent named after himself.

A little later on 15 January, *Endurance* came across a natural bay which had been formed by a glacier disgorging out into the sea. Worsley, the captain, wanted to seize the opportunity, land supplies and set up a base camp immediately. Shackleton disagreed. A base there would have added about 200 miles to their overland crossing and the proposed journey would be long and hazardous enough without adding to the mileage, he reasoned.

The ship pressed on, making good progress and raising hopes that Vahsel Bay would soon come into sight. A gale struck from the north on 17 and 18 January forcing the ship to seek shelter behind a mighty iceberg which towered over the ship like a floating mountain. The crew watched with considerable apprehension as smaller, highly dangerous bergs hurried past and crashed into each other in the swirling storm. Without the shelter afforded by the giant berg, *Endurance* would have struggled to survive the storm.

As soon as the gale abated, Worsley ploughed on, covering 20 miles (32 km) in a southwesterly direction and spirits were lifted at the prospect of making a landfall in a matter of days. However, these hopes were soon dashed when the pack ice suddenly reappeared and formed an insurmountable barrier.

The strong northerly gale had blown the ice pack against the land mass of Antarctica and *Endurance* was surrounded by an endless plain of ice which stretched as far as the eye could see in all directions. Only a similar gale from the opposite – southerly – direction offered any hope of opening the ice and releasing them.

It had taken almost seven weeks to reach this spot and the 28 men were now resigned to sit back and wait for the winds that would open up a pathway to the safety of Vahsel Bay. In maritime terms the landing spot was almost within spitting distance, barely 80 miles (130 km) across the horizon.

The party awoke next day to find that the ice had closed all around *Endurance*. The ship was stuck fast. It was 19 January 1915, at latitude 76° 34'. *Endurance* was a tiny, lonely speck of stranded humanity in a million square miles of frozen, treacherous and unmapped seas.

There was no immediate concern on board, partly because there was still perhaps six weeks of summer weather ahead for the ship to work herself free. Experience had shown that the ice frequently broke up towards the end of the season. *Discovery*, for example, had been imprisoned for two years and not freed until mid-February, the equivalent of late summer in the northern hemisphere. Also, the ship was drifting slowly in a southwesterly direction which, if it continued, would bring them nearer to their intended destination at Vahsel Bay.

But the weather was ominously poor for the time of the year and after ten days of captivity, Shackleton ordered that the ship's boilers, which devoured half a ton of coal a day, should be allowed to go out to save fuel. As the dull repetitive chugging of the engines died away, an eerie silence descended over the white plain, interrupted only by the idle chattering of the men and occasional yelping of the discontented dogs. Thoughts began to turn to the prospect of the ship remaining in the icy grip of the pack throughout the coming winter.

Winter routine, which men like Crean, Wild and Shackleton knew only too well, gradually took over as they began to reconcile themselves to perhaps months of captivity. Few could take their minds off their predicament. One crew member gloomily recalled that the German explorer, Wilhelm Filchner, was beset in the Weddell ice only a few years earlier and had drifted over 600 miles (1,000 km) before finding open water.

Endurance, though firmly ice-bound, was still drifting slowly in a southwesterly direction. Ironically, the ship was edging ever more slowly towards Vahsel Bay. But as the days and weeks passed by, it became necessary to make plans for the Stygian gloom of a dark, isolated winter before the sun disappeared for months. For some it would be their first time. For others like Crean, Wild and Shackleton it was all too familiar, but no less threatening.

Shackleton made one final strenuous attempt to free the ship on 14 February when he raised steam and ordered the men out onto the ice with picks and chisels to force their way through the encircling pack. They even employed a makeshift long-bladed saw in an effort to slice through the ice. For two days the ship strained and heaved and the men on the ice battled to carve out a channel which would free *Endurance*. It was, said Shackleton, 'terrific labour' but there were still 400 yards (365 m) of heavy ice blocking the ship's path.

Every opening won by tremendous physical effort by the men was soon wiped out as the sea immediately froze over in the very low temperatures. It was the moment when Shackleton and experienced hands like Crean realised that the game was up. *Endurance* was helpless, locked in for the winter. Shackleton wrote:

> '. . . reluctantly, I was compelled to admit that further effort was useless.'[1]

Understandably, the men were deeply disappointed and began to come to terms with the unpalatable prospect of a winter drifting ice-bound in the Weddell Sea.

They considered the obvious option of trekking what was now the 60-odd miles (100 km) across the ice to Vahsel Bay and building a hut for the winter. It was, by any standards, a short journey. Indeed, on clear days it was possible to glimpse the area from the crow's nest.

But travel would be very difficult, if not impossible. The ice was broken and hummocky and it was already late in the season, with temperatures set to plummet. Each return journey of 120 miles (190 km) with supplies and equipment over unknown terrain would take perhaps ten days, possibly more. There was no realistic prospect of carrying the tons of food, oil and equipment – enough to keep 28 men alive for at least one year – across the treacherous ice before winter set in.

In addition, there was no guarantee that the ice was solid all the way to Vahsel and they faced the possibility of meeting impassable channels of open water which might cut them off from the ship.

In short, the trek to Vahsel Bay was a non-starter.

The ship, meantime, continued its slow drift southwards and on 22 February reached 77°, which was to prove the expedition's 'furthest south'. But the summer had gone, the sun was dipping lower and the temperatures were sinking. At this point, *Endurance* began to change direction and change its drift from the south to northwards. The land near Vahsel Bay, which was so tantalisingly close, began to disappear across the horizon.

Two days later, the stranded party ceased to observe ship's routine and the *Endurance* officially became a winter station. A thorough review of stores and equipment was ordered and the men began to slaughter seals for winter rations.

Kennels – known as 'dogloos' – were built on the ice to house the dogs and on board the ship, living quarters were adapted for the winter routine. McNeish, the carpenter who was widely known as 'Chips', built neat little cubicles in the forehold after supplies were transferred to the now-empty coal bunkers. Crean found a home in cubicles in the wardroom alongside the other senior characters, Wild, Worsley and Marston.

He was also preoccupied with a set of four puppies born to one of the dogs. Crean adopted the pups and cheerfully posed for Hurley to take a memorable photograph showing the muscular Irishman, smoking his pipe and gently clutching an armful of furry wriggling animals.

Crean's dogs became a welcome diversion from the monotony of captivity and worry about their plight. Hurley laconically wrote that Crean had become 'foster father' to the pups, while Worsley felt the small animals looked upon the Irishman as their mother. One dog, he reported, raised a 'dismal howl' the moment Crean went out and only 'ceases his lament' when he returned.

In May, Crean began taking the pups for runs with the sledge and Shackleton observed that they just managed to keep abreast, 'occasionally cocking an eye with an appealing look in the hope of being taken aboard for a ride [with] their foster father, Crean'.[2] By August he was able to put the young dogs into harness for the first time and he was hopeful that they would mature into fully-fledged sledge-dogs. Worsley remembered:

'Crean has practically completed their education in sledging – but his language – it sounds terrible to my tender young ears.'[3]

Nevertheless, the ship's party was agreed that Crean's dogs were, as Worsley put it, 'wonderfully trained'. He explained:

'Crean places his box of hoosh between his double row of kennels and roars out an order – "Kennels". In a second every dog has retired into his abode and nothing but noses and appealing eyes is to be seen. Although the dogs are ravenous – as dogs always are – and the food within easy reach, not one attempts to help himself, but waits obediently till Crean capsizes a bowl of hoosh on their floor where it disappears with marvellous rapidity.'[4]

Crean's fondness of animals also provided him with an unusual moment, capturing the eccentric behaviour which occasionally enlivened the otherwise dullness of daily life on the slowly drifting ice. Worsley, an impulsive character, suddenly jumped up one morning and decided to take a 'snow bath', even though temperatures were 29° below freezing. He recorded the moment in his diary, writing:

'Poor Crean was taking his pups for their morning con-stitutional and on catching sight of me naked in the snow nearly fainted – thinking I'd "gone wrong in the napper". Now everyone except myself, is sorry for me and say it is a pity to see one so young go wrong.'[5]

There were far more serious moments for the Irishman and on one occasion he suffered another very close brush with disaster. Crean had joined two others on an improvised platform trying to break up a large chunk of ice which had forced its way alongside the ship. Suddenly the ice broke, pinning him between an 11-ft (3.3-m) iron ice 'pricker' and the platform. Frantic efforts by his colleagues freed the trapped man and Crean escaped with little more than a few bad bruises.

Crean had been in danger of having his legs broken or being pulled under the freezing water. Not for the first time in the South, Crean was very lucky and Worsley remembered:

> 'He was soon extricated, fortunately, with no worse damage than some bad bruises inside his legs, but the thick iron pricker had been bent against him to an angle of 45°.'[6]

On another occasion, he fell through a crack in the ice and was dragged into the freezing waters by his heavy clothing. After being pulled out, Crean stripped out of his soaking clothes and was hurriedly dressed in any spare clothing which could be found. Wild said that Crean was 'almost paralysed before he was reclothed and was some time before he recovered from the shock'.

Unlike the frigid atmosphere of Scott's cabins, the *Endurance* was a more relaxed, informal setting where class distinction and rank were observed more casually. Shackleton, in particular, was more approachable and although discipline was maintained, all the party felt more involved than was apparent on earlier expeditions. There was, like all polar expeditions, tension between individuals living on top of each other in cramped confinement, but on the whole the 28 men co-existed remarkably well, even if the mental strain became increasingly tough on some members. Attempts were made to keep the men as busy as possible and everyone was encouraged to join in regular games of football or hockey on a conveniently flat piece of floe.

An urgent requirement was food for the coming winter. Parties went out onto the slow-moving ice to find and butcher as many seals as possible. By mid-April they had accumulated 5,000 lb (2,265 kg) of meat and blubber, which was likely to last at least three months and avoid dipping into the provisions of tinned food, earmarked for the continental crossing.

Crean was placed in charge of sledges and sledging gear. It would be necessary to get the sledges ready for any emergencies which might arise, such as the crushing of the ship or a dash for land. In addition, the decision underlined Shackleton's determination to press ahead with the trans-continental expedition, despite the huge setback of seeing *Endurance* ice-bound and helpless.

Shackleton had not given up hope of completing the mammoth task of crossing Antarctica, regardless of their current plight. Indeed, the supreme optimist saw the entrapment as one of delay rather than abandonment. He believed that *Endurance* would drift north, clear the pack ice and return to South Georgia, where she would be restocked and equipped for a return to Vahsel Bay in the following summer.

Stores and clothing had been set aside for the great journey and six dog handlers were appointed to look after the animals. Significantly, these were the men originally chosen for the trans-continental crossing – Crean, Wild, Hurley, Marston and Macklin. The sixth was McIlroy, the surgeon, who stood in as the driver of Shackleton's team.

The reality of the situation was somewhat different. *Endurance* was adrift, like a cork in the ocean, moving slowly northwards at an average of about 1 mile (1.6 km) a day in a clockwise direction. But the ship was totally at the mercy of the ice. Indeed, *Endurance* was a ship only by name.

The nearest known land was a host of tiny uninhabited islands off the spindly Graham Land peninsula which stretches out like a finger from the Antarctic Continent pointing towards the southern tip of South America. But these islands, such as Joinville, Snow Hill or Paulet, were well over 600 miles (1,000 km) away to the north and there was no guarantee that, even if they reached an island, any rescuers would look there for a stranded party. The territory to the immediate west, Palmer Land, was uncharted and totally unknown. Nor was there even a remote prospect of relief, even if they succeeded in crossing the broken chaotic ice. Their best hope, assuming that they could reach the tip of Graham Land, was the slim chance of meeting a passing whaler. But the old saying of finding a needle in a haystack came to mind.

Apart from optimistically keeping alive his plans for the great journey, Shackleton also worked very hard to maintain morale and discipline as the *Endurance* party slipped deeper and deeper into the cold blackness of Antarctic winter. The scientists kept busy with their work, and endless tasks were found to keep the men occupied.

Routine was important. The party all rose sharply for breakfast at 9 a.m. and evenings were given over to informal discussions or sing-songs, a stark contrast to the rigidity of Scott's lectures. At one stage a dog race was run amid a flurry of frantic gambling. It hardly seemed to matter that the spectators, huddled in the inky blackness which prevailed even at midday, could barely see the outcome of the 'Antarctic Derby'. Wild, though, claimed victory, pushing Crean's team into third place.

Midwinter's day, true to custom, was celebrated as a substitute Christmas, with flags and streamers, ludicrous fancy dress and the usual excess of food and drink. True to tradition, the men retired to their bunks warm and satisfied, comforted by the fact that they had now passed the halfway point in their winter sojourn.

Another comfort was that, so far, *Endurance* had not been troubled by pressure from the ice-pack. But, soon after mid-winter, conditions began to deteriorate. Winds screeched to 70 mph and temperatures plunged to −35 °F (−37 °C). Worse still, the winds began to attack the ice and transform the once-solid ice-pack into a twisted, broken jumble of distorted ice hummocks. When caught by the fierce winds, the ice began to move and grind, creating the sort of deadly pressure which can crush a ship like a matchwork model.

Worsley said it was like an 'enormous train with squeaky axles' and was mingled with 'moans and groans of damned souls in torment'.

The men were both impressed and appalled at the awesome power of the pressure and on 1 August they were given a clear sign of just how powerful. There was a rumble and suddenly the ice began to scatter and break up, before forcing *Endurance* up out of the water. The pressure was cracking the floe, forcing masses of ice underneath the ship, lifting the vessel out of the sea and inflicting severe damage to the rudder. The ship listed about ten degrees and the men began to realise their vulnerability. It was exactly one year to the day that *Endurance* had sailed away from the London dockside full of hope.

As a precaution, the dogs were brought on board the ship and warm clothing was gathered together. Chips McNeish placed photographs of his loved ones inside his Bible.

By now thoughts were turning towards the very real prospect that *Endurance* was doomed and that the men would have to abandon ship in the desolate Weddell Sea, at least 1,000 miles (1,600 km) from other humans. The prospect of abandoning *Endurance* had been in the air for some time and Shackleton himself admitted that the vessel was probably lost during a brief discussion with Wild and Worsley in July.

But Shackleton was determined to remain on the ship for as long as possible, particularly as it provided essential shelter against the howling gales and sub-zero temperatures. No one wanted even to contemplate spending the remaining darkened winter months in a tent on the slowly moving ice, which might crack at any time.

Towards the end of August, Shackleton calculated that after months of drifting, the ship was now 250 miles (400 km) from the nearest known but uninhabited land to the west. It was at least 500 miles (800 km) to the nearest outpost where they might possibly find other humans and relief, but there was no guarantee and they could not afford to risk it. South Georgia, the only certain place of finding relief, was approximately 1,000 miles (1,600 km) away.

However, *Endurance* was now entering the most dangerous area of the Weddell, the region where thousands of square miles of ice press up against the Antarctic land mass to the west. *Endurance* was stuck, vice-like, and coming under repeated attack from the grinding pressure. It was as though the ice was slowly closing in on its prey.

In mid-October, *Endurance* briefly became a ship once again when, after a period of pressure, a narrow lead of open water suddenly emerged. Worsley even raised sail, but the ice closed in again on 17 October. On 24 October shock waves of the relentless pressure caused the first serious leaks and the ship began to list badly at an angle of 30°. Water poured in, McNeish struggled to plug the gaps and the pumps worked frantically. Others began packing Crean's sledges.

Endurance, languishing at a crazy angle halfway out of the water, was now in her death throes as wave after wave of pressure hit the stricken vessel against a background cacophony of creaking and groaning timbers. Hurley remembered that the ship was the 'embodiment of helpless futility' as the men scrambled to shift all the precious gear and food onto the ice.

Shackleton reported that huge blocks of ice weighing many tons were lifted into the air and tossed aside as other masses rose beneath the ship. The men, he recalled, were 'helpless intruders in a strange world'.

The three small life boats were untied and made ready for lowering. Below decks someone sang a sea shanty as the water continued to pour in and Green, the cook, dutifully made supper as though nothing was wrong.

Endurance finally submitted on 27 October, the ship being mercilessly squeezed on both sides and her beams cracking under the immense strain. The ship, arching like a bow, was letting in torrents of water. Macklin recalled that no one actually ordered the men to stop pumping out water, they just simply gave up. At about 5 p.m., Shackleton gave the order to abandon ship.

It was a sorrowful moment, the official end of the Imperial Trans-Antarctic Expedition. But it was the start of the most remarkable fight for survival in Antarctica's history.

The 28 men clambered off the ship and huddled together in a collection of tents on a relatively stable chunk of the ice a few hundred yards from the doomed and sinking vessel. Around them was an untidy jumble of hastily-salvaged gear, food, sledges, 60 barking dogs and three small boats.

The men had drifted almost 1,200 miles (1,950 km) in a semi-circular direction over the past ten months and were stranded at 69° 5' S in temperatures of –5 °F (–20 °C). It was 364 miles (585 km) to the uninhabited Paulet or Snow Hill Island to the northwest where, it was recalled, a small hut had been built and stored with supplies in 1902.

At this stage, the weary, disappointed men had not fully calculated how they would possibly haul supplies and equipment across the disorderly muddle of broken ice. Or whether anyone would bother looking for them when they were supposed to be tucked up 1,000 miles (1,600 km) away at Vahsel Bay.

It was 27 October 1915, and the outside world was not expecting to hear from *Endurance* until at least the following February or March, perhaps even later.

The reality was that the 28 men were stuck on the ice, they had no means of communicating with the outside world and no one was looking for them.

17
Cast adrift

On the ice the men could hear the dying agonies of *Endurance* as the ship groaned and creaked under the weight of the immense pressure which slowly strangled the vessel in its vice-like hold. If the ship had been a living thing, someone would have ended her misery.

Few managed a good night's sleep, partly because the ice floe beneath was constantly cracking and on three occasions they were forced to move the tents to a more secure-looking spot. Alongside the men were the three little boats which were lifted off the dying ship. They alone seemed to offer a tenuous chance of survival – if they could escape the ice and reach the open sea.

There were only five tents to accommodate the 28 men gathered together on the drifting ice floe as they sought shelter and comfort only 200 yards (182 m) from the doomed *Endurance*. Also there were only eighteen reindeer-fur sleeping bags and the unlucky ones had to sleep in woollen bags, which held the damp and offered less protection against the freezing temperatures. The unfortunate ten were wisely chosen by lot to avoid any unnecessary friction or claims of favouritism.

But Shackleton ensured that each tent had its own natural leader, aware that maintaining discipline and morale would be essential in the struggle ahead. A decline in morale could spread like wildfire and lead to anarchy. He chose leaders carefully and placed Crean in charge of Number Four, a small hoop tent which also contained two polar veterans, Marston and Cheetham, and the cheerful, banjo-playing meteorologist, Hussey.

Over the next few days, the men made repeated trips to rescue precious supplies and equipment from *Endurance* before she met her inevitable end. These were melancholic little excursions for the men who understandably saw the ship as their last link with civilisation. Psychologically the loss of the ship meant severing the umbilical cord and on one trek a party of men respectfully hoisted the Union Jack. At least the ship would go down with colours flying.

The men were ordered to prepare themselves for the coming journey across the ice and hopefully to the edge of the open sea, where they would launch the little boats. Crean had already arranged the packing of the sledges with as many rations as he could reasonably stow and along with others, he was also deployed on frequent trips to hunt for seals.

With a tough journey ahead, the men were issued with a completely new set of underwear, socks and Burberrys and asked to limit their personal possessions to a modest 2 lb (0.9 kg) in weight. It meant many heartbreaking choices as the men considered what to keep and what to throw away in the snow.

Shackleton emphasised that nothing was of value if it worked against their survival. As he spoke, he took out his own gold watch, gold cigarette case and a few gold sovereigns and theatrically tossed them into the snow. He then opened the Bible which Queen Alexandra had given the ship a little over a year earlier and tore out the flyleaf containing her personal message. He also ripped out a single page containing verse a from the Book of Job, which reads:

> *'Out of whose womb came the ice?*
> *And the hoary frost of Heaven, who hath gendered it?*
> *The waters are hid as with a stone.*
> *And the face of the deep is frozen.'*

There were exceptions. Hussey, for example, was ordered to keep his banjo even though it weighed about 12 lb (5.4 kg) because, as Shackleton explained, it was 'vital mental medicine'. The surgeons' medical instruments were kept for obvious reasons and those who kept diaries were allowed to hang onto them.

But all around them on the ice were scattered forlorn reminders of home and the ordinary trappings of a normal life – personal keepsakes, books, clothes, plus more practical reminders of their original purpose, like scientific instruments, telescopes and carpenter's tools. Tom Crean kept the scapular around his neck.

Before they prepared to leave, Crean was called upon to administer a particularly grim chore. There was no room on the trek for those who could not pull their weight so three of Crean's carefully nurtured pups and Chips McNeish's popular cat, Mrs Chippy, were shot. It was Crean, who was so fond of animals, who executed the animals. Even a tough polar hand like Crean was affected by the unhappy, but necessary task and Worsley recalled:

> 'Macklin, Crean and Chips seem to feel the loss of their friends rather badly.'[1]

It was decided to take only two of the three boats and the bulk of the gear was carefully loaded. Each boat, loaded with the vital food and supplies, was placed on specially prepared sledges and weighed nearly one ton (over 1,000 kg). With some trepidation, the party set out on Saturday 30 October.

It was obvious from the start that it would require prodigious effort to haul the boats across the tortured, broken landscape of ice hummocks which surrounded them on the drifting ice floe. A team of four man-haulers went ahead with picks and shovels, trying to smooth out the undulating surface and ease the path of the boat-pullers. There followed the dog teams pulling seven sledges, who went back and forth in a monotonous routine of relaying their dreadfully heavy loads. Behind them came fifteen men, yoked to the largest boat in a long sledging harness. After moving on a short distance, they regrouped and began the same process of hauling the smaller boat, which offered the prospect of only slightly lighter pulling.

The long procession of men, dogs, sledges and boats stretched for half a mile across the disturbed commotion of ice. They calculated that, at best, the most distance they could manage would be 5 miles (8 km) a day, which implied many weeks and possibly months of strenuous exertion to reach the safety of land or open seas. The cost in human effort would be enormous and another very real fear was that at any moment, the ice could open up and swallow them or separate them from the relative safety of their camp. Any realists in the party must have doubted their chances of survival.

The men received a painful reminder of their slim chances after the first back-breaking day in the wet, soft snow which made the going appalling. Occasionally the men sank to their waists in the soggy, slushy conditions. Each step was terribly heavy labour and after the most colossal effort, they were near to exhaustion when they stopped for the day.

To their utter dismay they discovered that they had covered barely one mile. They made the same distance on 31 October, arriving physically worn out after a day when they flogged themselves to the point of collapse. The next morning, the march was abandoned.

The 28 men were now camped on a sizeable, solid-looking floe about one mile across which offered some degree of stability in comparison with their ordeal during the slow death of *Endurance*. But they were still inside the Antarctic Circle, drifting slowly northwards on a chunk of ice which at any time might split apart. Shackleton appropriately named it 'Ocean Camp'.

The aim was to remain as comfortable as possible at Ocean Camp and let the floe travel gently northwards towards open seas before setting out in the boats to row for the safety of Paulet or Snow Hill Island off to the west. Since they had abandoned the march only 2 miles away from the broken hulk of *Endurance*, the men made repeated journeys back to retrieve supplies and equipment which might help sustain them through the coming months.

Two important decisions were taken at this time. First it was decided to return to the vicinity of the ship and recover the third small boat. Second, to bring back more lengths of timber and nails from the mother ship which would be used to build up the sides of the three small boats for the proposed journey across the ocean to dry land.

Wild also managed to bring back *Endurance*'s wheelhouse which was modified to make a useful galley and storehouse on the ice. From the patchwork roof they defiantly flew the Union Jack which King George had given to Shackleton on the eve of departure from London.

It was also decided to rescue some of Hurley's precious and memorable photographs, mostly glass plates which had been stored in metal cases on *Endurance*, now over 3 ft (1 m) under the mushy ice. It was not possible to keep all 600 plates and camera equipment so Hurley sat on the ice and calmly assessed the merit of each picture. As a negative was rejected, he summarily smashed the plate, thus ensuring that there would be no second thoughts. However, he retained one small pocket camera and about 120 plates which contain some of the most outstanding Polar pictures ever taken and are a fine memorial to a truly great photographer.

Crean, meanwhile, ensured that the sledges were kept loaded and ready for instant departure in case of any break in the ice and others were sent on a daily search for penguins, seals or anything else that might be eaten. Fortunately, there were sufficient supplies in the vicinity, although Shackleton was anxious not to stockpile too much food. He reckoned that storing large supplies of seal and penguin meat would send out the wrong signals to the men, suggesting that they were preparing to endure the unthinkable – another winter on the ice.

Above all, he wanted to keep up morale and hope. To counter any developing fears or loss of heart, Shackleton talked frequently about going home and the future expeditions on which they would all sail. He also moved Ocean Camp a little way onto firmer, more comfortable snow, which also helped make life a little more bearable.

The men filled their time with a mixture of duties like searching for food and maintaining the equipment, or alternatively with games of cards or a browse through the handful of books – like *Encyclopaedia Britannica* – which had been salvaged from *Endurance*. At night the twang of Hussey's banjo – the 'mental medicine' – could be heard drifting across the eerie landscape.

In early November, temperatures began to revive which was a mixed blessing. It was warmer but it also meant that the area around Ocean Camp became a slushy, waterlogged mess, with men's feet frequently sinking deep into the morass. Everything was wet through.

There was almost a sense of relief when, on 21 November, *Endurance* finally succumbed to the Antarctic. At around 5 p.m., Shackleton suddenly called out, 'She's going, boys' and everyone scrambled to snatch a final farewell to their ship. She went down, bows first, her stern raised in the air before the ice swallowed the broken vessel.

The loss of *Endurance* was the moment when the 28 finally cut their ties with civilisation. They were, officially, castaways at 68° 38' south, 52° 28' west, adrift in one million square miles of ocean and 1,000 miles (1,600 km) from the nearest human settlement.

It was also the moment when the morale of the men would be severely tested and Shackleton was coming to realise the full value of men like Crean and Wild who, in the face of the growing adversity, were becoming the mainstays of the party. Both men gave invaluable support to Shackleton at a time when the spirits of the party were under enormous strain from the loss of the ship and dreadful living conditions on the drifting ice floe.

Shackleton had already been forced to handle a minor mutiny from the carpenter, Chips McNeish, and there was simmering discontent from others as anxiety over their position began to take hold. Shackleton had threatened to shoot McNeish if he failed to obey orders and the mental condition of several others was deteriorating under the pressure of their isolation.

Shackleton's biographer, Huntford, concluded that, at this point, Crean and Wild were 'the only men he could absolutely trust'.[2]

An inventory of stores confirmed that the men had about three months' full rations, not counting the concentrated sledging rations which were originally earmarked for the expedition across the Continent. These were now on standby for emergencies such as a long boat journey or, at worst, another winter on the drifting ice. But with summer approaching, it was felt there would soon be ample supplies of seals and penguins to feed the men.

At one point, Crean performed an impromptu little act to help build up their larder. The Irishman was out with Worsley and three others searching for meat when they spotted an Emperor penguin. Without hesitation Crean sank onto all fours and began making noises like a fish and Worsley recounted:

'This brings the Emperor up in a hurry and a quarter of an hour later he is cut up for man meat.'[3]

The biggest concern was the direction of the drift. If it continued on its present northwesterly course, it would take them close to the northerly tip of the Graham Land peninsula and the relative safety of nearby Paulet or Snow Hill Island. The fear was that the drift would change direction towards the northeast which would send the slowly melting ice floe out into the vast open expanses of the South Atlantic between the land masses of South America and South Africa. It was vital to take to the boats before that happened.

Work on the three small boats was virtually complete and it was decided to give them names. Shackleton wanted to remember his key benefactors and called the whaler *James Caird*. The two smaller boats, both cutters, were called the *Dudley Docker* and the *Stancomb Wills*. McNeish, working with the minimum of tools and equipment, had performed a minor miracle raising the gunwales in the hopes of keeping out the waters of the Southern Ocean, skilfully using nails extracted from the sides of the *Endurance*.

With the work finished, Shackleton began final preparations for departure from the ice floe and on 19 December he recorded in his diary:

'Am thinking of starting off for the west.'[4]

Next day he took three of his most reliable and trusted colleagues – Crean, Wild and Hurley – on a short trip to survey the ice conditions to the immediate west. Taking dogs, the four men travelled for about 7 miles and were reasonably encouraged.

Spirits lifted and Shackleton, a great man-manager, decided to lift morale further by bringing forward Christmas Day celebrations to 22 December, just before they set out westwards. Large quantities of food would be left behind because it could not be carried. With great enthusiasm the men tucked into their remaining luxuries, scoffing ham, jugged hare, anchovies, baked beans, biscuits, pickles and jam and washing it down with ample mugs of tea and coffee.

The next day, 23 December, the men set off again in a replay of the back-breaking hauling of the boats across the hummocks of contorted ice. The procession was, as before, led by trailblazers and dog teams ferrying supplies at what seemed breakneck speed in stark contrast to the laborious plod of the struggling boat-hauling teams.

It was a tortuous process. The boats were now pulled in a relay by eighteen men at the rate of 60 yards (55 m) at a time, which meant the men walked 180 yards (165 m) for every 60 yards gained. The pulling was extremely heavy and even the toughened seamen in the harness could pull for only 200 or 300 yards (182–274 m) at a time before sinking to their knees exhausted and gasping for breath. They hauled the *Caird* a few hundred yards, then returned to pick up the *Docker* and hoped that her sledge runners had not frozen firmly to the ice in the low temperatures. When they did, it required three or four violent jerks of the harness to get the leaden weight moving across the ice, even before they began the terrible strain of pulling.

But, by general consent, it was better to be on the move, regardless of the heavy pulling in dreadful conditions. Anything was better than sitting in the cold, wet slushy snow passing the time. Also they all knew they were pulling for their lives.

There was concern among some that only two boats – the *James Caird* and the *Dudley Docker* – were to be taken on the new bid for freedom. The *Stancomb Wills*, the smallest vessel, would remain at Ocean Camp. Inside the little boat the expedition left a message for posterity, detailing the date and their position. Rather optimistically, it concluded: '*All well.*'

The reality was that the men were fighting a losing battle and despite immense effort, once again they were moving at barely one mile a day. At the current rate of progress, they would take 300 days – about ten months – to reach land in the west. But there was no question of their strength holding out for ten months.

On 29 December a quick reconnaissance of the immediate surroundings demolished all hopes of continuing with the march. For at least 2 miles ahead the terrain, in Shackleton's words, was 'quite unnegotiable' with a jumbled mess of broken ice and hummocks. More worryingly, the ice ahead appeared to be very thin and there were some narrow leads of open water which were not enough to take a boat but unstable enough to cause the ice to collapse under their weight. There was no prospect of hauling heavily laden boats across this surface.

It meant a retreat to firmer ice and another humiliation for the bitterly disappointed men. But they had no choice. Once again, they camped and waited for what the drift had in store for them. They were at the mercy of the drift and Shackleton called it 'Patience Camp'.

The failure of the escape march was a blow to the men's already strained morale. In general, spirits had been fairly high throughout the long drift on *Endurance* and despite some isolated difficulties, the mood overall had been reasonably optimistic. Shackleton still leant heavily on the support of men like Crean and Wild and somehow succeeded in conveying the belief that they would escape.

The new year, 1916, arrived with the more optimistic development that the drift was picking up speed, carrying them faster and faster on the journey towards open water. On 21 January they crossed the Antarctic Circle (66° 33') and the men climbed the tallest nearby fragment of ice in an attempt to pick out a faint glimpse of far-off land, which was the tip of Graham Land. Hope was briefly restored.

But food was becoming a problem. Seals were far less abundant and Shackleton was anxious to avoid breaking into the sledging rations until absolutely necessary. The alternative was to cut back on their food consumption and so, reluctantly, the decision was taken to shoot most of the remaining 50 dogs. Crean, who had devoted so much time to the animals in the past year, had the cheerless task of helping to lead the dogs away from the camp area where they were summarily despatched by Wild.

Soon after spirits were raised by, of all things, a howling gale. Although the winds roared to 70 mph, the men were delighted that it was a southwesterly wind which blew them further and further northwards towards open seas.

Shackleton said it was the 'most cheerful good fortune for a year' and estimated that the castaways were no more than 170 miles (270 km) from Paulet Island, a tiny volcanic outcrop little more than a mile in diameter. In six windswept days they covered 84 miles (135 km). But, crucially, there was no open water and therefore no hope of launching the boats. They were still imprisoned on their floating island of ice.

In early February, Crean and Macklin led teams across the ice to recover any remaining items of value from Ocean Camp, which was only about 7 miles away. They returned with some tinned fish, beef cubes and tobacco, which brought a welcome relief for the men whose digestion was struggling with the unrelenting diet of meat. It was causing horrid constipation and thunderous flatulence and Crean was among the men who suffered most. Worsley wrote:

> 'A number of our stomachs were rebelling against the excessive meat diet. I expect we will soon get used to it but I think it was better for us if we cooked some blubber with it. Personally I suffer from, to put it mildly, pronounced flatulence, which might almost be described as squeak gut.'[5]

At the same time, Wild returned with eighteen men to recover the other cutter, *Stancomb Wills*. Worsley, who had long argued that all three boats would be needed when they finally encountered open water, was delighted. He insisted that it would be 'a practical impossibility' to bring 28 men out of Antarctica in only two boats.

The following day, Crean, Worsley and Macklin set out for another foraging trip to Ocean Camp and found their path blocked by leads of open water. The trip was abandoned and it was apparent that they had only managed to recover the *Stancomb Wills* at the last possible moment. Had they left 24 hours later, the 28 men would have faced the boat journey crammed into only two small boats.

As the month of February wore on, the supplies of food began to dwindle and the men began scrabbling about in the waste dumps to retrieve scraps of seal or blubber for cooking. The last of the cheese – a one-inch cube apiece – was served out in the middle of the month. Later some Adelie penguins were caught and on 29 February – 1916 was a leap year – the hungry men drank their final cup of hot cocoa. Most of the tea was gone and the only drink soon would be powdered milk, laced with sugar.

On one occasion, a massive sea-leopard climbed onto the ice and tried to attack one of the men. Wild shot the beast and after cutting it open, found several undigested fish in its stomach. It was the only 'fresh' fish they managed to catch on their long drift.

They were still hungry, however, and the prospect of once again dragging the boats across the ice was a miserable one. In addition, they were short of exercise after idly sitting around on the drifting ice floe for many months and lacked the fitness and strength for the task. The only good news was that, despite their discomfort, there was no sign of scurvy, thanks to the fresh supplies of meat.

The castaways were now less than 100 miles (160 km) from Paulet Island and there was some hope that the ordeal was finally nearing an end. It was an end that could not come soon enough for many of the trapped men. Spirits were now deteriorating and the mood had changed. Meals were getting smaller, the daily servings of hoosh growing noticeably weaker. Hot drinks were rationed to one a day.

There was an air of depression about the camp, despite the constant optimism conveyed by Shackleton. The patience at Patience Camp was wearing thin.

On 11 March hopes were again briefly raised when the men felt a distinct movement of the pack and dark-coloured leads of open water began to appear in the distance. The boats, which had been strengthened and improved over the past few months, were made ready for launching. One particularly important task was to ensure that the boats were seaworthy, which meant an unusual piece of improvisation to block any leaks between the seams of the little vessels. To caulk and waterproof the seams, the men replaced the traditional pitch and oakum with seals' blood.

There was some cheer when, on 23 March, they made a definite sighting of land far off to the west, the first for five months. Again, however, their hopes were dashed. The land, probably Joinville Island at the northern tip of Graham Land, was an estimated 57 miles (91 km) away. It meant that Paulet Island, their intended destination, was now behind them to the south. Like a ship in the night, they had passed their hoped-for refuge.

In normal conditions it was probably no more than 24 or 48 hours' sailing to Joinville, the largest of the three small islands at the tip of the Antarctic Peninsula. But the ice was too broken and thin to march across and, equally, far too dangerous for their tiny boats. They had to watch helplessly as their floe slowly drifted northwards and the land receded away in the distance.

The sight of Joinville Island, instead of cheering the men, only confirmed the gravity of their plight, for they were now drifting past known solid ground and out into the enormous seas of the fearsome Drake Passage between the Weddell and Southern Ocean. South Georgia, over 900 miles (1,500 km) to the northeast, was probably the ideal destination. But in their weakened, demoralised condition, there was no realistic prospect of all 28 men surviving a lengthy journey in open boats across the world's most violent and dangerous stretch of water.

Instead, attention was focused on the much closer Elephant Island or Clarence Island, two small uninhabited dots of inhospitable rocks and mountains in the vast area of water that lay ahead.

Finding either island in the enormous expanses of water alone would be a massive task calling for a supreme act of navigation. But if they missed the islands, they were doomed. After Clarence or Elephant Islands, the nearest major landfall was Cape Horn, the southernmost tip of South America about 500 miles (800 km) to the north across the Drake Passage. But to reach South America, the little boats would have the improbable task of rowing or sailing against the powerful currents and winds which whip up the Drake Passage into the most fearsome expanse of water on earth. More likely was that if they missed Clarence or Elephant Islands, the men would drift into the vast uninhabited expanses of the South Atlantic.

While the men contemplated their fate, winter began to close in. It was late March, temperatures were dropping and the light was fading. More importantly, the supplies of seal and penguin were disappearing and the food shortage was becoming critical.

On 30 March the last remaining dogs and Crean's last pup were shot, a sorry occasion for many. But, without hesitation, the animals were immediately cut up and fried before being served to the hungry men who, more than anything else, were relieved for the welcome change of diet. With a flourish Crean delivered a dog steak to Shackleton in his tent, like a Master Chef serving his favoured guests at their table in a high-class restaurant.

The loss of the dogs also signalled the inevitable fact that they would not be marching across the broken ice hauling the boats to Graham Land. Shackleton realised how the men's condition had deteriorated and he knew that many were simply not up to weeks of heavy man-hauling the boats across the icy terrain. Instead they would be sailing or rowing to safety, which meant waiting for the drift to carry them northwards until they reached open water.

The ice floe, once about one mile across, had been whittled away by the constant weathering and battering on their long drift. It had now shrunk to only 120 yards (110 m) at its widest and was only large enough for their filthy, slushy home, Patience Camp.

But, frustratingly, the pack refused to budge open. All day and night the men kept a constant vigil, eager to detect even a slight sign of sea swell which would signal free-flowing water and an end to their captivity.

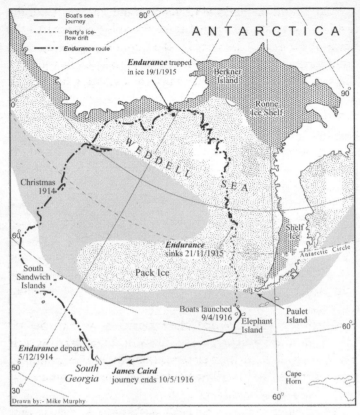

Endurance: *The drift of the* Endurance *through the Weddell Sea and the expedition's subsequent journeys to Elephant Island and South Georgia.*

Over the following days they picked up the crucial signals for which they had been longing. The sea was taking over from the ice, the thin dark grey lines of open water getting larger by day and the floes all around noticeably melting. Despite adverse northerly winds that should have pushed them back to the south, they were still drifting slowly northwards, which indicated that the currents had taken control. Birds could be seen flying overhead, an encouraging signal that land was nearby.

On 7 April the peaks of Clarence Island, the smaller of the two islands, could be sighted some 60 miles (96 km) to the north. A little later the winds picked up, driving their slowly disintegrating floe against other larger chunks of floating ice. The constant battering of their vulnerable floating home spelt disaster for the castaways and it became increasingly apparent that the time for launching the boats had arrived – whether they liked it or not!

On Sunday 9 April, the men ate a hearty breakfast and the tents were taken down. Everything was poised to go. All that was required was open water.

By lunchtime their prayers were answered as sizeable leads of open water began to emerge alongside and at 1 p.m. the order came to launch the boats. The *Dudley Docker* and *Stancomb Wills*, packed with food and equipment, were the first into the water, where a small skeleton crew held them steady while the bulk of the party man-handled the heavier *James Caird* into the sea.

Worsley's log recorded their position as 61° 56' S, 53° 56' W. The 28 men had spent almost six months on their fragile ice floe and drifted close to 2,000 miles (3,220 km) in a huge semi-circle around the Weddell Sea since *Endurance* was beset fifteen months earlier.

Miraculously, there had been no casualties. But as they pushed their boats into the bitterly cold, ice-strewn water the most hazardous part of their ordeal was ahead of them.

18
Launch the boats!

The three lifeboats pulled away from Patience Camp on 9 April 1916, the floe by now a small slushy little island of ice littered with the debris of humans who had spent almost six months attempting to make life as palatable as they could in the frozen wilderness. As they rowed, the ice around them began to close in again, shutting off lanes of open water and once again threatening their escape.

Some of the men rowed while others tried to push away great lumps of ice which drifted threateningly close to their vulnerable little vessels. It was soon clear that the men were dreadfully unfit and not up to the task ahead. The months of idleness at Patience Camp, coupled with the inadequate diet, had left them in no fit state for the hard work of rowing. At the same time, it was apparent that in raising the gunwales of the *Caird* and *Docker*, McNeish had inadvertently made them significantly more difficult to row.

But, to their profound relief, the little cavalcade of boats made some progress. The ice seemed to be receding and the amount of open, navigable water increased all the time. Moreover, although the men found the pulling very hard, the fatigue was to some extent offset by the warmth being generated by the exertion.

The *James Caird*, the largest and safest of the three, was in the lead. The boat, which was built in London to Worsley's specifications, was 22 ft 6 ins (7 m) long with a 6 ft (1.9 m) beam. Shackleton was in charge and he took with him another ten men, including Wild, McNeish, Hurley and Hussey. Next came the *Dudley Docker*, a 22-ft cutter built in Norway. There were nine men on board, led by Worsley and including Cheetham, Macklin and Marston.

Bringing up the rear was the *Stancomb Wills*, another cutter built in Norway, which was 20 ft 8 ins (6.3 m) long. Her beam was only 5 ft 6 ins (1.6 m) and she was barely 2 ft 3½ ins (0.7 m) from the inside of the keel to the top of the gunwale. Crammed inside her were eight desperate men, including Crean at the tiller.

In charge, nominally, was Hubert Hudson, navigating officer of *Endurance*. However, Hudson had struggled with niggling illnesses and the pressure of confinement on the ice floe, and was now heading for a nervous breakdown. Before the hazardous journey would finish, responsibility for the *Wills* would pass to the experienced hands of Tom Crean.

The imperturbable Irishman once again faced a crisis with equanimity and calmly rose to the occasion. As the difficulties worsened, he simply took control. It was, in many ways, similar to what he had done on the drifting ice floe to help rescue Bowers and Cherry-Garrard in 1911 and more recently, his heroic solo march to save the life of Teddy Evans in 1912. The difference was that previously Crean had displayed great courage by setting out alone to save other men. This time he was the leader, the skipper in charge of a tiny lifeboat struggling against the odds to combat the labyrinth of broken ice and ensure the safety of the seven other men in his charge.

What was particularly impressive, once again, was Crean's composure and mental toughness. His physical strength was, as ever, readily apparent. But at moments of great stress, it was his capacity to remain calm, think clearly and obey orders that served him. While some of the men in the little boat struggled to cope with the strain, Crean stood out like a beacon. Shackleton, who possessed a masterful ability to judge and direct people, could not have chosen a better person to take the helm of the *Stancomb Wills* on the hazardous journey.

Crean's seamanship was also to the fore as the little craft pulled away from their icy home. Hurley, who was in the *Caird* alongside Shackleton, remembered that the little flotilla was struck by an 'ice-laden surge' which threatened to capsize the more vulnerable *Wills*. He recalled:

> 'One of these reached to within a few yards of the *Stancomb Wills* which was bringing up the rear end; disaster was only averted by the greatest exertion of her crew and Crean's skilful piloting.'[1]

As darkness closed in, the men had rowed a total of 7 miles (11 km), an extraordinary achievement in the circumstances. Rowing in the dark was far too dangerous even to contemplate with so many icebergs blocking their path. Therefore, it was decided to tie up the three boats alongside a lengthy floe which, as luck would have it, contained a seal. The boats were hauled onto the ice and the seal made a welcome hot meal of fresh meat for the tired men.

By 8 p.m. the men, except two on watch, were into their sleeping bags. But at around 11 p.m. they felt the swell of the rolling sea beneath them and new disaster threatened. The floe suddenly lifted and cracked. The crack ran straight through one of the tents where some men were sleeping and they heard a splash as one of the party tumbled into the freezing black water. Shackleton rushed forward to see a frantic wriggling shape, trapped inside the sleeping bag and doomed to drown. In an instant he thrust a powerful arm in the direction of the writhing mass and hauled the man and sleeping bag back onto the ice. A second later the two halves of the broken floe crunched together. The wriggling man was Ernie Holness, a tough Hull trawlerman, whose sole concern was that he had lost his tobacco.

There were no dry clothes for Holness so volunteers marched him up and down the ice floe in the darkness to prevent him freezing to death in temperatures which had dropped to –12 °F (–24 °C). Throughout the night, the men could hear the crackling of his frozen clothing which sounded like a suit of clanking armour as he walked stiffly back and forth, grumbling about his lost 'baccy'.

All the men were cold, of course, and the incident with Holness had reminded them of their vulnerability. Few slept easily for the remainder of the night.

The party was up at 5 a.m. with the first hint of light. But the news was not good. Ice floes had moved in during the night, threatening to trap them once again. Nor was there any sign of Clarence or Elephant Islands. Worsley reckoned the distance was between 30 and 40 miles (48–64 km). Three hours later, to the relief of all, the pack began to disperse and once again the boats were launched.

It was another fraught day of heavy pulling on the oars while at the same time, the men had to keep constant vigilance against the threat of being struck by a passing floe. The men were exhausted, freezing, wet and hungry. The boats were heavily overladen and moved sluggishly through the choppy seas, while the men continually struggled for an inch of comfortable space among the packing cases and supplies which were strewn about their feet. They were continually wet from the spray, which frequently froze to their clothing and encased them.

To add to their woes, many of the party were struck by diarrhoea from the uncooked dog pemmican they had been forced to eat. Relieving themselves was a dreadful ordeal. It meant dangling their rump over the side of the heaving, swaying boat and exposing their most tender parts to a cold drenching from the breaking sea and painful frostbite where they would least want it to strike.

The *Wills*, whose gunwales had not been raised by McNeish, was undoubtedly the most exposed to the lumpy seas. Waves constantly poured over the sides and the weary men were occasionally up to their knees in the freezing water, though some reckoned that the sea water was warmer than the air. At the same time, the continuous salty spray left the makeshift canvas covering over the *Wills* smothered in a screen of ice, weighing her down even further into the sea. At regular intervals, men had to risk their lives by clambering forward in the rolling seas to chip away at the accumulations of ice.

Blackborrow, the stowaway, was developing severe frostbite in his toes because his leather boots offered no protection against the wet and Hudson had developed a mysterious and debilitating pain in his buttocks which was increasing his feelings of woe. Several others were showing emotional strain and the withering effects of exposure.

Shackleton realised that the *Wills*, despite Crean's experience, was highly vulnerable and might lose touch with the other two craft. Crean had been trained on large steel battleships and although he had some experience of small boats, it was not his natural area of expertise. As a result, Shackleton fixed a line between the *Wills* and the *Caird*. It was a lifeline, for the *Wills* would probably not survive alone in the high rolling seas, shipping water and weighed down with growing layers of ice which now covered the boat.

Concern about the fate of the *Wills* was shared by the men in the two other boats and Hurley recalled their fears:

> 'It seemed from moment to moment that we should have to part the line and leave her to her fate. Sir Ernest, in the stern, strained his eyes into the dark torrent and shouting at intervals words of cheer and inquiry: "She's gone!" one would say as a hoary billow reared its crest between us.
>
> Then against the white spume a dark shape would appear and through the tumult would come, faint but cheering, Tom Crean's reassuring hail, "All well, Sir".'[2]

The icebergs were a constant threat to all three boats and it was also apparent to the experienced sailors that the vessels were dangerously overloaded in these choppy seas. There was no alternative but to dump something and the only commodity they could jettison was food.

Shackleton slashed their supplies from three to two weeks. Green, the cook who performed wonders in the most trying circumstances, produced the best and largest meal they had eaten in nearly six months before they reluctantly left a pile of food on an ice floe.

They rose next day to find 20° of frost and great rolling seas. The ice floe on which they had spent a relatively contented night was being buffeted and broken by the angry seas. It was breaking up and disintegrating beneath their feet and they were unable to launch their boats because there were no leads of open water. The anxiety was acute.

It was not until late afternoon, with the light already beginning to dim, that they spotted a lead and could launch the boats off the floe and into the uninviting water. Shackleton was unnerved by the experience, fearing that they would become trapped on a disintegrating floe in waters where they could not launch the boats. As a result, he vowed never to spend another night on an ice floe.

Although they soon found some welcome open water, the *Wills* could not make the same progress as the other boats and once again fell away to the rear of the flotilla. The obvious concern was that the boat would be smashed against the ice so the *Docker* went back to provide a much appreciated tow to safety.

True to his word, Shackleton did not camp on the floe that night. The boats were tied up against a floe and the men landed while Green prepared a hot meal. The three 'skippers', Crean, Worsley and Shackleton, each remained on board their little boats to steady them and prevent collisions with any floe which might pass dangerously close.

But there was a shock awaiting the men when Shackleton asked Worsley, an experienced and highly capable navigator, to calculate how far they had travelled. Without checking he guessed about 30 miles (48 km) and everyone was relieved.

But, after working out his observations, Worsley found to his horror that they had travelled 30 miles in the wrong direction!

The little vessels had been carried away from the intended route by the strong-running current pouring out of the Bransfield Straits, the narrow strip of water between the Antarctic Continent and the South Shetland Islands. After three days of unrelenting labour and toil, the party was about 40 miles (64 km) further away from Elephant or Clarence Islands. Joinville Island, which they had left on their northerly drift a few weeks earlier, was now barely 80 miles (130 km) across the horizon.

Shackleton said the result of Worsley's sighting was a 'grievous disappointment' but he kept the information from the bulk of the party. Instead he told them that they had not made as much progress as expected and then changed course for Hope Bay, a desolate spot about 80 miles (130 km) away on the northern extremities of the Graham Land peninsula.

That night the men tried to grab a little sleep as the three boats, now tethered together, bobbed and swayed in the lee of a berg. Snow was falling, the temperature had dropped to 4° below freezing and the men huddled against each other for snatches of warmth. Their frozen clothing thawed where their bodies met and Shackleton recalled that, as the slightest movement exposed the 'warm spots' to the biting cold air, the men clung motionless to their nearest comrade.

By 13 April, the fifth day afloat, some of the men were starting to crack. The strain of the drift and now the exposure from the boat journey was taking its toll and their difficulty was increased by the knowledge that hot food and drink was out of the question unless they could land on a stable-looking floe to erect the primus stove. Cold breakfast after a broken night's sleep in sub-zero temperatures was hardly encouraging for the hungry, tired and freezing men.

Shackleton immediately took the bold decision of abandoning his plan to sail for Hope Bay. He realised that the depleted men needed to find land as quickly as possible.

Instead, he announced, they would make a run for Elephant Island, then about 100 miles (160 km) away to the northwest. He had been persuaded by a strong southeasterly wind which had risen that morning. They redistributed the food supplies to ease the pressure on the *Wills*, hoisted their little sails and set off, praying that the southeasterly wind would carry them to the safety of Elephant Island.

Good progress was made and at around noon, the three boats suddenly burst away from the pack and out into the open seas. The last time they had sailed in open water was December 1914, and now, sixteen months later, the men were free. Shackleton said that for a few hours they enjoyed 'a sense of the freedom and the magic of the sea'.[3]

Their joy, however, was short lived because the wind freshened and *Wills* in particular, began shipping dangerously large amounts of water. In choppy, windswept seas, the fear was that the three boats would become separated and the party had little choice but to hurriedly find a safe haven for the night.

However, there was little safety to be had. It was a dreadful night for the men, with temperatures sinking below zero and the wind penetrating their badly worn clothing as they struggled to grab a few hours' rest in the cramped, uncomfortable and constantly swaying boats. A further concern was the lack of fresh water because they had escaped the pack so suddenly that there was no time to grab ice blocks to melt for drinking water. Thirst was the last straw for some.

The men were a sorry sight, huddled together for warmth and comfort. For some it was to be the worst night of the expedition and Shackleton admitted that the condition of many of the exhausted men was 'pitiable'. Some were suicidal and Shackleton later wrote that he doubted if all of them would survive the night.

Blackborrow, the youngest in the party, was in an especially poor condition because of severe frostbite. His feet had 'gone' and there was little anyone could do about his plight in an open boat tossing around in the darkness in the Southern Ocean.

Most of the men had been struck by frostbite but Shackleton said it was interesting to note that 'old timers' – Crean, Wild, Hurley and himself – were all right. 'Apparently, we were acclimatised to ordinary Antarctic temperatures,' he added.[4]

Dawn on 14 April brought the welcome sight of snow-clad peaks on Clarence Island and a little later the bleak, but welcome mountains of Elephant Island suddenly appeared on the horizon. Worsley's navigation had been faultless. They were perhaps 30 miles (48 km) away from dry, firm land.

The *Caird* would have to tow the struggling *Wills*, a difficult task in the treacherous rolling seas. Shackleton shouted across to Crean that in the event that they became separated, the *Wills* should make for the nearest land, probably Clarence Island. It was a forlorn hope. If the *Wills* had drifted off it would have been fatal. To add to the gloom, Crean reported back that Hudson had finally collapsed.

The fervent hope was that they could make landfall by darkness but as dusk rolled in they dared not risk trying to land on an unknown beachhead in heavy seas. In the darkness, the *Docker* had become separated and the men on the *Caird* and *Wills* were worried that she had been lost. Perhaps the strong winds and currents had carried the little cutter through the channels and past Elephant Island into the sweeping expanse of the Southern Ocean.

The 28 men on the three boats spent a dreadfully uncomfortable night. Temperatures plunged to 20° below freezing and wind howled as they once again sought warmth from each other's bodies. The imperturbable Wild freely admitted it was the worst night he had ever known.

Dawn broke on 15 April 1916 to find the three boats reunited but buffeted by a raging gale. Above them towered the steep forbidding black cliffs of Elephant Island. The joy of reaching solid land was tempered by the very real concern that they might be smashed to pieces on the rocks which blocked their path to landfall. The men, many on the brink of collapse, strained their eyes to find a suitable landing place.

Crean in the *Wills* was ordered to come alongside Shackleton in the *Caird* and after a brief discussion it was decided to take the smaller, lighter cutter closer to land to investigate likely places to land. Shackleton joined Crean on the *Wills* and at around 9 a.m. they spotted a narrow rocky beach at the base of some cliffs which offered the hope of a landing.

The entrance they sought was guarded by a reef of threatening rocks which jutted out from the heavy rolling seas. A narrow channel was spotted which offered some hope of slipping through the protruding rocks and they carefully guided the *Wills* towards the inviting gap. Patiently they waited for the right moment and as the next wave rushed through the channel, the order was given to pull. In an instant, the *Wills* crossed the reef and the following wave carried the small boat to a grinding halt on the rocky, pebble-strewn beach.

Crean, Shackleton and the others in the *Wills* had made the first ever landing on Elephant Island. It was the first time they had felt firm ground beneath their feet since they left South Georgia 497 days earlier. They had spent 170 days adrift on an ice floe and 7 days in the open boat.

19
A fragile hold on life

The small pebble beach at Elephant Island provided the 28 men with only a tenuous grip on life. It was little more than 100 ft (30 m) wide and 50 ft (15 m) deep, surrounded on both sides by large rocks and steep cliffs, climbing sharply to over 2,000 ft (600 m) in places. The beach was exposed to the full rage of the Southern Ocean, which battered down incessantly.

Elephant Island is no place to be stranded. It forms part of the chain of South Shetland Islands, which were discovered in 1819 by the English merchant seaman, William Smith, who was blown off course while rounding Cape Horn. Smith did not land on the hostile-looking island, which sits at the north-eastern end of the chain of islands and rocky outcrops about 600 miles (1,000 km) from the tip of South America. It is 23 miles (37 km) long and about 13 miles (21 km) across at its widest, a remote, uninhabited and unfriendly world. The island is comprised almost entirely of rocks and mountains that rise steeply out of the sea, offering very little shelter or beaches.

No one knew they were there and they could not expect a chance meeting with a passing ship. It was not on any known shipping route and any rescue mission for the expedition was improbable. By all known information, the men were thought to be at Vahsel Bay, well over 1,000 miles (1,600 km) away on the Antarctic mainland. Without a radio to make contact with the outside world, the castaways would have to effect their own rescue.

These thoughts were far from their minds as the men first stumbled ashore, to feel the firm ground under their feet for the first time in many long months. Some simply sank to their knees while others picked up pebbles and ran them through their grubby hands as if to convince themselves that they had indeed reached land. A few of the men reeled about on unsteady rubbery legs like drunks and others simply sat on the stony ground, shivering uncontrollably. Someone recalled that the men did not know whether to laugh or to cry.

The boat journey from their ice floe had exacted a terrible toll on the men. They had been badly weakened by a combination of exposure to the cold and wet, the heavy work of rowing the boats in stormy seas, a shortage of hot food, severe thirst, a lack of sleep and above all, the enormous mental strain imposed by their captivity. Everyone was affected by the ordeal. Even the indomitable Shackleton, in the words of Macklin, looked 'gaunt and haggard'.

Many of the men under Crean's command in the *Wills* had cracked under the intense strain of six days in the open boat. McNeish wrote that Hudson had 'gone of [sic] his head'.[1] Blackborrow's feet were so frostbitten that he had to be carried from the boat and Stevenson had to be helped ashore. Many others from the other boats were on the point of collapse and several had developed severe cases of frostbite.

Hurley moaned that many had conducted themselves in a manner 'unworthy of gentlemen and British sailors'. Some who had expected to be bulwarks had 'stove in' and many of the cases of frostbite were, he concluded, the result of negligence. But there was full praise for the stalwarts like Crean and Wild who had been so prominent throughout their trial. Hurley wrote:

> 'Amongst those that stand meritorious, Sir E [Shackleton] has mentioned: Wild – a tower of strength who appeared

as well as ever after 32 hours at the tiller in frozen clothes, Crean who piloted the *Wills*, McNeish (carpenter) Vincent (AB) McCarthy (AB) Marston (*Dudley Docker*) and self.'[2]

The majority of the men were too exhausted or dejected to care about much. The fitter, stronger ones were immediately deployed to bring the stores and equipment onto the beach. With one last supreme effort, they managed to haul the three little boats onto the pebbles. The soggy sleeping bags were spread out across the beach in the hope they would dry. Green, ever reliable, quietly conjured up some steaming hot milk to toast their arrival and the blubber stove began to cook their first hot meal in days.

The most encouraging feature of the beach, soon called Cape Valentine, was that the many nearby glaciers provided ample supplies of fresh water and there were abundant signs of wildlife like seals and penguins to provide fresh meat. The men ate a hearty meal, which immediately spread some warmth through their chilled bodies for the first time in days. As soon as they had finished, the men settled down for a long, unbroken night's rest knowing that they had solid ground beneath them. Most were in their sleeping bags by 3 p.m. in the afternoon, desperately anxious to get their first good night's sleep in a week. Somehow they managed to ignore the roaring winds crashing into their little green tents with monotonous regularity.

But the weary, relieved men were not safe. It was clear from the water marks on the nearby cliffs that the beach would be swamped at high tide and there was the ever-present threat of a northeasterly gale sweeping down on them, sending mountainous waves to engulf their little haven. The men could not remain on the beach, though for many the prospect of another boat journey was almost too much to bear.

Next morning, Shackleton's two most trusted lieutenants, Wild and Crean, took the *Wills* around the coastline in search of a safer haven. They returned long after darkness at 8 p.m.

with the welcome news that a sandy beach, about 150 yards long and 30 yards wide, had been discovered approximately 7 miles away. It contained a sizeable amount of wildlife and a nearby glacier would yield abundant supplies of fresh drinking water. They would leave the next morning.

The men rose at 5 a.m. and packed their gear. Crean's task in the *Wills* was made a little easier by the transfer of Blackborrow and Hudson, his two major invalids, to the other boats. But as they departed, the weather closed in with a vengeance, the wind gathering speed from gale to hurricane force. It was as though the Antarctic was refusing to let them escape. The *Wills* was swept in to shore by one mountainous swell and came perilously near to being smashed onto the rocks as Crean struggled to retain control.

In the turmoil several of the boats' oars broke – Crean's party in the *Wills* was reduced to only three. The little boat, although now lighter after Blackborrow and Hudson's departure, began to fall behind and Worsley in the *Docker* dropped back to lend a hand. Worsley handed Crean an extra oar – the shortest – from the *Docker*.

Even in the depth of their current crisis Crean retained his sense of humour and Worsley cheerfully recalled:

> 'I dropped back and handed our shortest oar to Crean, who was over six feet tall. [sic] He thanked me emphatically. "Skipper, darlin'," he added, "what the hell's the good o' givin' me, the longest man, the shortest oar." Swap it, I shouted, which he did.'[3]

After two hours of strenuous labour, the three little boats found shelter behind a point of rock and the men hurriedly ate some cold rations. Soon they resumed their slog. Despite the cold and wet, they continued to pull against the strong winds and at about 5 p.m., they arrived off the small sandy beach found by Crean and Wild the previous day.

As before, Crean took the *Wills* in first and the men gratefully clambered or were helped ashore as soon as the boat ran to ground. As soon as they trod on firm ground, the first engineer, Louis Rickinson, collapsed with a heart attack, another victim of the strain.

The beach offered minimum protection but was safer than Cape Valentine. It was little more than a spit, extending steeply upwards about 100 yards (90 m) by 30 yards (27 m). Shackleton said it was 'rough, bleak and inhospitable' and Hurley said the beach was like the 'courtyard of a prison'. Macklin remembered that a 'more inhospitable place could scarcely be imagined'.

The beach was named 'Cape Wild' after Shackleton's deputy. 'Cape Bloody Wild', some called it.

The weather immediately gave them a typically hostile Antarctic welcome, an early reminder of their continued vulnerability. A gale started to blow and when snow followed, it soon developed into a full-scale blizzard. At one point the *Docker* was lifted from the beach and swung round by the violent winds and the men had to take down the tents, their only shelter, because of the fear that they would blow away. Shackleton was blown off his feet. In an emergency move, the *Docker* was turned upside down to provide some meagre shelter.

But, despite the savagery all around them, some of the men were forced out of their bags next day to find stocks of seal or penguin. Skinning the beasts was appalling and freezing work in the sub-zero temperatures and one man reported that only the warmth from the dead animals' bloody carcasses had saved their hands from severe frostbite.

The blizzard blew all night and most of the next day, confining the men to their bags for long periods and once again denting their already fragile morale. The shrieking blizzard had demonstrated that their little beach was relatively safe from the sea and not likely to be engulfed by the tides. In the circumstances, this was a major source of comfort and they were happy to clutch at such straws.

The main topic of conversation was rescue. It was abundantly clear that they could not expect help and equally, it was obvious that some of the men would not survive a long boat journey across the Southern Ocean to safety. Many were thoroughly beaten and despondent, almost resigned to their fate. The fatigue, exposure and stress had proved too much for some and their survival was in doubt. McNeish was especially gloomy about the prospects for the men on the beach and wrote:

> 'I don't think there will be many survivors if they have to put in a winter here.'[4]

Hurley was equally pessimistic about the ability of some to resist the elements much longer and later recalled that the first few days on Elephant Island were 'hell'. He did not believe they would all survive. Wordie, the geologist, estimated that a total of eight men were 'broken down and unable to work'. These would have to be rescued – they could not rescue themselves. It would mean that a party of the fittest and most capable would have to take one of the boats and sail across the ocean for rescue.

Shackleton decided that six men would take the *James Caird*, the most seaworthy of the three boats, and bring a relief ship. All that had to be decided was who was to go and where they would go.

There were three principal options for relief. The nearest was Tierra del Fuego at Cape Horn on the southern tip of South America, about 600 miles (965 km) away to the northwest. Next came Port Stanley in the Falkland Islands, which lay about 550 miles (885 km) almost due north. Lastly there was South Georgia, a little over 800 miles (1,300 km) to the northeast. Each journey presented immense obstacles.

To reach the closest points at Cape Horn or Port Stanley, the tiny boat would have to cross the fearsome Drake Passage and sail into the teeth of a strong westerly current and howling winds. Worsley observed that currents run at over 60 miles (96 km) a day and he added:

> 'This meant we had practically no hope of making Cape
> Horn, the nearest point; very little of reaching the
> Falklands but fair gales and favouring currents to S
> Georgia.'[5]

In theory, the prevailing winds would blow from behind the
little boat and push them along towards South Georgia. The
only realistic choice for rescue was South Georgia – the
starting place for their journey fifteen months earlier.

Shackleton began by calling for volunteers to man the
James Caird. Shackleton himself would lead the rescuers and
Worsley, a navigator who had already demonstrated supreme
skill, would be indispensable. Wild, the obvious choice for the
journey, was asked to remain behind on Elephant Island to
hold the remaining party of 22 castaways together.

Tom Crean was an ideal man for either staying behind
with Wild or crossing the Southern Ocean with Shackleton.
He would be invaluable to Wild on the spit at Elephant
Island, helping to maintain morale and leading by example
during what might be a long and stressful wait. Wild could
not ask for a better lieutenant. Equally, his immense physical
and mental strength and experience of the sea would be vital
on the boat journey.

Crean's outstanding record on two expeditions with Scott,
notably the rescue of Evans, provided the right credentials for
the task facing Shackleton. Moreover, Crean carried the
respect of his colleagues. There was nobody better qualified for
the daunting tasks ahead, whether on the beach at Elephant
Island or in the *James Caird* on the open seas.

Initially Shackleton asked the Irishman to remain behind
with Wild, sensing that his right-hand man would need strong
support. But Crean, in Shackleton's words, 'begged so hard to
come that, after consulting Wild, I promised to take him'.[6]

The biographer, Huntford, claimed that Shackleton took
Crean because he was a fellow Irishman while another writer,
Alfred Lansing had a different explanation. Lansing, who

wrote his book *Endurance* in the late 1950s after consulting many survivors of the expedition, said Shackleton was not sure that Crean's 'rough, tactless nature' would lend itself well to a period of enforced and perhaps long waiting.

Shackleton also chose another Irishman, Timothy McCarthy, a powerful and experienced seaman who was also popular with the other men. Then he picked Chips McNeish, who had blotted his copybook by a minor mutiny when under pressure on the ice floe some months earlier. Shackleton was impressed with McNeish's work in raising the gunwales but, more pertinently, he did not want a potential troublemaker disrupting the fragile peace among the unstable castaways left on Elephant Island. The last member was Jack Vincent, another experienced sailor who was also occasionally difficult and could be kept under closer supervision in the boat.

The party and destination now decided, the men went to work preparing the *James Caird* for the momentous journey. McNeish, once again, performed minor miracles. There are no trees on Elephant Island so the resourceful carpenter cut up the remaining sledge and found other bits and pieces of wood from the lids of wooden supply cases, a few planks from the *Dudley Docker* and the mast from the *Stancomb Wills*.

The main task was to cover the deck and to protect the little craft against the constant wash from the waves of the Southern Ocean. There was only enough spare wood to construct a frame, so McNeish finished the deck-covering with canvas. Without the covering, Shackleton admitted, the *James Caird* would never have survived the journey. The *Wills'* mast was jammed into the hull from one end to the other along the keel to prevent the boat breaking her back under the strain of the gigantic seas which would hit them in the Southern Ocean.

The preparatory work, in keeping with their ordeal so far, was a torture for the men. With winter setting in, temperatures had dropped and the winds picked up. Work was constantly interrupted and had to be abandoned altogether on 20 April because of a furious gale which beat down upon them.

Crean was engaged in rigging the canvas covering over the *James Caird*, a painful and demanding task on the exposed beach. To sew the canvas, volunteers had to hold the material foot by foot over the blubber stove until it thawed out enough to manipulate. The canvas was so tough and frozen that the men had to use a pair of pinchers to pull the sewing needle through.

Ballast was also needed for the voyage, so several of the less fit men were employed filling bags, which were hurriedly made from old blankets, with sand and shingle from the beach. Others gathered up large stones to place in the bottom of the boat and some were deployed to melt ice for the two casks of drinking water the men would take in the boat. For good measure, they would take along some extra blocks of ice.

The preparation took the best part of a week, interrupted frequently by the bouts of severe weather. The plan was to set sail on 24 April, weather and the ice pack permitting. The last night on Elephant Island was bitterly cold and uncomfortable, but the men rose to find the sun shining. For the 28 desperate men anxiously searching for any optimistic signs, this was a good omen.

Even their departure was not straightforward. The unladen *James Caird* was hauled down the beach and into the sea, moving quickly about 100 yards from the shore to avoid the breakers. But the little boat was heavily buffeted by the crashing waves and came close to being overturned even before the rescue attempt could be launched. Wild recalled that only the timely intervention of Crean and Worsley saved the *James Caird* from being wrecked in the heavy swell.

At the same time, the *Wills* ferried 30 days of food and supplies out to the boat. On the second trip, the *Wills* was driven against some rocks and one of the two water casks was punctured. Unknown to the men, salty sea water leaked into their drinking water.

On another occasion, McNeish and Vincent were thrown into the sea by the heavy swell and were forced to return to shore to swap their wringing wet clothes for dry garments with the men left on the beach. It was an opportune moment to remind the six men that they would not be wearing oilskins or sea boots for crossing the most turbulent ocean in the world.

By midday, the *James Caird* was ready to begin the perilous voyage. Shackleton said goodbye to the men, saving a special word of grateful thanks and good wishes for Wild, on whom a heavy burden was about to fall. The *Wills* came alongside for the last time and the two crews leaned across, exchanging a few feeble but well-meaning jokes to lift spirits. One crewman from the *Wills* told them to make sure that Crean behaved himself when they reached shore and Worsley recalled:

> 'As for Crean, they said things that ought to have made him blush; but what would make Crean blush would make a butcher's dog drop its bone.'[7]

Finally, the men leant across the sides, shook hands for the last time and prepared to get under way. On the shoreline, the castaways were a forlorn sight, though they waved hopefully and made sure that the parting cries of 'three hearty cheers' rose above the constant noise of the sea breaking around their feet. Hurley said the men felt confident about the 'six proven veterans, seasoned by the salt & experience of the sea'. He estimated that the journey to South Georgia would take fourteen days.

Slowly the *James Caird* began to pull away from Elephant Island, with the men on the beach straining for a final glimpse of the vessel as she rose and fell between the heaving swell. Very soon the tiny boat disappeared from view behind the dark menacing waves.

It was a toss-up which party faced the greatest ordeal – the 22 castaways stranded on the bleak inhospitable beach at Elephant Island, or the six men preparing to sail across the world's most dangerous seas in a 22 ft 6 ins (7 m) long open boat without proper navigating equipment. Worsley remembered:

'This was the beginning of the ordeal by water.'[8]

It was shortly after noon on Easter Monday, 24 April 1916, and South Georgia was 800 miles (1,300 km) away. On the same day on the streets of Crean's homeland, Irish Republicans launched the Easter Rising against British rule.

20
An epic journey

Right from the start, the Southern Ocean lived up to what Shackleton said was its 'evil winter reputation'. Although they safely navigated their way through the immediate pack ice surrounding Elephant Island, winds rose to 30 mph and the sea picked up as evening approached. The only visible light in the vast expanse of ocean came from the occasional glow of Tom Crean's pipe.

The party had been split neatly into two groups who took turns with four-hour watches, with Shackleton, Crean and McNeish taking one and Worsley, McCarthy and Vincent the other. The men on watch had to be particularly vigilant against the ice, since a collision with a sizeable floe would spell disaster. Darkness brought the greatest danger of collision and the men on deck strained their eyes to spot any looming danger.

Each man took spells at the tiller while the others pumped or bailed out the floods of water which constantly entered the boat. A man could hold the brass cylinder pump under the water for only five minutes before his hands went numb with the cold. By the time their watch had finished the men were exhausted and wet through. They all longed for waterproof oilskins.

Indeed, the men were poorly dressed for their 'ordeal by water'. They wore a heavy suit of Jaeger underwear and a large, loose-fitting Jaeger sweater, plus a suit of Burberry overalls, woollen helmet and a Burberry over-helmet. Their hands were covered by a pair of Shetland wool mitts and a larger pair of dog-skin mitts. On their feet there were two pairs of woollen socks, felt shoes and finnesko boots made from reindeer skin. However, the Burberry outer-wear was designed for dry cold and was not waterproof – the very opposite of what they needed in the Southern Ocean.

Those not on watch crawled into their wet reindeer sleeping bags in the hopes of snatching a few hours' precious rest on the uncomfortable packing cases, bags of ballast and rocks. The men had to wriggle into the narrow space between the ballast-lined floor and the oarsmen's thwart which Worsley said was like a 'dungeon cell'. Worsley remembered that more than once he awoke in sheer panic thinking he had been buried alive.

The jagged edges of the rocks and ballast was especially hard on the men's worn bodies which by now had developed severe boils on the wrists, ankles and buttocks caused by the combination of salt water, cold and continual friction from their rough clothing. To add to the discomfort, the men from the next watch were usually wriggling their way out at the same time and it required one person to direct the two-way flow of bodies like a traffic policeman.

Cooking was especially difficult in the rolling and tumbling seas which added a new soaking with every crashing wave that came pouring over the sides. The hardest task was to keep the hoosh from splashing out of the pot as the little boat pitched and rolled.

Crean was the cook, a vital task for men who badly needed hot, warming food and drink to counter the bitter cold and constant soaking. But a simple task on dry land was beyond the capacity of one man in the heaving Southern Ocean and it soon developed into a team effort.

The tortuous routine involved Crean bending double over the primus stove because there was not enough room to sit up straight. He sat crouched opposite Worsley, their backs jammed against the side of the boat and feet pointing towards each other. The precious stove was then stuck between the pair's legs to avoid being tipped over by the lurching seas. Worsley said he was the 'scullion' to Crean's 'chef' and had to hold the 'sacred hoosh pot' to prevent it toppling over.

Others fished out the reindeer hairs which fell from the heavily worn sleeping bags and gathered everywhere. Every meal or drink was laced with hair from the bags. On one occasion, Worsley was idly watching Crean stir the hoosh. To his amazement, 'a filthy black paw shot out, seized a handful of reindeer hair from the hoosh, squeezed it out so as to waste nothing and then threw it away'.[1] The men could cope with a little dirt but drew the line at reindeer hair.

McCarthy dispensed chunks of ice into the pot and Crean stirred in the dried meat, usually about half a pound per man. Worsley described the routine:

> 'All eyes, except the helmsman's, were fastened on the cooker. Mugs & spoons were ready. As soon as it boiled Crean shouted "Hoosh" & blew out the primus. All [mugs] were held out, Crean rapidly filling them in turn. We took it down scalding hot . . . The first man to finish his hoosh jumped outside & relieved the helmsman for his while still hot.'[2]

Crean took special care to ensure that everyone had the same amount of hoosh but there was a price to be paid for being a cook and Worsley added:

> 'The hands of all of us were scarred with frostbite, but Crean's hands and mine, in addition, were marked with burns from the primus.'[3]

Eating was an ordeal in itself as there was not enough space to sit upright in the confined space. Worsley said it was distressing, because 'the chest is pressed down on the stomach, one swallows with difficulty & the food appears to have no room to go down'.

Despite the discomfort, one small consolation on the boat journey was that the six men were generally well fed. After the hoosh, the men also ate a chunk of 'nut food', a sweet nougat which had been brought along as part of the sledging rations for the trans-continental crossing. In between meals, hot milk was served regularly and supplemented with biscuits or sugar lumps. Worsley recalled that they trained themselves to guzzle the milk at scalding heat.

However, even hardened sea dogs like Crean and Shackleton were affected by the constant heavy swell. Everyone was seasick, except Worsley and McCarthy, as the little boat rose and fell, swayed and listed in the rolling seas.

The Southern Ocean, Worsley wrote, rolls 'almost unchecked' in the vast space between Antarctica and the land masses of South America, Australasia and South Africa. The waves rise 40–50 ft (12–15 m) and sweep forward in 'fierce and haughty majesty' and he added:

> 'These blue water hills in a very heavy gale move as fast as 27 statute miles an hour but striking the banks probably attain a speed of 60 miles. The impact of hundreds of tons of solid water at this speed can only be imagined.'[4]

Astonishingly, the men retained their sense of humour, particularly Crean and Shackleton. Worsley reported a 'quaint sort of mimic bickering' between the two Irishmen which intrigued the others. Worsley explained:

> 'It was partly chaff & partly a comic revolt against the conditions. Tom Crean had been so long and done so much with Sir E that he had become a privileged retainer. As these two watchmates turned in, a kind of wordless rumbling, muttering, growling noise could be heard issuing from the dark & gloomy lair in the bows, sometimes at things in general, & sometimes at nothing at all. At times they were so full of quaint conceits & Crean's

remarks were so Irish that I ran the risk of explosion by suppressed laughter. "Go to sleep Crean & don't be clucking like an old hen." "Boss, I can't eat those old reindeer hairs. I'll have an inside on me like a billygoats neck. Let's give 'em to the Skipper [Worsley] & McCarthy. They never know what they're eating". & so on.'[5]

On another occasion, Worsley provided a none too flattering critique of Crean's singing talent, a habit he often practised at the most testing moments. He recorded:

'[Crean] was making noises at the helm that we found by a Sherlock Holmes system of deduction represented "The Wearin' o' the Green". Another series of sounds, however, completely baffled us.'[6]

Initially, they headed due north to get as clear as possible from the pack ice and pick up the westerly winds which, it was hoped, would carry them to South Georgia. Despite everything, they made remarkable progress. By noon on 26 April – two days after leaving Elephant Island – the *James Caird* had carried them 128 miles (206 km) away from captivity. But, as if to remind them of the constant threat from the vicious seas, they also caught sight of two small pieces of wreckage from an unknown and presumably unfortunate vessel. Shackleton now reckoned they were far enough north to be away from the pack and he turned the vessel to the northeast. South Georgia lay ahead.

Determining their precise position by 'shooting the sun' – using a sextant to line up the sun and horizon – was a difficult task in the turbulent seas and required a four-man effort. Worsley, the navigator, could barely stand still and upright in the swell to catch a steady glimpse of the sun, so Vincent and McCarthy had to hold him firmly round the waist. Crouched under the canvas, Shackleton struggled with the chronometer, pencil and paper, desperately trying to keep everything dry as readings were yelled out.

Worsley had served a long apprenticeship for this moment, having been at sea for almost three decades. His first command was a three-masted sailing ship which ploughed the more inviting waters around the South Sea Islands and his varied career had taken him through the merchant service to the Royal Naval Reserve. Even as a young second mate, Worsley had been spotted as a 'careful and exact navigator'.

While accuracy was crucial, the observations were inevitably haphazard, particularly in the first few days as the little craft dodged the ice. At night, Worsley steered by the feel of the wind and by observing the angle at which the little pennant at the masthead blew. The compass was also affected by the iron plunger of the pump which worked up and down a few inches away.

But, in spite of everything, Worsley became increasingly adept and surprised himself with the accuracy of his sightings. Even a small margin of error would mean sailing past South Georgia and out into the yawning expanses of the South Atlantic, with no realistic possibility of fighting back to land against the prevailing winds. There was little, if any, room for error.

Until this point, the boat was assisted by the strength of the southwesterlies which on 29 April propelled them along at good speed. They covered 92 miles (148 km) in a single day and although it was still a long way to South Georgia, they had covered a good slice of the distance.

But the gathering Antarctic winter was tightening its grip and temperatures sank by the day. At one point during a gale, Crean and McCarthy bravely clambered forward on the fragile deck covering to take down the sails which threatened to freeze solid in the low temperatures. Worsley laconically described the seas as 'very big' or 'heavy, lumpy'.

The constant wash and spray from the freezing sea was coating the little vessel with ice and posing a new threat. They woke on 1 May to discover to their horror that the ice covering was about 6 inches (15 cms) thick and the boat was in grave danger of toppling over. They took it in turns to creep forward on their knees, chipping away at the layers of ice with an axe. Standing up on the pitching, rolling boat would have been suicidal and none of the men could tolerate the ordeal for more than a few minutes before crawling back under the canvas to recover. Vincent came perilously close to sliding over the edge when the boat lurched violently and he almost lost his grip on the slippery surface.

No sooner had they finished than the ice began to form again, the sea spray freezing as it washed onto the *Caird*'s makeshift decks. For a second time, they had to crawl out on the decking and chip away at the accumulations of ice.

Throughout the night, a gale raged and McNeish uncovered a new and unexpected twist in their battle to survive. After investigating a peculiar, fetid smell on the boat, he realised that the reindeer sleeping bags had begun to rot.

The men, too, displayed signs of the strain. They were exhausted from exposure to the penetrating cold and the constant battle against the freezing water which poured in with every wave. Worsley recalled that as a result of the thorough soakings their legs began to swell, turn white and lose much of their feeling. Shackleton called it 'superficial frostbite'.

Worsley also recalled that their hands were 'awful objects' to look on and wrote:

> 'I remember Crean's and mine in addition to being almost black with grime, blubber and soot were ornamented with recent frostbites and burns from the primus. Each successive frostbite on a finger was marked by a ring where the skin had peeled off, so that we could count our frostbites by the rings of skin – something after the woodman telling the age of a tree by counting the concentric rings.'[7]

Helped by a gale from the southwest, the little boat continued to make progress and by 3 May a sighting showed them to be 403 (nautical) miles from Elephant Island, or more than halfway to South Georgia. They had another good day on 4 May but were not prepared for what happened on 5 May.

At around midnight, Shackleton caught sight of a line of clear sky between the south and southwest, which he thought was a rift in the clouds. He called Crean and McNeish to tell them the sky was brightening. Suddenly he realised that the line of clear sky was advancing menacingly towards them. It was, in fact, a gigantic wave.

Shackleton shouted for the men to hold on as the wave swept down on the small boat. The vessel, caught by the impact of the enormous wave, was catapulted forward and almost lifted out of the sea. The boat, said Shackleton, was lifted and flung forward 'like a cork in a breaking surf' and they found themselves in a 'seething chaos of tortured water'. For an instant no one was sure whether they were still upright. The boat shuddered but almost as quickly as it had appeared, the wave was gone. They had survived, somehow.

The vessel was half-full of water and Crean and McNeish grabbed anything that would carry water and began bailing for their lives. Worsley's team quickly scrambled from their dungeon and joined in, knowing that another big wave would undoubtedly sink the dangerously overladen boat.

Shackleton said that never in 26 years' experience of the sea had he encountered a wave so large. It was, he said, a 'mighty upheaval of the ocean' and Worsley guessed it had been caused by the 'calving' of some vast unseen iceberg many miles away.

The next day's sight confirmed them less than 100 miles (160 km) from South Georgia, but the strain was beginning to tell on the weary men. Vincent was close to breaking down and McNeish, the eldest man in the party, was also suffering badly. But Crean remained unmoved and indomitable. Shackleton's diary recorded:

> 'One of the memories that comes to me from those days is of Crean singing at the tiller and nobody ever discovered what the song was. It was devoid of tune and

as monotonous as the chanting of a Buddhist monk at his prayers; yet somehow it was cheerful. In moments of inspiration Crean would attempt "The Wearin' o' the Green".'[8]

By now the pressure was also getting to Shackleton, who at one point exchanged a sharp word with Crean over the water. As Crean was preparing an evening meal, he tasted the water from the second cask and found it salty. He called Shackleton, gave him a sip and asked what he should do. Shackleton snapped back that there was nothing they could do so the Irishman should go ahead and make the hoosh. But when cooked it was almost unpalatably salty.

The damage to the second water cask was the latest in a long line of setbacks which had bedevilled the expedition from the outset. While they had about two weeks' food, their only supply of water was now brackish and barely drinkable. The six men had barely managed to cope with the heavy seas and cruel weather, but they would not be able to survive without fresh water. The need to find South Georgia was now critical.

The original plan was to head for Willis and Bird Islands at the western end of South Georgia, then swing eastwards to the whaling station at Leith Harbour on the north side of the island where they would find men and ships. But now it did not matter too much where they landed – so long as they landed as quickly as possible and slaked their growing thirsts. To underline their plight, Shackleton ordered the daily allowance should be cut to half a pint per man on 6 May. 'Thirst took possession of us,' he wrote.

Dawn broke on 8 May in stormy, squally conditions with the men feeling the thirst acutely. Their lips were cracked, tongues swollen and mouths dry, an incongruous predicament when surrounded by endless amounts of water.

But, by Worsley's reckoning, they were nearing South Georgia and suddenly their hopes soared at the sight of small birds flying overhead, a clear indication that land was not far away. The men peered into the distance through their heavily salt-rimmed eyes, hoping to catch a glimpse of land through the hazy squall and billowing clouds which obscured their vision.

Shortly after midday, McCarthy let out a mighty yell – '*Land*!' As the clouds and mist broke, right ahead lay the rugged black mountains of South Georgia. One glimpse, though, and it was gone as the clouds and mist closed in again and shut out the wondrous sight.

Worsley's navigation had been impeccable and he remembered:

> 'We looked at one another with cheerful foolish grins of joy. The feelings uppermost were "We've done it".'[9]

Shackleton said:

> 'It was a glad moment. Thirst-ridden, chilled and weak as we were, happiness irradiated us. The job was nearly done.'[10]

However, they had reached the southern coast of the island, not the western end which offered the easiest route to Leith or any of the other harbours of safety on the northern side. Nor was the weather prepared to release them from their torment. As they neared land, winds raced to about 60 mph and drove them dangerously close to the rocks. Worsley saw hazardous blind rolling waves, indicating shoals and reefs that would smash the *James Caird* to little pieces. It was far too risky to attempt a landing in the howling storm and the boat was taken back out to sea to stand off until the winds died down. It was so near, yet so far.

Daylight faded in the short winter's day and the winds rose in intensity. Throughout the miserable storm-tossed night, the men had to bail and pump the water which flooded into the *Caird*. At one stage the little boat was caught on a cross sea, battered one way and then the other. The men were painfully thirsty and that night's hoosh was badly tainted by the brackish water near the bottom of the damaged casket.

Shackleton privately doubted whether they would survive. It was the longest night of the journey and for the men probably the longest night of their lives.

Dawn on 9 May broke with winds screeching to hurricane force (over 73 mph on the Beaufort Scale) in the violent cross seas which threw up waves 40 ft high. Worsley said no one had seen anything like it before and added that the conditions 'seemed to have been loosed from the infernal regions'.

By noon the wind had grown even stronger, racing to over 80 mph in a last desperate bid to prevent them from making their landfall. Some miles away in the same storm, an Argentinian vessel, *Argos*, sank off the coast of South Georgia with the loss of all hands.

Cooking was by now out of the question and the men gnawed on cold sledging rations, though they could hardly generate enough saliva to swallow. The water supply had dwindled to about a pint of murky liquid which had to be strained repeatedly through a fragment of gauze to remove the hairs.

The storm raged unbroken for ten hours but through one break in the clouds the men could pick out more rock formations as land neared. It was perhaps only 1 mile (1.6 km) away but again the boat was being dragged onto the shoals and reefs – so again they had to turn away.

The weather was appalling and Worsley's log was short, sharp and straight to the point in a matter-of-fact way. He recorded:

'Mountainous westerly gale and swell. Wind rose to hurricane force.'[11]

At the height of the crisis, Crean and Worsley were forced to crawl on their stomachs out onto the decking and hoist the sail to allow the little vessel a chance to get away from the dangerous rocks. It took several minutes before they were able to drag themselves to their feet, clinging onto the mainsail in the roaring storm and finally fixing the sail. They then had to repeat their hazardous trip, crawling on their stomachs in the pitching, rolling seas. It was another act of calm bravery and it almost certainly saved the *Caird* from destruction.

At around 4 p.m. the clouds lifted enough for them to catch sight of Annekov Island, a black 2,000-ft mountain which emerges from the sea about 5 miles (8 km) off the coast of South Georgia. The risk of running aground on reefs loomed again but, miraculously, the little boat cleared the danger and men faced up to the dreadful prospect of spending another night in the open sea. Worsley reported a 'very heavy swell' as they laboured to avoid the rocks.

Daylight broke on 10 May to find that the storm had abated and the wind was blowing gently. They were now free to make a run for dry land, but there was another shock for the men as Crean crawled out from the bows. As he emerged, his large frame struck the thwart and the pin which held the mast clamp in place was dislodged. The pin had worked loose in the hurricane and Worsley observed that, had it dropped out during the storm, the mast would have 'snapped like a carrot and no power on earth could have saved us'. Luck had been with them, after all.

By noon they were close to Cape Demidov, the entrance to King Haakon Bay on the south of the island of South Georgia. But shortly afterwards, the winds began to blow in their faces, driving the boat away from land. They had no option but to lower sails and take to the oars. Two at a time, the men pulled and pulled, but after the privations and exhaustion of the past weeks, they were in no fit state. It was a hopeless task and the prospect of another night on board the boat looked likely.

They had already spent seventeen days in the open boat and were near the end of their tether. Another winter's night in the Southern Ocean without water or hot food might have been the last for some.

By late afternoon, with the light fading, they could just see a narrow passage, too narrow for sail. It required another supreme effort to row up to the channel. They pulled and then as they neared the gap, the oars were withdrawn and the boat passed through the small entrance like threading a needle.

Almost immediately, the little craft was carried on the incoming waves and ground to a halt in a small cove. Shackleton leapt onto the shore and held the boat fast. The others clambered ashore and to their relief immediately found a welcome stream of fresh water, probably from a glacier. In an instant, they all fell to the knees and drank.

The little cove, about 360 ft (110 m) long and 180 ft (55 m) wide, was surrounded by imposing black cliffs rising to over 100 ft (30 m) and topped off with a layer of snow. At the head of the cove was a rocky beach and the sharp eyes of Crean soon spotted a small cave which he believed would provide them with shelter for the night.

It was late evening on 10 May 1916, and 522 days since they had last set foot on South Georgia.

21
Crossing South Georgia

There was little rejoicing as they hauled themselves slowly onto the beach at the end of their remarkable boat journey. Never before had men accomplished such a feat in the Southern Ocean but it was hardly a thought that occupied them as they struggled up the stony beach, drained of energy and suffering badly from exposure and thirst.

The six men were a pitiful sight. They had paid a heavy price for their seventeen days in the open boat and were shocked to find that they could barely walk up the beach. Worsley said they had almost lost the use of their limbs through the continual wetting and cramped conditions which for much of the time prevented them from even the basic task of standing up straight.

The first consideration was to get the remaining food and equipment out of the boat, but it was soon apparent they were too weak to lift the boat to safety beyond the grasp of the sea. To lighten the load the rocks and bags of ballast were dumped, though this hardly helped. Normally six men would have managed to manhandle a small boat with some ease, but their strength had been sapped by the trials of the past seventeen days and they could barely move the boat, let alone drag it up the beach. Further struggle was useless so a rope was hastily tied around a nearby rock to hold it steady while the men refuelled themselves with a much-needed hot meal and rest.

The modest 12 ft (3.6 m) cave at the top of the beach was, in fact, little more than a hollow in the cliff-face. The entrance was blocked by a curtain of huge icicles, each about 15 ft (4.5 m) long, which might have deterred some from entering. But after seventeen days in the Southern Ocean it offered all the comfort of a five-star hotel.

Crean, resuming his duties as cook, prepared a meal, their first hot food in days. Shortly afterwards they collapsed into their sleeping bags, with Shackleton somehow finding the resolve and energy to take the first watch and keep an eye on the *James Caird*. They could ill-afford to lose the craft now with the journey around the island to Leith Harbour still ahead. But disaster was never far away.

Crean happened to be on watch at about 2 a.m. when the boat was suddenly caught by a heavy swell and broke loose from her makeshift mooring. Without thinking about his own safety, Crean plunged into the cold black water to catch the rope before it was carried out to sea. At one stage the Irishman was up to his neck in the foaming seas, clinging onto the boat before the others could scramble to his aid.

But, as before, the men were still too weak to drag the boat high up the beach and beyond the grasp of the rolling waves. It meant that the desperately tired men had to sit up for the remainder of the night to ensure that the precious boat was not lost to the ocean. The hostile environment denied the men even the simple pleasure of a few hours' much-needed sleep.

In the morning, they decided to lighten the boat further by cutting down the top-sides and decking which McNeish had so carefully built three weeks earlier. Even then, it still took the tired little group much of the day to drag the *James Caird* inch by inch slowly up the beach beyond the high-water mark.

Towards the end of the day Crean and Shackleton went scouting for fresh meat and managed to find an albatross and a chick, which provided the hungry men with an excellent evening meal and badly needed inner warmth. McNeish pronounced it 'a treat' and for the first time in many weeks, the men could relax a little. With the *Caird* safe, they all crawled into their bags and indulged themselves in the sheer luxury of twelve glorious hours of unbroken sleep on firm ground. For the moment, their humble refuge was all they required.

The little beach, called Cape Rosa by Shackleton, was clearly not intended to be their final destination. It was merely the first suitable landfall before making their way around the island to Leith Harbour or any of the cluster of whaling stations to be found on the north side.

Vincent and McNeish, in particular, had suffered badly during the fraught boat journey and were probably incapable of completing another sea journey. However, any lingering hopes of sailing around South Georgia to the north side were quickly dispelled when they awoke after their long sleep. In the previous night's incident, the boat's rudder had been lost. The vessel, which had crossed 800 miles (1,300 km) of the worst seas on the globe, was now reduced to little more than a humble rowing boat.

It meant a hurried revision of their options. Leith Harbour, the intended destination, was about 130 miles (210 km) away by sea, although there was some doubt that the whaling station was manned in the depths of winter. The alternatives were Stromness and Husvik, about 150 miles (240 km) away, which were known to be operational all year round.

By land the distance was estimated to be about 30 miles (48 km) as the crow flies. No one, however, had ever attempted to cross South Georgia before and the interior was largely unmapped and unknown. Shackleton knew there was little choice. They would have to travel where no one had been before. It hardly seemed to matter that they did not have adequate equipment, food and clothing or that the already exhausted men would have to rely on willpower alone.

South Georgia is a hostile wilderness, unremittingly bleak and forbidding. Its spine of mountain peaks, the Allardyce Range, runs through the centre of the island at an average height of over 5,000 ft (1,500 m) and stretches up to the 9,000 ft (2,750 m) Mount Paget. The rugged interior is a jumble of rocky cliffs, snow fields, treacherous crevasses and steep icy slopes. Glaciers cover over half the crescent-shaped island, which is little more than 100 miles (160 km) long and less than 25 miles (40 km) across at its widest point.

Without hesitation Shackleton selected Tom Crean and Frank Worsley to make the challenging journey with him. McCarthy, the fittest of the others, would stay behind to look after the ailing McNeish and Vincent.

Worsley, as an outstanding navigator, picked himself for a journey into the unknown. His achievement in taking the *James Caird* across the Southern Ocean is one of the greatest feats of seamanship ever recorded and without his skills the trek would have been impossible. In addition, he had picked up some valuable experience of Alpine mountain climbing and had undoubtedly coped well with the fatigue and deprivations of the past few weeks.

There was inevitability about the choice of Crean, even if his experience of climbing had been limited to strolling the rolling hills of County Kerry, Ireland. But no one was more experienced at travelling across the ice.

Now approaching his thirty-ninth birthday, Crean had spent almost half of the past fifteen years exploring in the South and was better equipped than most to cope with the trials and tribulations of the coming journey. Crean's astonishing endurance and fortitude had been demonstrated before and Shackleton also knew Crean would not break down. Crean had repeatedly shown that he was both mentally and physically tough and that, equally important, he was demonstrably a man for a tight spot.

First, though, the men badly needed proper rest and warm food to recover from the past few weeks. Hot meals were prepared and sledging rations, initially intended for the crossing of Antarctica, were assembled.

The men, though physically drained from the boat

journey, soon settled into a routine. Some found tussock grass for the floor of the cave and driftwood for the fire, others hunted for birds or anything else which could be eaten and McNeish and McCarthy worked at cutting down the sides of the *James Caird*. McNeish wrote in his diary:

> 'We have not been as comfortable for the last five weeks.'[1]

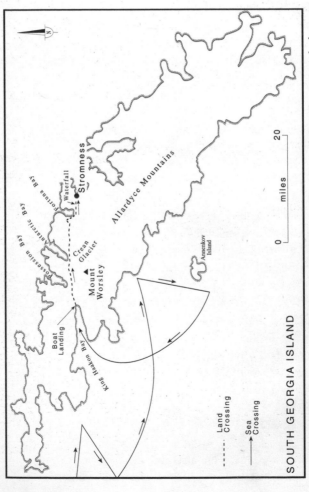

South Georgia was largely unexplored when Shackleton, Worsley and Tom Crean marched across the mountainous, glacier-strewn island in 1916. The map shows the path taken by the James Caird approaching the island and the route across the island.

Stricken. Frank Hurley's famous photograph of the doomed Endurance, *lurching at a crazy angle as the ice of the Weddell Sea tightens its deadly grip. (SPRI)*

Dry land. After 497 days on the Endurance or adrift on the ice, the party reached the uninhabited Elephant Island. The men barely had the strength to lift the three little boats – the James Caird, Dudley Docker and Stancomb Wills – onto the rocky beach. (SPRI)

Hurley's evocative picture of Tom Crean taken on board Endurance *and showing the Irishman's great determination and resolve. (SPRI)*

Launching of the James Caird. *The men on Elephant Island prepare to launch the 22-ft* Caird *on her epic 800-mile journey to South Georgia, April 1916. (SPRI)*

South Georgia. The mountainous, unexplored island had never been crossed before Tom Crean, Shackleton and Worsley conquered it in 1916 to bring rescue to the men on Elephant Island. (SPRI)

Back from the dead. Tom Crean (left), Shackleton (centre) and another (presumed to be Worsley) caught on camera by a Norwegian whaler soon after their memorable forced march across South Georgia. (SPRI/Alexandra Shackleton Collection)

The entire Endurance *party reunited at Puntas Arenas, Chile, September 1916, after the rescue from Elephant Island. Crean stands (6th from left) alongside Frank Wild (8th left) and Shackleton (10th from left wearing hat). (SPRI)*

Tom Crean and his bride, Eileen Herlihy, photographed on their wedding day, September 1917. In their home village of Anascaul the couple were affectionately known as Tom the Pole and Nell the Pole. (Crean family)

The family man. Crean photographed in the late 1920s with his wife Nell and daughters, Mary (left) and Eileen (centre). (Crean family)

The South Pole Inn, Tom Crean's pub in the village of Anascaul, County Kerry. (M. Smith)

The inscription on Tom Crean's grave features the appropriate words of Robert Louis Stevenson: 'Home is the sailor, home from the sea'. (M. Smith)

A memorable link with the past. The skis Tom Crean wore on Scott's last expedition. The skis spent many years hanging over a doorway in the Gordon Lennox Club at Merthyr Vale, Wales, and were later donated to the Cyfarthfa Castle Museum in Merthyr Tydfil.

However, it was clear that a more suitable camp was needed to accommodate the weakest pair, McNeish and Vincent. The spot chosen was about 6 miles away across King Haakon Bay where their rudimentary charts indicated that the terrain was slightly friendlier. It was decided to move as quickly as possible.

As they prepared the boat, Crean suddenly leapt up and began to wade out into the water to investigate an object he saw bobbing about in the waves. To their astonishment he returned clutching the missing rudder. It had been lost in the ebbing and flowing tide for six days and yet, with the enormous area of the Southern Ocean at its disposal, the rudder had miraculously chosen to land back at their feet.

The weather, too, was kind as they skipped through the little passage guarding Cape Rosa and headed westwards in a comfortable breeze to cross King Haakon Bay. Shortly after noon they came across a gently inclined beach of sand and small stones. As they neared the beach, they caught sight of many sea-elephants, which it was reckoned would provide enough food and blubber for as long they wanted. It was exactly what they were looking for and Shackleton called it Peggoty Camp after the matronly figure in Dickens' *David Copperfield* who lived in a house made from a boat.

With considerable effort, the boat was hauled up the beach and turned over to provide an improvised shelter against the winds. McCarthy shored up the boat with some large stones and the few remaining bags and equipment were stored inside. When finished, it was almost the lap of luxury after their experiences of the past months on the ice floes and in the open boat.

There was no time to indulge. Shackleton, Worsley and Crean were anxious to start their overland journey, fully aware that it had been over three weeks since they had left their comrades on the beach 800 miles (1,300 km) away at Elephant Island. But on 16 May the weather was appalling and the six men huddled underneath the boat for most of the day. There was little let-up until late on 18 May and Shackleton decided to start the next day.

At 2 a.m. on Friday morning, 19 May 1916, they ate a large meal of steaming-hot hoosh and prepared to set off in their attempt to cross South Georgia. The moon shone brightly, a good omen.

Initially, they intended to take a sledge which McNeish had made from scraps of wood. It was to be packed with five days' food and sleeping bags and abandoned halfway across the island. However, the sledge proved to be 'heavy and cumbrous' and was not suitable for the snow plains, glaciers and peaks which they had to cross.

After a brief conference, they decided to travel light, making the trip as quick as possible. They took three days' rations and to save weight they decided to leave behind their sleeping bags. It was a huge risk. The men did not possess a tent and without shelter they would be highly vulnerable in a blizzard. The fact that it was approaching midwinter only increased the risks of getting caught by the severe weather in the region.

Each man carried his own ration of three days' food in a sock and there was a primus stove with enough fuel for six meals. They had two compasses, a pair of binoculars, 50 ft (15 m) of rope, a half-full box of matches and a carpenter's adze which would double as an ice-axe. McNeish, in one final inspired piece of improvisation, yanked numerous brass screws from the *James Caird* and fixed eight into the sole of each of their snow boots to give a better grip on the slippery ice fields. The one 'luxury' was Worsley's log of the *Endurance*.

Their clothing was sparse and badly worn after five months' constant wear. What had been heavy-duty Jaeger underwear, for example, was now little more than a light covering of fabric more suitable for warmer climates. Over this they wore a pair of ordinary trousers and a Jaeger wool sweater. The outer clothing was a set of windproof Burberrys, a blouse and trousers securely fastened around the neck, waist, wrists and ankles to prevent cold air getting in. They protected their heads with a wool balaclava helmet and wore two pairs of mitts. The footgear was two pairs of heavy wool socks in felt-lined boots.

Finally, the three had sown an 8-inch (20-cm) piece of blanket into their badly-worn Jaeger wool sweaters to make a rough pocket for little personal items, such as a spoon, tobacco and papers and some biscuit. For men who had nothing these were treasures. Around his neck, Crean wore his little treasure, the scapular.

Shackleton left a note in McNeish's diary saying that he was heading for Husvik and recommending that, if he did not return, the three men should sail round to the northern coast of the island in a few months after the winter had passed. He concluded:

'I trust to have returned in a few days.'[2]

They all shook hands, then took their first steps into the unknown. McNeish walked with the three men for the first 200 yards (180 m), shook hands a second time and watched as the three men began the climb up the steep snowy slopes towards the ominous black, snow-topped mountains. It was shortly after 3 a.m. and the moon provided a welcome splash of light to guide their steps.

Fortunately, the weather remained fine and clear as they began their first ascent, reaching a height of around 2,500 ft (760 m) after about two hours of steady climbing in the eerie moonlight. The track ahead was formidable. In their pathway, Shackleton recalled, stood a collection of five high peaks, impassable cliffs, steep snow-slopes and sharply descending glaciers. The interior, he concluded, was 'tremendously broken' and peaks resembled the knuckles on a clenched fist.

As dawn neared a fog swept down and they encountered their first brush with disaster as they stumbled close to the edge of a massive crevasse in semi-darkness. In the half-light they could not see each other clearly and each feared that one of the party might have plunged unseen to his death. Suddenly they felt highly exposed and Worsley recalled the moment of sheer relief when they found all were safe:

> 'The relief of hearing Shackleton's voice, and then that of Crean, who was cursing softly, was indescribable. Never have I felt so puny, nor realised so clearly the helplessness of Man against Nature. For a brief moment I felt that curious weakness about the knees that comes upon one when one has just gone through some fearsome ordeal.'[3]

It was a stark lesson and the men quickly roped themselves together as insurance against one of them crashing through thin ice or toppling over a concealed precipice. In the same way that Evans, Lashly and Crean had bonded together on the last returning journey from the Polar Plateau in 1912, the fate of the three now rested with each other.

Shackleton took the lead, striding into the wall of fog with Crean in the middle and Worsley at the rear of the little column. It was essential to steer a direct course for Husvik or Stromness and Shackleton was guided from behind by the sharp tongues of Crean or Worsley who kept him on the straight and narrow with suitably robust instructions of 'port', 'starboard' and 'steady'.

A little later the fog began to lift and the men saw an enormous snow-covered inland lake slightly off to the left which offered the cheering prospect of a smoother surface and easier travel. Anxious to make haste while the weather was in their favour, they descended onto the frozen lake and, as expected, found the going much easier. But they had been fooled.

The 'lake' stretched as far as the eye could see and it soon dawned on them that they were gazing out at the open sea. It was Possession Bay on the northern coast of South Georgia, which meant they had crossed the island at its narrowest point in a south-to-north direction. But there was no shoreline and no inhabitants.

They had no choice but to retrace their steps, climb back up the heights where they could gain a clearer view of the terrain and resume their path to the knot of manned whaling stations in the east. It was a bad mistake, but the weary men could be forgiven for trying to find the quickest, simplest route. Nevertheless, it was precious time they could ill-afford to lose.

By 9 a.m., after an unbroken march of about six hours, they stopped for the first hot meal. A 3-ft (0.9-m) hole was dug in the soft snow and Crean and Worsley took turns to spread-eagle themselves over the primus to prevent the sharp winds blowing it out. When the meal was cooked, they each dipped their spoons into the scalding cauldron of steaming hoosh and gulped it down as hot as possible. The effects of the warm food swept through their bodies, reinvigorating them.

Despite their precarious position on the edge of the unknown, the three men somehow managed to keep up their spirits with gentle banter which showed that, whatever the elements threw at them, they had managed to retain their humour. Worsley remembered one incident as they gulped down their welcome first hot meal. He said:

> 'At our first meal Shackleton, who was always fond of a leg-pull, said: "Crean, you've got a bigger spoon than we have."
>
> "Doesn't matter," said the imperturbable Crean, "The Skipper [Worsley] has a bigger mouth".'[4]

The men wasted little time and within 30 minutes had resumed their march, conscious that they had to progress as quickly as possible before the notoriously changeable weather of South Georgia deteriorated.

Ahead lay the imposing barrier of five mountain peaks, which looked like the knuckles of a clenched fist. They chose the easiest-looking pass, climbing a steep face with the aid of McNeish's adze. But fresh disappointment waited the men as they reached the 1,500-ft (450-m) peak after three hours' steady uphill climbing.

At the crest they discovered that the slope broke away sharply in precipices and ice cliffs that were impossible to negotiate. Going ahead was too dangerous to contemplate and for the second time that morning, the three disappointed men were forced to retrace their steps. It was another bitter moment and for those who did not have time to spare, it was more valuable time lost.

The weather, so far, had been remarkably calm and stable. But it was the depths of winter in South Georgia and they knew that a sudden change could hit them at any moment.

At the bottom of the slope they warmed themselves with another helping of hot hoosh which helped take their minds off a frustrating and disappointing morning. Soon they were back on the march and ascending another steep pass in hopes of better luck at the next crest.

The climb was steeper than the first and the snow was soft, which made the going terribly heavy as they sank up to their knees with every step. It was also apparent how weak they had become. While the rest and fresh food at Cape Rosa and Peggoty Camp had been welcome, it was far too little recuperation for the seriously weakened trio who now moved ever more slowly. As they climbed higher in the increasingly rarefied air it became necessary to halt every twenty minutes and lay flat out in the snow gasping for breath.

At the second peak an even bigger blow awaited the men. The land ahead was just as menacing as the first, possibly worse. To carry on would be highly dangerous and again they faced the grim prospect of retracing their steps to find a safer route through the peaks. Worsley wanted to chance it but Shackleton vetoed the idea. They would have to go back – again. It was a third, bitter blow for the men who had wasted almost the whole day trying to find a pass through the knuckles of mountains.

The most pressing problem was that they were about 4,500 ft (1,400 m) up and swirling banks of fog were closing in from all sides. In the gathering gloom of twilight, darkness approached and they had no shelter against the sub-zero temperatures of the South Georgia night. Without a tent or sleeping bags, they would probably freeze to death during the night.

As speedily as possible, the dejected trio began to zigzag down the icy slope and scurried across the snow towards the next pass as the sun began to set behind the snow-topped mountains at their backs. After half an hour of tortuously slow travel, with the light fading fast, they found the soft snowy banks very hard going and it was apparent that it would take many hours of arduous struggle to reach a safer more sheltered spot for nightfall.

Progress, Shackleton soon realised, was far too slow and the risk of being caught high up the mountain in the rapidly sinking temperatures of the night was growing by the minute. They had to descend much faster.

The three men huddled together on a ledge which had been hacked from the snow with the aid of McNeish's adze. As the fog closed in around them, Worsley recalled a brief conversation which summed up their plight. He wrote:

> 'Crean said, quaintly, "You won't be able to do much navigating in this, Skipper", but Shackleton, who was usually amused by his remarks, did not smile. He said tersely, "I don't like our position at all. We must get out of it somehow; we shall freeze if we wait here until the moon rises".'[5]

The situation was desperate and Shackleton, who normally preferred not to take chances, offered a desperate solution. They would slide down the ice slope.

Below the men was a precipitous slope and in the gathering gloom they were unable to see what precisely waited them at the bottom. If they crashed into a rock it would mean certain disaster and there was always the possibility that the slope might give way to a yawning crevasse. Only desperate men would contemplate such a risky move.

For Crean the moment brought back the hair-raising episode four years earlier on the Beardmore Glacier with Evans and Lashly. Then, against his better judgement, they had climbed aboard their sledge and tobogganed down the glacier at speeds of up to 60 mph. Luckily they had survived.

As then, Crean could see there was little choice. Both he and Worsley agreed with Shackleton, though Worsley admitted it seemed 'a most impossible project'.

The 50-ft (16-m) rope was coiled into three circular 'mats' and each man sat on the makeshift toboggan. Shackleton sat at the front, then Worsley and Crean at the rear. Worsley wrapped his legs around Shackleton's waist and his arms around his neck, while Crean did the same to Worsley. They were locked together as one.

In an instant, Shackleton kicked off and the trio hurtled downhill, the wind whistling past their ears and the snowy landscape becoming a white blur as they rushed along. Crean, at the rear, had great difficulty preventing the adze cutting tool swinging round and slicing into the men as they plummeted downhill. They all clung to each other for dear life as they sped down the slope and Worsley recalled:

> 'We seemed to shoot into space. For a moment my hair fairly stood on end. Then quite suddenly I felt a glow and knew that I was grinning! I was actually enjoying it. It was most exhilarating. We were shooting down the side of a most precipitous mountain at nearly a mile a minute. I yelled with excitement and found that Shackleton and Crean were yelling too. It seemed ridiculously safe. To hell with the rocks!'[6]

The trio's downward descent began to slow as they reached softer snow and the toboggan suddenly came to an abrupt halt in a bank of snow which mercifully softened the impact of their crash landing. Slightly dazed, disoriented and relieved, the men hauled themselves to their feet and rather solemnly shook hands. A quick inspection found the biggest casualty was their trousers, which were now in rags.

Their rapid descent had lasted two or three minutes and in the darkness it was unclear how far they had travelled. Shackleton estimated only 900 ft (275 m) while Worsley speculated that they had descended 3,000 ft (900 m). But the madcap scheme had worked. Luck had smiled upon them.

The heartily relieved trio enjoyed a quick meal and promptly resumed their slog across the soft snow, keeping a watchful eye for hidden crevasses, a constant danger in the gathering darkness. Very soon the moon appeared overhead, casting a ghostly light to help guide them over the treacherous but undeniably beautiful terrain. The scene was 'majestic' according to Worsley.

Today the 'majestic' place is called the Crean Glacier in honour of the Irishman who, with Shackleton and Worsley, crossed it first.

By midnight the men had been on the march for 21 hours, broken only by short rests and a meal every four hours. Now they were about 4,000 ft (1,200 m) high and suddenly began to see the land fall away before them on a downward slope. In the freezing temperatures, the snow would be firmer and the going a little better. At the bottom, they believed, lay Stromness Bay.

Cheered by their discovery, the men stopped for a meal, lit the primus and talked optimistically about reaching their goal. Shackleton recalled:

> 'Worsley and Crean sang their old songs when the primus was going merrily. Laughter was in our hearts, though not in our parched and cracked lips.'[7]

Within half an hour they were back on the march and once again confronted with utter dejection. They found themselves embroiled in a mass of dangerous crevasses which meant they were travelling across a glacier. But there is no glacier at Stromness. The disappointment, Shackleton remembered, was 'severe'.

Not for the first time, the increasingly tired men had to turn around and retrace their steps in the snow. For two weary hours they plodded back where they had been and at 5 a.m., with dawn approaching, they stopped for a breather. They had been on the march without sleep for 26 hours and badly needed a far longer rest.

It is also likely that they were suffering from dehydration because they did not have enough spare fuel to melt snow for drinking water. Lack of adequate fluid intake in the cold, dry Antarctic environment is a constant threat and today doctors recommend drinking at least a gallon of water every day. In 1916, on the freezing South Georgia landscape, Crean, Worsley and Shackleton were drinking only a fraction of the necessary water intake.

As they huddled together for warmth behind a protective rock, Crean and Worsley succumbed to the growing fatigue and instantly dropped off to sleep. Shackleton was also on the brink of dozing off when he realised that sleep would be fatal. They would freeze to death in the open. After five minutes he woke his two comrades telling them they had slept for half an hour. It was a bare-faced lie that saved their lives.

Ahead lay another steep climb of about 1,000 ft (300 m). The men were understandably apprehensive at what they would find at the summit. At around 6 a.m. they reached the peak just as the dawn was beginning to shed light on the day. For a change, what they saw was highly promising. There were no threatening precipices or impassable cliffs, just a comfortable-looking slope down to a valley. Beyond the valley they could pick out the high hills which, they remembered, surrounded the whaling stations at Stromness and Husvick. Their goal was in sight.

Shackleton ordered a warming meal of hoosh to galvanise the men for the final leg of their journey. As Crean prepared the food, Shackleton went ahead to survey the terrain. It was about 6.30 a.m., the curtain of darkness was being slowly lifted and Shackleton suddenly thought he heard a noise in the distance. It sounded faintly like a whistle but he could not be sure and he was aware that intense fatigue can play tricks on the mind. However, he assured himself that 6.30 a.m. was the time when the men at the whaling stations were woken up for work, probably by the sound of a factory whistle blowing.

Breakfast was gulped down and the men gathered around Worsley's chronometer and stared silently as the hands moved round to 7 a.m. – the moment the whistle at Stromness would definitely ring out again to summon the men to work. The tension was unbearable as the seconds ticked by.

Right on time at seven o'clock they heard the toot of the far-off steam whistle. The men looked at each other, smiled and shook hands. It was the first sound from civilisation they had heard for almost eighteen months.

Worsley began to yell and Shackleton said it was a moment which was 'hard to describe'. He recalled that all the pain and ache, boat journeys, marches, hunger and fatigue seemed to belong to the limbo of forgotten things.

The journey to safety was far from over though, and the men had to compose themselves quickly and grasp the reality of the situation. They were in the advanced stages of exhaustion, thirsty and they had to cross more unknown snow fields to reach Stromness.

The empty primus, which had provided vital hot food at regular intervals over the past hours, was dumped and they gathered together the last scraps of food. Each man was down to one last sledging ration and a single biscuit.

Although the men were fairly well fed on their overland trek, fatigue was taking over. They had not slept for nearly 30 hours and their steps became a weary plod as they frequently sank deep into the soft snow. Each step was a test of their resolve. At the back of their minds was the constant fear that the weather, which had been so kind, might take a vicious turn for the worst. They were in no condition to fight back.

Soon they came across a steep gradient of blue ice which threatened to halt their immediate passage. Crean and Worsley lowered Shackleton down the full length of the 50-ft (15-m) rope, cutting steps with the adze as he moved down. There he cut a small platform and the others climbed slowly down. Then the process was repeated over and over again as they slowly and purposefully lowered themselves down the sharp gradient.

Worsley said the slope was nearly as perpendicular as a church steeple and they were terrified that the weather might suddenly deteriorate. Exposed as they were on the cliff face, they would probably not have survived. But, despite the gnawing fear of a sudden break in the weather, it took two painful hours for the severely drained men to slowly descend a mere 500 ft (150 m).

At the bottom of the gradient, the ground led easily to the valley. Slowly they moved across to the welcome flatter ground and soon began another climb up yet another ice slope. It was about 3,000 ft (1,000 m) to the top and the going was terribly heavy.

The danger was ever present, even when they came across a piece of flat, firm ground which made the going somewhat easier. It turned out to be another frozen lake and suddenly Crean broke through into freezing water. He sank up to his waist, the final indignity for a man who had already endured so much. But Worsley recalled:

'Crean was a bit cold, but otherwise none the worse for his ducking.'[8]

They had no dry clothes to give their dripping colleague and all they could do was to plod on, hoping that continuous movement would warm Crean's body and that the chilly wind might dry his clothes. By 1.30 p.m. in the afternoon they had managed to clamber up the ridge and gazed down on the wondrous sight below – in front of them, about 2,500 ft (760 m) below, was the Stromness Whaling Station.

They could see ships, buildings and, thankfully, the tiny figures of men hurrying about their work. Instinctively the three men began yelling and waving but their voices were lost in the wind and, of course, no one was looking in their direction. No one in their right mind would have expected men to be approaching Stromness from the interior of South Georgia. Only desperate men would have contemplated travelling from the interior of South Georgia.

They began to descend, hopefully for the last time. The slope was steep and soon they found themselves tramping along in a stream of very cold running water which rose to their knees and chilled them further. To their dismay, the stream came to a sudden halt and the bitterly cold water tumbled over the edge in a cascading little waterfall.

Shivering with the cold and on the point of exhaustion, the men stared in disbelief. The waterfall poured down about 30 ft (10 m) below and on either side there were impossibly steep rocks and cliffs. For a brief moment they contemplated doing what they had done so many times in the past day and a half and retrace their steps.

But the shivering, hungry, thirsty men were in no condition to make another uphill climb and more importantly it was now nearing 3 p.m., with darkness approaching and temperatures set to drop sharply as the sun disappeared. The three men had now been out in the open without sleep for 36 hours, their food was all gone and they had no means of melting ice for drinking water. A night in the open would probably be fatal.

Shackleton said it was 'scarcely thinkable' to retrace their steps. The only option was to climb down through the waterfall.

Hurriedly they found a suitable boulder and fixed the rope as firmly as possible. According to Shackleton, Crean, the heaviest of the three, went first. Slowly and cautiously Shackleton and Worsley lowered the Irishman through the bitterly cold running water. He disappeared altogether in the flowing torrent of water and came out gasping for air as his feet finally touched the rocks 30 ft (10 m) below.

All three endured their own cold shower as they climbed down through the waterfall. But they were unable to release the rope, which therefore remained behind lashed to the boulder as a memento of their remarkable journey.

Once on the bottom the men were barely a mile from the whaling station. Despite the freezing cold, intense fatigue and growing thirst, their spirits were lifted by the prospect. The end was in sight.

They faced one last hazard before they completed their momentous journey. The eight, 2-inch (5-cm) brass screws which McNeish had fixed in the soles of their boots at Peggoty Camp, had been worn away by the constant scrapes with rocks and packed ice in the past 36 hours. By now they were flush against the soles and without the extra grip, each of the men suffered some heavy falls on the glassy ice which shook them badly. Crean took a painful tumble and fell onto the blade of the carpenter's adze, narrowly avoiding a dangerous cut. Undeterred they picked him up and plodded on.

By now, as the end of the amazing journey approached, they began to ponder what people would make of the three ragamuffins who had come back from the dead. Worsley, in particular, became concerned that there might be women at Stromness who would be shocked at the appalling state of the three men.

The weary, bedraggled men were indeed a ghastly-looking sight. They had not washed for three months, their hair hung down onto their shoulders and their beards were matted with soot and blubber. Their haggard faces, which were blackened with grease, had been ravaged by a combination of frostbite, wind and exposure. They gave off a disgusting smell and their clothes, which they had worn for over a year, were wet and ragged. They had been on the march almost without a break for 36 hours and had probably covered around 40 miles (64 km) on their trek. Worsley said they were a 'terrible looking trio of scarecrows'.

After leaving South Georgia eighteen months earlier with 28 fit men and a fully stocked ship, Crean, Worsley and

Shackleton were returning to civilisation with just the clothes they stood up in.

They could not have imagined the welcome awaiting them as they turned the corner and walked slowly towards some outbuildings of the whaling station. The first humans they saw were two boys, aged about ten or twelve. They took one look at the 'scarecrows' and fled in terror. Soon after they entered a building and found an old man who, like the young boys, turned on his heels and hurried away in alarm.

They moved onto the quay where they found a man called Matthias Anderson, who looked as though he was in charge of something or other. Shackleton, in a weak reedy voice, asked to see Anton Anderson, the station manager at Stromness.

It was 20 May 1916, and apart from their *Endurance* colleagues, some 532 days since they had last spoken to another human. Matthias Anderson shook his head and said Anton had left and been replaced by Thoralf Sorlle. By coincidence, Shackleton knew Sorlle.

Anderson was suspicious of the sight before him, but went into an office and told Sorlle that there were 'three funny looking men outside' who claimed to have walked across the island from the interior. As a precaution, Anderson asked the trio to remain outside while he spoke to Sorlle.

After a moment Sorlle, a tall imposing man with a large moustache, emerged from the building and stared in utter disbelief at the three unkempt wrecks of humanity who stood before him. He did not recognise them.

In fact, they were unrecognisable. But Sorlle knew Shackleton well and had entertained the party at South Georgia before the departure south. However *Endurance* had been out of touch for over 18 months and it was assumed all hands were lost. Shackleton recalled the first conversation:

'Mr Sorlle came out to the door and said, "Well."

"Don't you know me?" I said.

"I know your voice," he replied doubtfully. "You're the mate of the *Daisy*."

"My name is Shackleton," I said.

Immediately he put out his hand and said, "Come in, come in".'9

Anderson turned away and wept.

22
Beyond belief

The scale of the achievement by Shackleton, Worsley and Crean is breathtaking by any standards. Indeed, it is almost beyond belief bearing in mind that the three men were hopelessly ill-equipped for either the 800-mile (1,300-km) journey across the Southern Ocean in an open boat or the forced march over the uncharted interior of South Georgia.

They were poorly protected from the bitter elements, with their badly worn clothing and inadequate food supplies scarcely enough to sustain even modest physical effort – let alone the traumatic ocean crossing and the trek of about 40 miles (64 km) in 36 hours over the glaciers and icefields of South Georgia. The physical demands were immense and so, too, were the psychological strains which the ordeal imposed on the three men.

Duncan Carse, the explorer who retraced their steps almost 40 years later in 1955, was astonished by what the three men had achieved and almost lost in admiration. He could barely understand how they survived and wrote a memorable assessment:

> 'A man may travel on foot from the head of King Haakon Bay to the whaling station of Stromness, keeping either high or low. The high level route is circuitous, a gradual rise and fall via the spacious crest of

the Kohl-Larsen Plateau. The low-level route is direct, a saw-tooth thrust through the tortured upheaval of mountain and glacier that falls in chaos to the northern sea. In distance, they are hardly comparable.

We today are travelling easily and unhurriedly. We are fit men, with our sledges and tents and ample food and time. We break new ground, but with leisure and opportunity to probe ahead. We pick and choose our hazards, accepting only the calculated risk. No lives depend upon our success – except our own. We take the high road.

They – Shackleton, Worsley and Crean – were desperate castaways with sick companions and their only asset a boat that would never sail again. They travelled under headlong duress, reduced by long privation to exhausted starvelings destitute of all but their own worn out clothing – no sledges, no tents, little food, and less time. They broke new ground in a race against falling reserves of strength. Their only safety lay in speed and the short cut regardless of danger; they dared not fail because "22 men were waiting for the relief that we alone could secure for them." They took the low road.

I do not know how they did it, except that they had to – three men of the heroic age of Antarctic exploration with 50 feet of rope between them – and a carpenter's adze.'[1]

It may be easier to guess the physical effect of the months of hardship, isolation and immense endurance, climaxing in the remarkable crossing of South Georgia in winter. The photographic evidence immediately after their arrival is limited, although some pictures taken in the following weeks still reveal gaunt, haggard faces.

The journey had clearly exacted a heavy toll and it says enough of their unkempt appearance that station manager,

Sorlle, did not recognise any of them. Or that a toughened Norwegian whaler should spontaneously burst into tears at the sight of the bedraggled men.

The effect which is obviously less easy to detect is the mental strain imposed by the months of physical hardship and the ever-present knowledge that they were so close to a miserable death. The three men had tapped deep reserves of mental strength as they fought against one seemingly fatal hazard after another and after all these years, it is extremely hard to estimate what impact this had made.

Shackleton's inner strength and resolve were well known from two earlier expeditions to the South. But Crean, too, possessed special qualities of mental toughness and resilience which marked him out from the bunch and this was why Shackleton, a superb judge of character, chose the Irishman to accompany him on the boat journey and the South Georgia crossing.

On no occasion is there is any suggestion from the recollections of Shackleton or Worsley that Crean had weakened, either mentally or physically. Amazingly, he also retained his sense of humour and, to the occasional irritation of his stressed-out colleagues, even found the capacity to break into song.

But there was, in addition, another more surprising and inexplicable side effect of the men's journey – a spiritual dimension that perhaps reveals more about the psychological effect of the ordeal than the more easily apparent physical damage. All three men confessed, at separate times, to a highly unusual experience on the South Georgia crossing. All three, it emerged, believed there was a fourth person accompanying them on the crossing.

Worsley, writing in his book, *The Great Antarctic Rescue*, revealed:

> 'Three or four weeks afterwards, Sir Ernest and I, comparing notes, found that we each had a strange feeling that there had been a fourth in our party and

Crean afterwards confessed to the same feeling.'[2]

In his other book, *Endurance*, published in 1931, Worsley was slightly more expansive:

> 'There was no doubt that Providence had been with us. There was indeed one curious thing about our crossing of South Georgia, a thing which I have never been able to explain. Whenever I reviewed the incidents of that march I had the sub-conscious feeling that there were four of us, instead of three. Moreover this impression was shared by both Shackleton and Crean.'[3]

Shackleton describes much the same feeling of a fourth presence in his book, *South*:

> 'When I look back at those days I have no doubt that Providence guided us, not only across those snowfields, but across the storm-white sea that separated Elephant Island from our landing place on South Georgia. I know that during that long and racking march of 36 hours over the unnamed mountains and glaciers of South Georgia, it seemed to me often that we were four, not three. I said nothing to my companions on the point, but afterwards Worsley said to me, "Boss, I had a curious feeling on the march that there was another person with us." Crean confessed to the same idea. One feels "the dearth of human words, the roughness of mortal speech" in trying to describe things intangible, but a record of our journeys would be incomplete without a reference to a subject very near to our hearts.'[4]

Unfortunately, no documentary evidence has survived to show that Crean believed in the fourth person. But years later he told friends exactly the same story and evidently believed that he, too, had shared the experience. According to the recollections of his friend, Bob Knightly, Crean simply said:

'The Lord brought us home.'[5]

Equally the comments of Shackleton and Worsley are both unequivocal in showing that the Irishman shared their belief. In the circumstances, it might have been worthy of more comment from Shackleton and Worsley if Crean had confessed to not believing in the presence of a fourth person.

Shackleton also provided another brief insight into the psychological effects of the journey while he was compiling his book on the expedition, *South*. Shackleton did not write his own books, preferring to dictate his version of events to a New Zealand journalist, Edward Saunders, who dutifully and painstakingly took down his every word. Shackleton's adviser, Leonard Tripp, was present during the dictation session when the subject of the fourth presence came up and he thoughtfully recorded the strain which showed on Shackleton.

Tripp gave an account of the session, with evidence of the severe emotional strain, to Shackleton's friend and biographer, Dr Hugh Robert Mill in 1922, shortly after Shackleton had died. He told Mill:

> 'I shall never forget the occasion. I was sitting in a chair listening; Shackleton walked up and down the room smoking a cigarette and I was absolutely amazed at his language. He very seldom hesitated, but every now and then he would tell Saunders to make a mark because he had not got the right word; but that was only occasionally. I watched him, and his whole face seemed to swell, and I could see the man was suffering. After about half an hour he turned to me and with tears in his eyes he said, "Tripp, you don't know what I've been through, and I am going through it all again, and I can't do it." I would say, "But we must get it all down".
>
> He would go on for an hour and then all of a sudden would say, "I can't do it – I must go and talk to the girls or play tennis". He walked out of the room as if he

intended to go away, lit a cigarette and then in about five minutes, he would come back and start again. The same thing happened after another hour or so. I could see that he was suffering when he came to his sensation of a fourth presence, when crossing the mountains, he turned around to me and said, "Tripp, this is something I have not told you". As far as I can remember, his account of crossing South Georgia has practically not been altered in revision.'[6]

Although no similar account exists for the other two, it is a strain that must have been shared equally by Crean and Worsley who had, after all, been through the same ordeal.

The story of the mystical fourth presence inevitably created some controversy, with some suggesting that it was no more than a publicity stunt and even modern writers dismissing it as a hoax. Some saw it as reminiscent of the 'Angel of Mons', a mythical angel riding a white horse wielding a flaming sword who is said to have appeared to British troops on the battlefields of the First World War.

Myth or not, the battle-weary soldiers at Mons shared several important things with Crean, Worsley and Shackleton – they were exhausted and under great stress. Contemporary reports of the dreadful Mons retreat speak of troops hallucinating with fatigue and that 'very nearly everyone was seeing things . . .'

Whether the story of the fourth person was fact or fiction, it helped inspire the poet, T.S. Eliot to write *The Waste Land* in which he also told of another presence. With the knowledge of their ordeal in mind, Eliot's words are strongly evocative of the epic journey undertaken by Shackleton, Worsley and Crean. The relevant passage of the poem reads:

> *Who is the third who walks always beside you?*
> *When I count, there are only you and I together*
> *But when I look ahead up the white road*

There is always another one walking beside you
Gliding wrapt in a brown mantle, hooded
I do not know whether a man or a woman
– but who is that on the other side of you?[7]

We shall, of course, never explain the 'fourth person'. It may have been a simple case of wishful thinking on the part of three exhausted men nearing the end of their tether who in their darkest hour were involuntarily seeking some comfort from their God. At the depths of their plight, they would have called on any source for the last dregs of strength to carry them through their extraordinary journey. The instincts of survival have no bounds.

However, it is known that exhaustion, hunger, thirst and inadequate diet over a long period can contribute to hallucinations. It may well be that the debilitated, underfed, parched and slightly disorientated men were simply hallucinating.

Perhaps there is no adequate explanation.

23
Return to Elephant Island

There was a quaint Englishness about the greeting for the two Irishmen and the New Zealander as they were taken to comfortable quarters by the Norwegian station manager. Tea was served.

Shackleton, somehow, had the presence of mind to ask Sorlle to take a photograph of the three men. Unfortunately no one had any film, so the world was robbed of an opportunity to record the historic moment that Shackleton, Worsley and Crean stepped back from the dead. Or, as Worsley put it, the world lost a picture of 'its three dirtiest men'.

Their first concern was the war. Shackleton wanted to know when it had finished and Sorlle shocked them by reporting that millions were still being killed in the slaughter. It astounded the men and also underlined the fact the explorers had been out of contact with the rest of the world since December 1914. There were few people from the civilised world so out of touch with the momentous events elsewhere.

The men also picked up the first hints that their sister ship, the *Aurora*, had run into trouble on the other side of Antarctica. According to the whalers, the *Aurora* had broken clear of her mooring at McMurdo Sound and drifted north, eventually reaching New Zealand. Ominously, there was no news of the landing party, scheduled to winter at Scott's old quarters at Cape Evans before depoting supplies on the Barrier for the scheduled Trans-Antarctic Crossing.

The next act of kindness from the Norwegians was to offer the three men a welcome and sorely needed bath. Shackleton had warned their hosts that, after months without changing clothes or a wash, the men smelt badly. It was then, as they peeled off their worn and tattered garments and looked into the mirror, that the realisation of their appalling state began to dawn on the trio. The men were filthy, their hair matted and their scraggy beards had grown uncontrollably. The dirt and grime helped obscure another side of their ordeal.

Beneath the layers of dirt, the three men were gaunt and hollow. They had the look of men who had come face to face with death.

After their hot bath, they ate a hearty meal and prepared to spend their first night between clean sheets for close on two years. Shackleton shared a room with Crean in Sorlle's house and he recalled that the pair were so comfortable and unaccustomed to luxury they could hardly sleep.

While Crean and Shackleton prepared to wallow in the comfort of a well-made bed, Worsley elected to fetch McCarthy, McNeish and Vincent who were still under the *Caird* at King Haakon Bay on the other side of the island. Worsley climbed aboard the steam-driven whaler, *Samson*, for the eleven-hour trip around South Georgia to Peggoty Camp, where McCarthy, McNeish and Vincent were waiting patiently.

The exhausted Worsley slept through a raging gale on the stormy trip and landed on the beach to a surprising welcome. The three castaways, who had spent almost two years living close alongside Worsley, failed to recognise the well-dressed, clean-shaven man who stood before them. At first they thought it was a stranger and indignantly demanded to know why Shackleton, Crean or Worsley had not bothered to come to pick them up!

Worsley also recovered the *James Caird* from the beach and took it back to Stromness Bay with the three men, where they were greeted with a touching little ceremony from the sailors. The whalers – hardened, experienced Norwegian seamen – were almost overwhelmed in their admiration for the three men. Their journey, especially the crossing of the Southern Ocean, had astonished these highly proficient seafarers and the Norwegians insisted on bringing the *James Caird* ashore themselves as a symbol of their deep respect. Every man at the whaling station wanted to share in the honour of touching the boat and personally hauling it up the shore.

They refused to allow any of the *Endurance* party to touch the little vessel. It was a spontaneous gesture which, Worsley admitted, was 'quite affecting'.

In the evening the dingy smoke-filled local club room was packed with well-wishers who simply wanted to pay tribute to the remarkable men who had sailed the Southern Ocean in an open boat and made the first crossing of South Georgia. Worsley said the reception was 'full of captains and mates and sailors and hazy with tobacco smoke'.

One of the veteran whalers stepped forward from the crowd, saying that he had spent 40 years in the stormy Southern Ocean and had never heard of such a wonderful feat. According to Worsley, he said it was an honour to meet Shackleton and his comrades and finished with a dramatic gesture by declaring:

'These are men!'[1]

One by one the seamen stepped forward and shook hands with Shackleton, Worsley and Crean. It was a simple, informal gesture without the added ritual of the medals and fanfares which characterised the later, more formal celebrations of their achievements. But for the three men, it probably ranked higher than any other acclaim they would receive. Worsley spoke for all three when he wrote:

'Coming from brother seamen, men of our own cloth, and members of a great seafaring race like the Norwegians, this was a wonderful tribute and one of which we all felt proud.'2

'I think I enjoyed this more than any honour bestowed upon us afterwards; for these fine seamen were men of the Viking brand who for years had been weathering the same storms through which we had come in our little boat. Congratulations from them meant something.'3

But there was no time to dwell on events while their comrades remained in captivity 800 miles (1,300 km) away. While Worsley had been away, Shackleton had arranged for the British-owned whaler, *Southern Sky*, crewed by eager volunteer Norwegian sailors, to sail down to Elephant Island to pick up the 22 stranded men. On board would be their rescuers, Crean, Worsley and Shackleton himself. At the same time, McCarthy, McNeish and Vincent were placed aboard another vessel heading back to England.

Because there was no telegraph on South Georgia in 1916, Shackleton had not been able to inform anyone at home about the fate of the *Endurance*. Or cable the owners and ask for permission to take the *Southern Sky* on the risky trip down to Elephant Island in the depth of the winter. But there was no time for courtesies and Shackleton assumed personal responsibility for the ship as the rescuers set off from Husvik.

The *Southern Sky*, heavily laden with coal for the 1,600-mile (2,600-km) round trip, set off to cross the Southern Ocean on 23 May 1916, to the noise of factory whistles from the whaling station and rousing cheers from the seamen on the quay. It was almost a month since they had sailed from Elephant Island carrying the hopes of their comrades.

After a largely uneventful passage across the Southern Ocean, the vessel ran into heavy, impassable pack ice about 60 miles from Elephant Island. Attempts were made to force the ship through the ice, but the *Southern Sky* was not built with a steel reinforced bow and it was useless to persevere. Mile after mile the ship sailed up and down the ice looking for a way through, using up precious supplies of coal in a fruitless search for a safe channel. Even if they had managed to find a navigable lead, there was no guarantee that the ice would reopen to allow them safe retreat away from the island. Reluctantly, the ship turned and went back to the north.

Shackleton headed for the Falkland Islands, which are a little closer than South Georgia and had the added benefit of cable facilities. It would enable the *Endurance* party to re-establish contact with the outside world.

It was 31 May when Shackleton, Worsley and Crean entered Port Stanley in the Falklands. A cable was despatched to London announcing their return from the South and the loss of the *Endurance*. In London the news was a welcome diversion from the misery of the war. One missive was sent to the King, who took time off from the worsening conflict to respond:

> 'Rejoice to hear of your safe arrival in the Falkland Islands and trust your comrades on Elephant Island may soon be rescued.'[4]

Shackleton also wrote to his wife, Emily, with a brief outline of their 'year and a half of hell' and the inestimable support of close colleagues. He added:

> 'It was Nature against us the whole time . . . Wild and Crean were splendid throughout discipline was always good: but towards the end about ten of the party were off their heads.'[5]

At Port Stanley, the Governor Douglas Young invited the three men to stay with him while they searched for a new ship to go south to Elephant Island as quickly as possible. But Falkland Islanders, in general, were indifferent to the remarkable story of the *Endurance* party. The local newspaper, *John Bull*, reported:

'Not a soul in Stanley seemed to care one scrap, not a flag was flown and no one seemed to care a cuss about him [Shackleton], are the words which describe Shackleton's arrival at Port Stanley.'[6]

One Falkland Islander, quoted in the same publication, said the men should have been at war long ago '. . . instead of messing about on icebergs'.[7]

A little closer to the icebergs, the 22 men under Frank Wild were still stranded on the bleak rocky beach, eking out a life in the depths of the Antarctic winter.

Cables were sent to Britain and surrounding South American countries pleading for a suitable vessel to rescue the men, although the Admiralty was among the first to throw a wet blanket on their hopes. No suitable vessel was available because of the war and the first relief from Britain could not be expected until October. It would mean at least another five months, possibly more, before rescuing the men on Elephant Island.

Finally, the Uruguayan Government generously lent a steam trawler called *Instituto de Pesca No 1* which duly reached Port Stanley on 10 June. The ship sailed on 16 June with Shackleton, Worsley and Crean on board, increasingly anxious about the welfare of their comrades. But their hopes were soon dashed.

It was now approaching midwinter in the Southern Ocean and the weather was foul. Dawn broke on the third day with the sight of Elephant Island rising above the horizon far away in the distance. A little later the ship came to within 20 miles of shore but the pack was impenetrable and after another search for an opening, which consumed vital supplies of coal, they had to turn back. The disappointment was acute.

After arriving back at Port Stanley on 25 June, the three men took a steamer to Punta Arenas, on the western side of the Straits of Magellan in Patagonia, Chile. Punta Arenas was still a major gateway for the constant stream of ships rounding Cape Horn, although the opening of the Panama Canal two years earlier in 1914 would eventually mark its rapid decline. The bustling little port on the Pacific flank of the South American continent flourished from the thriving wool and fishing industries and Shackleton knew it was the type of place where he might find a suitable vessel for the trip to Elephant Island.

The three men were greeted like celebrities. They were heroes, particularly in the eyes of the sizeable local British colony and found themselves invited to an endless stream of parties and receptions and making frequent appearances in the local newspapers. But they were also greeted with great warmth and admiration by the Chileans. Over the years, Britain and Chile had developed fairly close links, partly because of trade and partly because they seemed like-minded people. Indeed, the Chileans have been described as the 'English of South America'.

Shackleton, who fully understood the value of good public relations, ensured that their names – and therefore the plight of the Elephant Island captives – would not be forgotten. It was essential to maintain a high profile throughout the search for a rescue and so the men were constantly in the public eye. Shackleton gave a series of lectures and all three attended various functions and gatherings which all helped ensure that nobody lost sight of the fundamental issue.

The men frequently appeared in the newspapers, notably the local English-language newspaper, the *Magellan Times*, which faithfully recorded their comings and goings on the busy social circuit. While the priority was to arrange a rescue for their trapped colleagues, they did not lose their playful sense of humour.

On one public occasion, Shackleton warmly thanked the Norwegians on South Georgia for their hospitality and generosity and pointed out that Crean was still wearing a suit donated by one of the whalers. Crean, not to be outdone, drew uproarious laughter from the audience by pointedly gazing at Shackleton's boots and honours were even.

His instinct was right and after raising £1,500, the three men chartered a 40-year-old oak schooner, *Emma*, at a rate of £18 per day for the third rescue attempt. Luckily the Chilean navy provided a steam driven vessel, *Yelcho*, to tow the *Emma* as far south as possible, which would conserve coal until they had to navigate through the pack.

With all due officialdom, Shackleton was appointed Master, Worsley First Mate and Crean Second Mate for the voyage. The seamen were drawn from eight different countries. They included a sailor from landlocked Andorra who had recently been released from jail for seal-poaching and therefore had something in common with the three explorers who had survived only because of their skills at poaching.

At dawn on 21 July the schooner came to an abrupt halt about 100 miles (160 km) from Elephant Island. The vessel, Shackleton remembered, was tossing about like a cork in the swell and it soon became apparent that further progress was impossible. Reluctantly, *Emma* returned to Port Stanley.

Slightly better news awaited the men as they arrived in the Falklands on 8 August after three failed attempts to rescue their comrades. *Discovery*, Scott's old ship, was preparing to leave England, but would not arrive until mid-September. It had already been over three months since Shackleton, Worsley and Crean had sailed away from the beach. The men on Elephant Island had endured the scourge of a southern winter huddled under the boats on their bleak rocky foothold. Another six or eight weeks of privation would surely be too much.

Crean played a vital role during the long frustrating weeks in the Falklands and on the South American mainland while the men anxiously searched for suitable vessels to carry their colleagues out of captivity. Although Shackleton was very much the frontman, negotiating and pleading with the authorities for help, the support of Crean – and Worsley – was very important.

Crean was a tower of strength for his leader. He went everywhere with Shackleton during these frustrating weeks and kept him from exploding over the irritating delays or drowning his sorrows in a bottle. One man who testified to Crean's quiet influence was Tom P. Jones, a local English businessman who many years later remembered the pair in his book, *Patagonian Panorama*. Jones got to know the men very well during their stay at Punta Arenas and he wrote:

> 'Tom Crean seemed to be his [Shackleton's] bodyguard and at cocktail parties he would watch over him, even to the extent of warning him not to have another drink.'[8]

Crean, who had proven beyond any doubt that he possessed truly remarkable qualities as a polar traveller, was now displaying the other side to his character – the more mature qualities of support and guidance.

Crean was a straightforward and simple man who considered loyalty and obedience as paramount. These were features which had attracted Scott fifteen years earlier and were now giving Shackleton vital help to cope with the great challenge ahead to rescue the men on Elephant Island. Without the support and loyalty of Crean at this stage it is unlikely that Shackleton, after the draining ordeal of the open boat journey and crossing of South Georgia, would have been able to cope with the frustrations of battling with seemingly endless bureaucracy to find a suitable vessel. Crean had become indispensable in the physical ordeal over the past few months and he now became indispensable in the diplomatic and personal mission to find a vessel to rescue their comrades.

The Irishman had also taken time off to write a few consoling words of hope to Hazel Marston, the wife of George Marston, the artist who was still stranded on the beach at Elephant Island. Crean, perhaps writing at the request of Shackleton, contacted the expedition's agent, Ernest Perris, in London, who forwarded the letter to the Marston family home in Petersfield, Hampshire.

The letter was written on 3 July while Crean, Shackleton and Worsley were onboard the British mail-boat, *Orita*, crossing from Port Stanley to Punta Arenas in their search for a rescue ship. It was about ten weeks since they had left Marston behind on Elephant Island but Crean was unequivocal about liberating his colleagues. He told Mrs Marston:

> **'Just a few lines to inform you about the welfare of your husband which no doubt you are anxiously awaiting for. But I must tell you, you don't want to be alarmed for I am positive we shall get them safely back.**
>
> **And I must inform you when I parted from him he was looking fit and well and he wanted very much to accompany us on our journey. But never mind we shall all be home soon. Please [God].'[9]**

The three men once again passed through the Straits of Magellan to Chile, where Shackleton begged the Government to let him have the *Yelcho* for one more rescue attempt. The Chileans, who much admired the indomitable fighting spirit of the men, readily agreed.

On 25 August, the 150-ton steel-built steamer chugged out of Punta Arenas, through the Straits of Magellan and headed south. The crew, mostly volunteers, were drawn from Chile's navy and the Captain, Luis Pardo, was content to allow the peerless Worsley to navigate. Shackleton quickly assumed overall responsibility and faithfully promised the Chileans that he would not risk the *Yelcho* by taking her into the ice.

For once in the two-year *Endurance* expedition, luck was with the men as they progressed southwards in reasonably favourable seas. As they closed in on Elephant Island, the pack ice began to prise open. Even a bank of fog, which descended shortly afterwards, did not deter them and they slipped through the pack to the clearer ice-free seas which normally appear near to land.

With impeccable timing the fog soon lifted and the bleak cliffs and glaciers of Elephant Island came into full view. Crean, Shackleton and Worsley scanned the coastline for familiar features and a hopeful sight of their lost comrades. After a tense period scouting back and forth, Worsley suddenly spotted the camp about 1 1/2 miles away, though it was barely visible under a covering blanket of winter snow.

The rescuers and the rescued spotted each other almost simultaneously. Through binoculars it was possible to see tiny black figures scampering around the shore and waving frantically. Shackleton counted the animated little figures until he reached 22 and shouted that they were all there.

Standing on the gently rolling deck, Shackleton, Worsley and Crean looked at each other, each moved by the moment when their ordeal was finally over and the men had been saved. It was an outstanding achievement but Worsley said they were 'all unable to speak'. Alongside them, some of the *Yelcho*'s crew broke down and cried.

Within minutes a boat was lowered and they began to pull towards the shore. Crean and Shackleton were on board, standing up, eagerly trying to identify the dark shapes moving about on the beach. As they rowed nearer to shore, Shackleton anxiously yelled out:

'Are you all well?'[10]

Wild, the faithful lieutenant who had held the men together for so long, shouted back:

'We are all well, Boss.'[11]

As the Chilean sailors rowed the boat to shore, someone threw a packet of cigarettes which, Shackleton remembered, were leapt upon like 'hungry tigers'. It was 30 August 1916, or 128 days (4½ months) since Shackleton, Worsley and Crean and the three others had sailed for help in the *James Caird*.

24
Life and death

L ife on the beach at Elephant Island was close to becoming intolerable for the 22 men when they caught sight of their rescuers. Early optimism of rescue had slowly evaporated, food supplies had declined alarmingly and morale had faded. Hopes of a rescue had all but gone and some were in sorry decline.

Each morning Wild raised the men with the cry: '*Lash up and stow, boys, the Boss may come today.*' At first the call was greeted with some enthusiasm, but this began to evaporate as the days, weeks and finally months began to pass.

Initially, the little group was optimistic that Shackleton, Worsley and Crean would reach South Georgia and bring help. Hurley had estimated that the trip would take only fourteen days, which was not very far wrong. In fact the *James Caird* had taken seventeen days, but it took another ten days for recuperation, preparation and the incredible crossing of South Georgia.

But as time wore on, a mood of increasing despondency began to take hold and by August, three months after the *James Caird* had sailed, spirits had sunk very low. Many feared that the rescuers had been swallowed by the Southern Ocean and that the survivors under the boats on Elephant Island would have to make another open boat journey to Deception Island, where the whalers were known to gather in the summer months. It was a dreadful prospect for the weakened men.

The boats, the *Dudley Docker* and *Stancomb Wills*, had been turned upside down and scraps of old tent and some hurriedly arranged stones were utilised to make a crude shelter against the violent winds which tore down upon them almost every day. Winds of up to 100 mph were recorded and blizzards kept them confined to their sleeping bags for days at a time.

Five men slept 'upstairs' on the thwarts of the *Wills* and four in the *Docker*, while the other thirteen were laid cheek-by-jowl on the floor. In these closely confined quarters, the 22 men had little option but to adjust to the foul-smelling environment, where the unpleasant stench of unwashed bodies and filthy clothing mixed with the rancid odour of rotting animal flesh and droppings. The smoke from the permanently lit stove stung their eyes until the resourceful engineer, Kerr, made a simple chimney with the lining from a biscuit tin, improving the atmosphere a little.

Food was in reasonable supply until early August when they were forced to dig up discarded seal bones and for a while there was the welcome diversion of a highly potent concoction of hot water, sugar and methylated spirits, which briefly helped blot out some of the misery and deprivation. But by August the meths had been drunk and the men were reduced to boiling seaweed for their sole pleasure.

Wild, who modelled his leadership on Shackleton's style, maintained a regular routine and tried to keep the men as busy as possible. But there were long periods of idleness which offered them full scope to speculate about rescue or the most popular of all subjects – food.

Many of the men suffered badly from the ordeal, but there were three particular patients. Hudson had suffered a breakdown and developed a severe abscess on his left buttock which eventually had to be drained of two pints of stinking fluid. Rickinson had a heart attack soon after reaching Elephant Island. But the most severe case was Blackborrow, the young Welshman who had stowed away on *Endurance* and whose feet were struck by acute frostbite. In mid-June the doctors, McIlroy and Macklin, amputated the toes of his left foot. Thankfully there was just enough chloroform to put Blackborrow out for the 55-minute operation in the half-light under the two little boats.

30 August dawned, just like the countless other days on Elephant Island, with some men scrambling around on the shoreline for limpets to help enliven the hoosh and others sweeping away the snowdrifts. Food supplies had dwindled and at that time of the year, seals and penguins were in short supply. Initial preparations were already being made for sailing to Deception Island.

Marston and Hurley were out on the nearby rocks shelling limpets for supper, occasionally taking a perfunctory look at the horizon. Suddenly Marston yelled out: '*Ship O!*' and pandemonium broke out.

Macklin made a dash to the flagstaff to hoist a signal and Wild put a pick through the last tin of petrol to start a fire from old damp woollen socks and mitts which were cluttering up the floor. In the rush to catch sight of the *Yelcho*, the lunchtime pot of hoosh was sent flying. Hard-man Wild was close to tears.

Macklin recalled seeing a boat being lowered from the *Yelcho* and rowed ashore, with the familiar beaming faces of Crean and Shackleton clearly visible to the ecstatic castaways. The two men, he said, were looking 'very well and to our eyes, very clean'.

However ecstatic the men felt at being rescued, the greetings were kept brief as possible because of the threat that the surrounding ice would close in and trap them. The men were swiftly brought aboard the *Yelcho*. The rowing boat, with Shackleton and Crean supervising proceedings, made three excursions inside an hour to bring the 22 men off the beach and by 2 p.m. on 30 August the entire *Endurance* party had been reunited onboard the Chilean vessel.

Soon after, the *Yelcho* was under way, her precious cargo of castaways safely on board and tucking into a hearty meal. Shackleton, Worsley and Crean passed on all they knew about the war and the men also absorbed every item from some old newspapers which someone had thoughtfully remembered to bring along for the occasion.

The ship ran into severe weather on the return to civilisation through the Southern Ocean, but it seemed almost irrelevant. By 2 September the *Yelcho* had reached the Straits of Magellan and early next day anchored off Rio Seco, a few miles from Punta Arenas. Shackleton, aware of the value of good publicity, went ashore with Crean to telephone ahead with the news that the party had been rescued.

Their arrival was not without bitter irony. As Shackleton and Crean rowed towards the quay, an excitable onlooker rushed forward and shouted:

'Welcome, Captain Scott.'

According to an eyewitness, Shackleton was not amused and could point out that while Scott had perished, he had both survived a terrible ordeal on the ice and saved his men. Jones recalled the incident and reported Shackleton's icy response as:

'. . . Shackleton replied: "Captain Scott be so-and-soed! He's been dead for years!"'[1]

A few hours later the *Yelcho* steamed into Punta Arenas to a tumultuous welcome. It seemed as though the entire population had turned out, with flags flying, sirens blowing and people cheering wildly. Macklin remembered that the 'noise was deafening' and the Chileans declared it a festival day. There were several German ships in the harbour, but they, too, hoisted flags in celebration. The headline in the *Magellan Times* screamed: '*Indescribable Enthusiasm*' and the paper reported:

'Never before in the history of Magellanas has a crowd been seen such as that which gathered to witness the entrance of the *Yelcho*.'[2]

The men, slightly bewildered by the raucous noise after so long in isolated captivity, stepped off the ship and walked through the little town to the energetic music of a local brass band. Worsley, who like Crean and Shackleton, had already made friends with the Chileans, said the local hospitality knew no bounds.

The men were led to the Royal Hotel where they were presented to the thronging crowds from one of the upper windows. As speedily as the festivities would allow, the bedraggled men were fixed up with clean clothes, a welcome shave and a haircut. In the evening everyone gathered for a noisy jostling reception at the offices of the British Association.

Once again, Shackleton took the opportunity to thank people for their support and hospitality but he reserved special praise for the two companions who had endured the greatest ordeal with him. His simple, straightforward comment was:

> 'I cannot speak too highly of Crean and Worsley, who have seen this through with me.
>
> My name has been known to the general public for a long time and it has mostly been as leader, but how much depends upon the men! What I do would be small, did we not work together. I appreciate my men on Elephant Island and the two I have on my right are fine fellows.'[3]

The Chileans were determined to celebrate in lavish style, especially as it had been one of their ships and its sailors which had finally plucked the men off Elephant Island. The proud Chileans would allow no slacking in their endeavour to celebrate. At one lavish dinner, Worsley went outside for a breath of fresh air and was surrounded by a group of armed men with fixed bayonets. Asked why he was being threatened, Worsley was told that 'no sober *gringo* [foreigner] leaves the building'.

The generous hospitality of the Chileans and local expatriates continued for about twelve days until the party rejoined the *Yelcho* and cruised up the coast to Valparaiso, to the north of the capital Santiago. When they arrived on 27 September the party were greeted with another rapturous reception from huge crowds of cheering people and it took the men 30 minutes to walk the 50 yards (45 m) from the ship to the local Naval Club because of the crush.

The Chilean president personally entertained the men and a few days later they set off by special train to cross the Andes for Buenos Aires, Argentina. Another rapid journey took some of the party to Montevideo where they could personally thank the people of Uruguay for their invaluable assistance.

But the attraction of continual celebration was beginning to wear thin and the men had their own plans. Many, notably the seamen, were anxious to get home as quickly as possible and join the fight against Germany. In contrast, Shackleton's concern was now focussed on the men from the *Aurora* in the Ross Sea party at Cape Evans on the other side of Antarctica. It was time to disband the expedition.

On 8 October 1916 the *Endurance* expedition finally came to an end on the concourse of a railway station in Buenos Aires as the men shook hands and went their own way. Shackleton and Worsley had decided to head for McMurdo Sound via San Francisco and New Zealand, while Crean, Wild and the majority of the others turned for home.

The same could not be said of the *Aurora* party in the Ross Sea, which was cut off from the outside world for over two years and suffered appalling hardship as the men struggled to fulfil their obligation of laying supply depots for Shackleton's crossing of the continent. Three of the ten-man party died laying supplies of food and equipment for men who would never come.

The ten men knew nothing about the loss of *Endurance* and ploughed on regardless with their task of supplying the trans-antarctic party. Dutifully they set about laying depots on the Barrier and up to the foot of the Beardmore Glacier for Shackleton's team, which was originally scheduled to make the land crossing from one side to the other from Vahsel Bay to Cape Evans via the South Pole, the Beardmore and the Barrier.

The party was ill-equipped for the huge task and Joyce, a veteran of the *Discovery* and *Nimrod* expeditions, was the only person with experience of sledge travelling. But, in the face of remarkable odds, they travelled over 1,500 miles (2,400 km) in 169 days, which is among the most formidable man-hauling achievements ever recorded.

Some of the men went almost five months without fresh food and were inevitably struck by scurvy. The padre, Arnold Spencer-Smith, had died within sight of safety at *Discovery*'s old quarters, Hut Point; two others, Mackintosh and Hayward, were lost trying to cross the dangerously thin ice between Hut Point and Cape Evans.

The Ross Sea party's achievements were quite astonishing and without the more widely publicised heroics of the men on *Endurance*, it is likely that history would have granted the men far greater recognition for their considerable efforts. Sadly, history has forgotten the men of the Ross Sea party whose tortuous depot-laying journeys onto the Barrier were all to no avail.

It was also the last of the great man-hauling escapades of the Heroic Age of polar exploration.

25
War, honour, marriage

Tom Crean's hair had turned iron grey by the time he arrived back in Britain. It was the only visible sign of damage from the two year ordeal on the *Endurance* expedition. Physically the Irishman had come through the experience in remarkably good condition and displayed no other outward marks of wear and tear.

Crean travelled back to Britain from Buenos Aires on the liner *Highland Lassie*, arriving back in early November 1916. Just across the channel in northern France, the Battle of the Somme was finally drawing to a close after over four months of bloody slaughter.

Crean wasted no time in joining the war effort, returning to the naval barracks at Chatham on 8 November. Six weeks later he was promoted to Acting Boatswain in recognition of his outstanding service in the South.[1] He was also awarded the Silver Polar Medal, his third.

Crean, however, remained characteristically modest about his own huge contribution to the expedition. In one classic piece of understatement, he wrote to Apsley Cherry-Garrard, his colleague on Scott's last expedition:

> **'We had a hot time of it the last twelve months when we lost *Endurance* and I must say the Boss is a splendid gentleman. And I done my duty towards him to the last.'**[2]

His contribution to the *Endurance* expedition earned special praise from the grateful Shackleton who knew the value of the Irishman's support at many crucial moments during the previous two years. He was genuinely grateful.

Shackleton's highly personal and straightforward judgement of Crean is contained in a private letter to Ernest Perris, his close confidante and agent for the expedition, which he wrote in October 1916 en route to Cape Evans to learn the fate of the Ross Sea Party.

His confidential verdict on Crean is notably brief and frank. It is also somewhat begrudging in view of the Irishman's outstanding contribution to the expedition and particular heroics in the long drawn out rescue of the stranded men. Shackleton's curt judgement reads:

> 'Loyal and good. Splendid in the boats and all through. Hyper-sensitive.
> I have written to Balfour urging his promotion to lieutenant boatswain. Do your best to help this along.
> Ask him to defer his pay for some time if you have not sufficient to pay him up.'[3]

Shackleton's terse assessment of Crean, of course, reflects the time at which it was written. He had, after all, suffered a terrible ordeal in the previous months and was now increasingly concerned about the fate of the men trapped at Cape Evans, who were unaware of the plight of *Endurance*. Shackleton was undoubtedly under terrible strain, but he might have been a little kinder to a man who stood steadfast beside him and provided invaluable support.

In finalising the details of the failed expedition, Shackleton had to decide how to pay off the men, particularly as the money had largely run out. Wild and Worsley had offered to defer their entire salaries and Shackleton asked the scientists to do the same. The crew, who perhaps needed the money more than the rest, would be paid in full, although some who had performed badly in Shackleton's eyes were only paid up to the moment

Endurance was abandoned. However, Crean and a seaman, Walter How, were placed in a different category. Shackleton did not want to make promises he could not keep to men he respected and admired and therefore he told them they would get paid when the money was available. As Shackleton's letter to Perris shows, he was merely asking Crean to defer his wages until money was available. Mary and James Fisher, his biographers, who had spoken to many survivors of the expedition, said this was Shackleton's way of paying a compliment to the two men.[4]

Shackleton undoubtedly trusted Crean, both as a fellow traveller and perhaps more surprisingly, as a straight-talking representative for the expedition back in Britain. In particular, Shackleton was concerned that his wife, Emily, should get a first-hand report of events rather than rely on speculation and gossip which had inevitably encircled the expedition. As he was making his way to Cape Evans, Shackleton wrote to Emily:

'I want you to see Wild, McIlroy and Crean – see Crean separately.'[5]

Crean was also looking for a different form of recognition. He was 39 years of age and nearing the end of his naval career as he returned from the expedition. First he wanted the money owed to him from the *Endurance* expedition and then he wanted promotion to a higher rank, which would improve his immediate earnings and, more important for the long term, improve his pension. Crean was looking beyond the day when he would leave the navy and thankfully he had an influential ally in Sir Ernest Shackleton.

Shackleton fully supported Crean's ambitions and took the unusual step of appealing to the highest levels to win promotion for his colleague. Shackleton wrote personally to Lord Balfour, who was First Lord of the Admiralty in 1915–16 shortly before becoming a more famous British Foreign Secretary. His letter recommended Crean for promotion. He had also asked Perris, a distinguished journalist who later became editor of the *Daily Chronicle*, to use his influence to press Crean's case.

The immediate target was the rank of Warrant Officer, the level between commissioned and non-commissioned officers. But Crean had a problem. He was nervous and concerned about passing the necessary written examination. While he was an experienced seaman and held gunnery and torpedo qualifications, his weakness was undoubtedly his poor education.

Crean was a practical man, someone used to handling physical problems. He had left school at a very young age after a rudimentary education in his hometown village of Anascaul which provided him with little more than the ability to read and write. This hardly equipped him for written tests, such as the Royal Navy exams which included some tricky mathematical questions.

The written test, for example, typically asked questions like: 'What fraction and decimal of half-sovereign is 7½d?'; or 'If 50 casks of flour are sufficient for 400 men for 30 days how long will 15 casks suffice for 200 men if the rations are reduced by one fourth?'[6]

The lack of schooling would have been glaringly apparent in the South, where Crean had to spend months in close confinement with officers, scientists, doctors and many others who had the benefit of university or some other private education. It may be that the hypersensitivity which Shackleton mentions in his letter to Perris reflects Crean's sense of inadequacy in the company of well-educated men.

Unsure of himself, Crean contacted Shackleton, seeking guidance and reassurance. Shackleton, though busy in the post-*Endurance* days, took time to encourage and console his old colleague. In one letter, written in June 1917, Shackleton emphasised that it was 'absolutely necessary' to pass the 'easy examination' before being considered for the commission. But Shackleton realised that Crean's confidence needed a boost and explained:

'You are sure to get it if you only do this: why don't you buck up and tackle it. Go ahead old son it means a lot to you. You say that the others are getting army commissions. They are not the same as the navy. The training is not difficult. A soldier is made in a few months and a sailor in years. You are not frightened of any seafaring job so don't let a little exam beat you.'[7]

Crean was also given valuable morale support by Emily Shackleton, who had seen his letters to her husband while Shackleton was away from home. She, too, recognised that Crean needed reassurance and responded by writing:

'. . . no one in the wide world deserves it [promotion] more and everybody knows the Admiralty want good men like yourself.'[8]

In the event, Crean passed the examination and on 11 August 1917, less than a month after his fortieth birthday, he was promoted to the rank of Acting Boatswain.[9]

Meantime, Shackleton had found some money to reward Crean. The Irishman had initially signed up for *Endurance* at a salary of £166 a year and during their many months together on the ice, Shackleton had privately agreed to raise this substantially to £260 (today: £13,000). In June he sent Crean £100 (today: £5,000) and promised to cable a further £100.[10]

Crean was also surprised to discover that his old *Terra Nova* comrade, Apsley Cherry-Garrard, had tracked him down and sent a small sum of money. Like Evans, perhaps Cherry-Garrard had special call to remember Crean's powerful presence on Scott's last expedition, in particular, the raw courage he displayed in 1911 to alert Scott to the plight of Cherry and Bowers who were cast adrift with the ponies on an ice floe. Crean was touched by Cherry's gift and promised to 'buy something' with the present.

The money from Shackleton and Cherry-Garrard had

arrived at a particularly opportune moment for Crean, who was now getting married.

Crean's early career in the navy and his long years exploring in the frozen wilderness of Antarctica had clearly made it difficult for the Irishman to establish long-term relationships. He had been away from home for 24 years since running away as a youngster to enlist and the only permanent feature in his life during this time was the occasional period of leave back home at Anascaul. It was no surprise therefore that he would marry a local woman.

His bride was Eileen Herlihy, the 36-year-old daughter of a local publican in Anascaul, who had known Crean since childhood. They had one other important thing in common. Eileen, who was invariably called Nell, had been born and raised in a pub in the centre of Anascaul and Tom Crean had already signalled his intentions of entering the licensed trade after leaving the navy. The liquor licence he had bought in 1913 with the old run-down bar in the village now assumed even greater importance.

Tom and Nell were married at Anascaul on 5 September 1917. It was a notable event in the village and Shackleton showed his affection for his old comrade by giving the newly-wedded couple a delightful silver tea service engraved from himself and Emily. Crean's naval colleagues in the chief Petty Officers' mess at Chatham presented him with a ceremonial sword.

Marriage was a temporary reprieve from the war, which in the autumn of 1917 was still locked in deadly stalemate on the European mainland. But Crean was luckier than many during the war. He escaped the horrors of the Western Front and remained in the relatively quiet backwaters of the navy for the final two years of the conflict. According to military records, Crean probably never saw any major hostile action in the two years which followed his return from the South.

He remained at Chatham Barracks from November 1916, until 2 March 1917, where he was engaged in routine, mundane tasks on the fringe of the war, such as helping to take a dredger, *St Giles*, from Immingham on England's east coast, to Rosyth, Scotland, in early February. It was a long way from the rigours of *Endurance* or the *James Caird* but after two years' living life on the edge, Crean probably welcomed the comparative serenity.

In March, 1917, he was transferred to the auxiliary patrol ship, HMS *Colleen* at Queenstown, Cork, in his home country of Ireland for another relatively quiet time. His duties took him to the Bere Haven patrol base in Bantry Bay on Ireland's southwest coast and, once again, his task was far from arduous.

While posted in Ireland, Crean was also awarded a further decoration. In February 1918, he was given a clasp to his Polar Medal. His next appointment, to the battle cruiser HMS *Inflexible*, took effect on 14 November 1918 – three days after the war ended. Crean's war was a quiet one.

Not so lucky were some of his comrades from the *Endurance* expedition. Tim McCarthy, the popular fellow-Irishman who had helped sail the *James Caird* across the Southern Ocean, was killed at his gun in the Channel and Frank Wild's brother Ernest, who had served so nobly in the Ross Sea Party, died from typhoid while on active duty in the Mediterranean. Alf Cheetham, a veteran of four Antarctic voyages and months under the boats on Elephant Island, was drowned when his minesweeper was torpedoed only a few weeks before the Armistice in 1918. Another five members of the expedition were wounded, some severely.

A month after the end of the war, in December 1918, Nell gave birth to their first child. They named her Mary. Soon after, on 14 March 1919, Crean was transferred to the 4,300-ton light cruiser, *Fox*.[11] It would be his last meaningful naval appointment.

In April 1919, Crean was Boatswain on board *Fox* for a routine trip from Chatham to the strategic ports of Murmansk and Archangel in northern Russia where Britain and other Allies were still attempting to stop the advancing Bolsheviks.

By coincidence Shackleton had been there a few months earlier on a British mission to prevent the Germans seizing control of Murmansk, which is highly valuable as the only port in Arctic Russia which remains ice-free throughout the year.

Fox left Chatham on 27 April and, after an uneventful short journey up England's east coast, arrived at Rosyth late on 29 April.[12] What happened next is not clear and important parts of *Fox*'s records have since been lost. But while *Fox* was berthed at Rosyth on 29 April 1919, the long and distinguished naval career of Tom Crean effectively came to an end.

While the ship was being anchored at Rosyth, Crean mysteriously suffered a bad fall and was severely injured. According to medical records, he tumbled down the cable hatch and struck his head above the left temple, opening a one and a half inch wound which needed three stitches. He also suffered heavy bruising to his legs, left arm and side. The fall was so severe that for a time he lost the movement of his left arm. The medical certificate does not divulge any further details of the injuries, but dryly records that Crean was 'sober at the time'.[13]

The *Fox* continued her journey into Arctic waters, but Crean was never the same again. The wound to the head had damaged his vision, though the precise details of the injuries have been lost. Despite the impediment, he continued to serve with distinction and his conduct earned full praise from the wardroom. Crean left *Fox* on 31 October 1919, and his Captain said he was:

'A capable and zealous warrant officer.'[14]

By the end of the year he had joined the 5,600-ton special torpedo depot ship, HMS *Hecla*, in the Nore Reserve. It was to be his last naval appointment.

The fall at Rosyth proved to have a more lasting effect than anyone could have anticipated, particularly for a toughened character like Crean who had suffered countless falls in the hostile terrain of Antarctica and had always come up smiling. A few months later Crean retired from the Royal Navy, declared medically unfit with 'defective vision'.[15] It was 24 March 1920, or less than four months short of completing 27 years' service.

In the official record, his commanding officer on *Hecla* said Crean had conducted himself 'to my entire satisfaction'. But, perhaps aware that he was writing for posterity, the officer added the fitting testimonial for a famous son of the sea:

> 'An officer of great ability and reliability. He is in all respects thoroughly deserving of all considerations of the service to which he is a great loss through being invalided.'[16]

26
Tom the Pole

Tom Crean quickly put his naval career behind him and embarked on a new course of building a home and a family. Although this was unfamiliar territory to a man who had spent almost three decades roaming away from his homeland, he was reasonably well equipped for the new life.

Crean had left the navy with two pensions – a statutory retirement pension and a special disability pension resulting from his injury at Rosyth. In 1922, the disability pension alone had been increased to £72 a year, which today is worth the equivalent of £2,300.[1] This would supplement any income he might generate from his proposed life in the pub trade.

Nor had he forgotten the £100 gift from the *Terra Nova* expedition for saving Evans' life on the Barrier in 1912. It was a useful injection of money as he contemplated building a new life and in August 1920, just five months after retiring from the Royal Navy, he wrote to Scott's widow, Kathleen, to thank her for the donation. He said:

> **'I will never forget your kindness towards me, for the £100 I received from the Secretary of the Expedition. It is a great help indeed.'[2]**

At around the same time, Crean took the crucial decision to retire from his life of exploration and adventure. While some explorers found it difficult to adapt to the routine of a quiet domestic life after returning from their travels, Crean was happy to hang up his snow boots. His roving days were over. Even the personal appeals of Shackleton, a character he respected more than anyone else, could not persuade him to go South again.

All the evidence suggests that his love for Nell and the attractions of a family and a more settled life in Anascaul outweighed even his passion for the South, once regarded as his adopted home. Crean was approaching his forty-third birthday when he left the navy. He was only three years younger than Shackleton, a restless soul who by now was planning another expedition. The legacy of Crean's eye injury undoubtedly played a part in his decision, although it did not have a lasting effect on his life. Shortly after retirement, he told Kathleen Scott that his eyes were 'going on all right'.[3]

More likely is that Nell, a strong-minded and determined character, was the major influence on his career change and the arrival of their three children added fresh responsibility. Mary, born in December 1918, was followed in 1920 by Katherine and Eileen in 1922.

Nonetheless the decision to retire from polar exploration was something of an about-turn for Crean. He had earlier set his heart on undertaking another journey, despite the rigours of many years with Scott and Shackleton. Even after the escapades on *Endurance*, Crean had not lost his appetite for adventure.

Soon after returning from the *Endurance*, Crean had given his friend, Captain Dodds at Bere Haven, the clearest possible indication that he was once again fully prepared to set sail for the South. In a letter to Dodds, probably written around 1918, he wrote:

'I have now fulfilled three expeditions but will look forward to a fourth.'[4]

But by 1920 he had changed his mind, despite a personal approach from Shackleton who was putting together a new polar expedition.

At around the time Crean was leaving the Royal Navy in March 1920, Shackleton was completing a dreary series of twice-daily lectures on the *Endurance* expedition to audiences at London's Philharmonic Hall. A month earlier, in February 1920, Crean had attended the 100th performance and was doubtless briefed about Shackleton's new ambitions.

Crean joined several other former *Endurance* hands – Wild, Worsley, James, Wordie, Hussey, and Orde-Lees – to relive the experience with Shackelton. Hussey played his banjo and newspapers reported that the men received 'a very special reception' from the audience.

The audience, who paid between 1s 3d (6p) and 8s 6d (42½p) to see the explorers in the flesh, were invited to ask questions from the floor and Shackleton was taken aback when one man asked: 'Was there not any use for a proper trained nurse?' The innocent question must have struck a chord for men with painful memories of almost two years of sexual deprivation and Shackleton diplomatically pointed out that women had so far not taken part in Antarctic exploration.

The lecture season was purgatory for Shackleton and he longed for the real thing. Initially he had plans for a trip to the Arctic north. He later changed his mind and declared his intention to circumnavigate the Antarctic Continent in a special ice ship. He bought a ship, renamed her *Quest* and began recruiting his tried and trusted comrades from *Endurance*.

First he wanted his two most loyal lieutenants, Crean and Wild, to accompany him on his latest adventure. Shackleton was so convinced that Crean would agree that he submitted the Irishman's name in a list given to the Admiralty in London of people prepared to join the expedition. The list included Wild, Worsley, Macklin and several others from *Endurance*.[5]

Shackleton told the Admiralty that he had picked a body of experienced men, who were 'ready to go with me'. Crean was to be 'In charge of boatwork' and he gave the Admiralty a brief rundown on his long Antarctic career. Indeed, Shackleton was so enthusiastic that he mistakenly claimed that

Crean had accompanied him South on the *Nimrod* expedition, during 1907–9, when he came to within 97 miles of the Pole.

But Tom Crean said no.

Crean, now a father and a prospective businessman, politely declined. His second daughter had arrived in 1920 and with a mixture of playful blarney and typical firmness, he told Shackleton that his wife and family now came first. Crean simply said:

'I have a long-haired pal now.'[6]

Quest, without the reassuring and formidable presence of Crean, sailed southwards in September 1921, with old *Endurance* colleagues forming the backbone of the expedition. On board with Shackleton and the faithful Wild were the instantly recognisable names of Worsley, Macklin, McIlroy, Hussey, McLeod, Kerr and Green. Three months later, on 5 January 1922, Shackleton died of a heart attack while the *Quest* was moored at the familiar setting of Grytviken, South Georgia.

In the period of only ten years, Crean had prematurely lost the two men – Scott and Shackleton – who had been so influential in his own life. Their loss aroused different emotions in Crean. He respected Scott but understood his weaknesses. In contrast, he worshipped Shackleton.

Crean had now decided where his priorities lay. First there was the matter of a family. His second child Katherine was a weak, sickly youngster who needed much care and attention from her concerned parents. Even today generations of Creans insist that the child was another unfortunate victim of Ireland's Troubles.

Nell was heavily pregnant with Kate when she became embroiled in an incident with the hated irregular soldiers of the Black and Tans. Nell, an independent and resolute woman, had attended a parade in honour of the martyr Thomas Ashe, who hailed from Kinard a few miles from Anascaul. It was a relative of Ashe who had left Anascaul with Crean in 1893.

Ashe, a prominent supporter of nationalist leader, Michael Collins, had died while imprisoned by the British and Collins turned his funeral into a great national demonstration against British rule. Ashe's funeral was an important episode in generating mass support for popular rebellion and his continuing popularity had a particular resonance for the British.

The Black and Tans, who were feared for their ruthless brutality, retaliated by raiding Crean's home in Anascaul to search for any evidence which might link the Crean family to Ireland's armed struggle. All they found was a Union Jack, a souvenir of Tom Crean's honourable 27 years' service in the British navy.[7]

However, Nell always swore that the rough treatment and harassment she received that day was the cause of Kate's subsequent sickness. The young child, who suffered from epilepsy, struggled through a short life.

In 1924, Tom and Nell found enough money to take her on a pilgrimage to the holy shrine of Lourdes, the small town in southwest France where in 1858 a vision of the Virgin Mary is reputed to have appeared to Bernadette, a peasant girl, in a grotto. Millions of Catholic pilgrims have since visited the grotto for the waters from an underground spring which, it is claimed, have miraculous powers of healing the sick and infirm. But shortly after returning from the pilgrimage to Lourdes in December 1924, Kate Crean died, aged four.

At around this time, Crean's plans for his own business, a pub in Anascaul, were beginning to come to fruition. It was more than a decade since he had bought the old thatched building adjacent to a forge at the western end of the village, alongside the stone bridge which crosses the Anascaul River. He demolished much of the structure and in 1927 opened a new pub which was given a name synonymous with his adventurous past. He called his pub the 'South Pole Inn'.

The pub was a favourite haunt of locals, partly because of Crean's fame and partly because he and Nell were popular figures in the village. To the people of Anascaul they were affectionately known as 'Tom the Pole' and 'Nell the Pole'.

Although the pub trade was his chosen profession after leaving the navy, Crean was not ideally suited to pulling pints and running a business. He enjoyed the profile but disliked bar work and Nell, who had been born and brought up in an Anascaul pub, soon assumed full control. She was a natural publican, while he was a traveller, a seaman at peace when on the move. As a result, the thriving business of the South Pole Inn was managed almost entirely by the resolute figure of Nell.

It was a good marriage. The two were well suited. Equally, the division of labour at the South Pole Inn worked well. Tom fully recognised that Nell was the brains behind the business and he respected her business acumen. While she ran the business, Tom could be found in the small snug bar chatting with his close friends or perched on the nearby stone bridge over the Anascaul River, smoking his familiar pipe and passing the time of day with his neighbours. Crean's simple lifestyle rarely ventured beyond a glass of stout, a glance at the newspapers or a bit of gardening. In particular, he liked to stroll up to his old home, the farm at Gurtuchrane, where his two brothers still lived. The prodigious traveller rarely ventured any further.

Crean never lost his love for animals. Each day he went for a long walk accompanied by two dogs, which he named Fido and Toby after two of the pups he had reared on *Endurance*. One of the dogs was accidentally killed after slipping down a cliff on the daily walk and Crean, the man who had seen and endured so much in his life, broke down and wept for the dead animal.

Nell also had to come to terms with her husband's past life, sometimes with unexpected results. On one occasion she encountered Tom in the kitchen cooking bacon, sausages and eggs for his pals. It was a Friday, the day when Catholics are traditionally forbidden to eat meat. Nell began to chastise her husband for his sins and Crean, with his customary robust mixture of bluntness and ready wit, shouted back:

'If you had been where I had been on some Fridays, I'd have eaten a slice off your arse.'[8]

At one stage he bought a large house in a Dublin suburb near the famous Croke Park sports stadium where he and Nell planned to spend their retirement. But the man who had spent so much time in vast open spaces disliked the clamour and bustle of big cities and after some further thought, he abandoned the idea of moving. The house was subsequently rented out before being sold off many years later.

He did, however, like to keep up with the comings and goings in the navy and each day he walked to the now-closed railway station at Anascaul for a chat with his close friend, Bob Knightly, and buy English newspapers as they arrived from Tralee. He particularly liked the *Daily Mail* because, said friends, it published a list of naval appointments and retirements and he could keep up with events and the progress of old friends. But that was as far as he allowed his old life to intrude on the new.

It was almost as though he had closed the book on his great days and adventures with Scott and Shackleton. He was, of course, rightly proud of his achievements and the massive contributions he had made to the three famous expeditions of the Heroic Age. But, surprisingly, he rarely spoke about his old life.

Crean's surviving daughters and other contemporaries all share one common recollection of Tom Crean: that he seldom, if ever, talked about his exploits. When people, especially strangers, raised the subject of his polar exploration – as frequently happened in the South Pole Inn – he would politely change the subject. People would travel some distance to visit the pub and discuss his exploits over a pint of stout but Crean would not be drawn.

Crean was a modest man, as he frequently showed on his three expeditions, and in later life, by eschewing the many opportunities to turn himself into a local celebrity. He deliberately chose not to promote himself with tall tales of hair-raising adventures or exaggerated claims of famous feats. Nor did he seek fame in books or newspaper interviews. Indeed, there is no entirely reliable evidence that Crean ever gave a single interview to a writer. His ambitions had been largely fulfilled in three trips to the South and after enduring enough hardship for any lifetime, he was not ashamed to content himself with a quiet life.

However, there was another good reason for keeping a low profile. Ireland was in a state of turmoil in the years immediately following Crean's retirement from the Navy. While the Anglo-Irish Treaty in 1921 had ended almost 800 years of British rule over the majority of Irish people, the partition of the country led to a bitter Civil War in 1922. The country was split between those who accepted the partition of Ireland and those who pressed for a united independent Ireland.

Crean was inevitably vulnerable in staunchly Republican Kerry because of his links with the British navy and the political climate had deadly consequences for his brother. Cornelius Crean, a sergeant in the Royal Irish Constabulary, was shot dead near Ballinspittle, County Cork, on 25 April 1920, just one month after Crean's return to Kerry.

In the circumstances, it was not the appropriate time for Crean to be publicising his exploits on three major British-led Polar expeditions, even if there was no political links between the two. It was easier to say little that could be associated with British colonial rule, even though Crean was certainly no political animal.

There seems little doubt the political tensions of the era prompted him to maintain a discreet silence about his remarkable feats. In that sense, Crean, too, was a victim of Ireland's Troubles.

He had very little contact with old polar comrades after his retirement, except by the odd letter. Few made the journey to the west coast of Ireland and Crean himself made few trips outside of Kerry.

But one notable exception was Teddy Evans, who always remembered the man who had so courageously saved his life on the Barrier in 1912. Evans had made rapid progress in the Royal Navy and in 1926 was given the prestigious command of the battleship, *Repulse*. It was a special moment in Evans' action-packed life and he chose to share the celebrations with Tom Crean and Bill Lashly.

Soon after his appointment, the pair were among the principal guests at a special reception on board *Repulse* at Portsmouth. Despite the stark difference in rank and social background, Evans always regarded the two sturdy seamen as special. His son, Broke Evans, said his father always spoke fondly of the two men and he confirmed:

> 'He always called them his friends, he thought the world of them.'[9]

Oddly enough, Crean had his reservations about Evans and his famous episode when commanding the destroyer HMS *Broke* during the First World War. During an engagement in the Straits of Dover, Evans rammed a German ship and refused to pick up survivors, yelling from the bridge, 'Remember the *Lusitania*' after the passenger liner sunk by U-boats in 1915 with the loss of 1,198 lives. Evans was acclaimed for his action and became famous as 'Evans of the *Broke*'.

But Crean was a naval purist and respected the etiquette of the sea, even if such customs are also victims of war. In later life, he told friends that one ship should never ram another and that he was uncomfortable with the fact Evans did not rescue the drowning German sailors.[10]

Outwardly Crean did not display any signs of the toll inflicted on his ample frame from years of hazardous living in the South. His daughters only recall that his ears were 'stiff' from the effects of frostbite. However, his feet had also been badly damaged by the severe cold of endless journeys in sub-zero temperatures in inadequate footwear. He had his boots specially made.

Two elderly residents of Anascaul recalled that as young girls they would sometimes accompany Crean on his daily walks into the nearby hills. On occasions he would take off his boots to dip his feet in the cool running water of the Anascaul River. His feet, they remember, were black. But, typical of his modesty, Crean urged the young girls not to tell anyone his secret.

Life passed quietly and pleasantly for Tom and Nell. The South Pole Inn and Tom's pensions provided a decent living and the surviving children, Mary and Eileen, were afforded a reasonably comfortable upbringing in a quiet rural setting.

His fondness for his family also extended beyond the living and, around this time, Crean did something unusual. He personally built a large tomb for past and present members of his family in the little cemetery at Ballynacourty, a quiet but historic spot alongside the Anascaul River up the hill from Anascaul and not far from his birthplace at Gurtuchrane. Ballynacourty once stood at the crossroads of various pathways across the surrounding hills and tradition has it that it was once the site of an ancient Brehon law court.

Crean was doing more than returning to his Irish roots in building his own tomb at Ballynacourty. It was a powerfully symbolic gesture which showed how much Crean had come to terms with his own mortality. The man who had faced death on many occasions in his perilous Polar career now faced his final journey with the same equanimity. The tomb survives to this day.

But his peaceful, contented life came to an abrupt halt in the summer of 1938. At around the time of his birthday on 20 July, Crean suddenly complained about severe stomach pains and began to vomit. He was taken to hospital in Tralee, about 16 miles from Anascaul, where acute appendicitis was quickly diagnosed. But there was no surgeon available at Tralee to perform the necessary operation and Crean was transferred to the Bon Secours Hospital, Cork, over 75 miles away, where his appendix was removed.

The delay was fatal. Crean's appendix had perforated and infection set in. The seemingly indestructible character had been felled by an illness which today is usually treated as a relatively minor problem.

He drifted in and out of consciousness for a week, with Nell in permanent vigil at his bedside as he clung to life. Tom Crean lapsed into unconsciousness for the last time and died on 27 July 1938, exactly a week after his sixty-first birthday. Nell was at his side.

The funeral a week later was among the biggest ever witnessed at Anascaul. He had commanded particular respect among the villagers and they were intent on paying a special homage. After a solemn requiem mass, Crean's body was proudly carried on the shoulders of friends and old naval comrades in a long relay from Anascaul church through the village and over a mile up the hill to the tiny cemetery at Ballynacourty overlooking the Kerry hills.

He was laid alongside daughter Kate and other members of the Crean family in the tomb he had built with his own hands. Around his neck Tom Crean was still wearing the scapular which had been with him all his life.

One of the host of floral tributes came from Admiral Sir E.R.G.R. Evans, better known as Teddy Evans. The tribute of porcelain flowers, set in a clear glass case, contained a simple heartfelt message which read:

'In affectionate remembrance from an Antarctic comrade.'

A few feet away from Tom Crean's last resting place the peaceful Anascaul River flows gently down the hill and past the South Pole Inn.

27
Memories

Tom Crean's memory has not been allowed to fade away, particularly among the devotees of polar exploration history and especially in Kerry where they are rightly proud of his achievements.

The South Pole Inn, for many, remains a notable commemoration of Crean. The pub will forever be associated with Crean and, like the man himself, it has a colourful history. Nell Crean kept the South Pole Inn for ten years after Tom's death, finally selling the pub in 1948 when she was 67 years of age.

By coincidence, 1948 was also a year in which Nell and her daughters briefly relived part of Crean's exploits on the *Terra Nova* expedition when they travelled to Cork to watch an early showing of Charles Friend's reverential film, *Scott of the Antarctic*. Tom Crean was portrayed by John Gregson and sitting alongside the three women in the cinema was Robert Forde, the Petty Officer from Cork who had served with Crean on Scott's last expedition almost four decades earlier.

Nell lived until she was 86 and, when she died in 1968, was buried alongside Tom in the family tomb he had built at Ballynacourty. Tom's daughters, Mary and Eileen, married two brothers called O'Brien who had their own building business. After moving a few miles to Tralee, Mary and Eileen had their own houses built next to each other. Appropriately one is called

'Terra Nova' and the other 'Discovery'. Perhaps if young Kate had lived her home would have been called 'Endurance'. . .

The pub had mixed fortunes after passing from Nell's hands in 1948. The celebrated director, David Lean, came to Anascaul in the late 1960s when making the film *Ryan's Daughter* and bought the pile of stones from the old forge that had originally stood on the site of the South Pole Inn. The stones, which had been collected by Crean when he was building the pub in the 1920s, were used by Lean to help construct authentic Irish cottages for the film sets.

But the pub itself changed hands several times in the years following Nell's retirement and became badly run down before finally closing in 1987. It remained empty for about five years but was then happily restored by the new owner, Tom Kennedy, a distant relative of Crean's mother. After considerable refurbishment, the South Pole Inn is now thriving once again and serving the people of Anascaul and passing tourists alike.

A further recognition of Crean's exploits came in 1987 when his daughters and relatives from around the world attended a simple ceremony to unveil the memorial plaque, which still stands above the doorway of the South Pole Inn.

Sir Edmund Hillary, the great twentieth-century adventurer who shared a birthday with Crean, opened an exhibition on the Irishman's life at the Kerry County Museum in Tralee. The display contains his many Antarctic medals, some photographs, a few letters, a naval uniform and ceremonial sword, and the silver tea service which Shackleton generously gave the Irishman on his wedding in 1917.

Another more ambitious attempt to commemorate Crean's life came in 1997. A team of five leading Irish mountain climbers and sailors attempted to follow in the footsteps of Crean, Shackleton and Worsley by sailing 800 miles (1,300 km) across the Southern Ocean from Elephant Island to South Georgia and then repeating the famous crossing of the island.

Their boat was named *Tom Crean* in special remembrance of the Kerryman. Unfortunately, the violence of the Southern Ocean defeated the party and after overturning three times in ferocious Force 10 storms, the *Tom Crean* had to be abandoned.

Perhaps the most touching tribute to Tom Crean is to be found in the family of Teddy Evans. Evans never forgot the man who saved his life in Antarctica. Years after the heroic rescue, he framed one of Ponting's photographs of a smiling Crean and placed it in a prominent spot in his home as a constant reminder of an outstanding man. Today the photograph still holds pride of place in the home of Broke Evans, son of Teddy Evans.

But the most permanent celebrations of Tom Crean can be found in his adopted home of Antarctica. The four-mile long Crean Glacier on South Georgia and Mount Crean, which rises 8,360 ft (2,550 m) above Victoria Land on the Antarctic mainland, will forever perpetuate the memory of polar exploration's unsung hero.

Endnotes

Chapter 1
1. Steve MacDonogh, *The Dingle Peninsula*, p37.
2. Royal Navy service record.
3. *Ibid.*
4. *Ibid.*
5. *Ibid.*
6. Quoted Denis Barry, *Capuchin Annual*, 1952.
7. RN service record.
8. *Ibid.*

Chapter 2
1. Sir Clements Markham, *Antarctic Obsession*, p1.
2. Robert Scott, *The Voyage of the* Discovery, p24.
3. *Ibid*, p66.
4. Tom Crean, Royal Navy service record.
5. Log book, HMS *Ringarooma*, 29 November 1901, PRO.
6. *Ibid.*
7. Robert Scott, letter to RGS, 18 December 1901, RGS.
8. *Ibid.*
9. *Ibid.*
10. Markham, *Antarctic Obsession*, p90.
11. *Ibid*, p175.
12. Log of HMS *Ringarooma*, 19 December 1901, PRO.
13. Scott to RGS, 18 December 1901, RGS.

Chapter 3
1. Robert Scott, *The Voyage of the Discovery*, p84.
2. William Lashly, *Under Scott's Command: Lashly's Antarctic*

Diaries, pp19–20.
3. Scott, *The Voyage of the* Discovery, p84.
4. Lashly, *Under Scott's Command*, p20.
5. James Duncan, Antarctic journal, McMG.
6. Scott, *The Voyage of the* Discovery, p86.
7. Duncan, McMG.
8. Scott, *The Voyage of the* Discovery, p98.
9. L.C. Bernacchi, *Saga of the* Discovery, p27.
10. *Ibid.*
11. Thomas Williamson, Antarctic diary, SPRI.
12. Frank Wild, papers, SPRI.
13. Lashly, *Under Scott's Command*, p21.
14. Scott, *The Voyage of the* Discovery.
15. Williamson, diary SPRI.

Chapter 4
1. British National Antarctic Expedition records, RGS.
2. Robert Scott, *The Voyage of the* Discovery, p170.
3. Louis C. Bernacchi, *Saga of the* Discovery, p40.
4. James Duncan, Antarctic journal, McMG.

Chapter 5
1. Michael Barne, Antarctic diary, SPRI.
2. Robert Scott, *The Voyage of the* Discovery, p466.
3. *Ibid.*
4. Barne, diary.
5. *Ibid.*
6. Scott, p539.
7. Louis Bernacchi, *Saga of the* Discovery p107.
8. William Lashly, *Under Scott's Command*, p64.
9. Scott, pp566–7.
10. Barne, diary.
11. Charles Ford, diary SPRI.
12. *Ibid.*
13. Scott, p667.
14. *Ibid*, p672.

Chapter 6
1. British National Antarctic Expedition records, RGS.
2. Tom Crean, Certificate of Service, Royal Navy.
3. BNAE records, RGS.
4. *Ibid.*
5. Crean letter to R. Scott, 10 October 1905, SPRI.
6. Crean, RN service record.
7. Recorded in several books and based on memorandum from Dr Edward Atkinson among papers for the British Antarctic Expedition, 1910–13.
8. *Ibid.*
9. Robert Scott letter to Crean, 23 March 1910.
10. Sue Limb & Patrick Cordingley, *Captain Oates: Soldier & Explorer*, quoted from recollection by Oates' sister, Violet Oates, p95.

Chapter 7
1. Victor Campbell, diary, 29 November 1911, *The Wicked Mate*.
2. Robert Scott, diary, 25 December 1910 (Quotations are taken from the facsimile edition, *The Diaries of Captain Robert Scott*).
3. William Lashly, *Under Scott's Command: Lashly's Antarctic Diaries*, p20.
4. Scott, diary, 2 February 1911.
5. Tryggve Gran, *The Norwegian With Scott*, p52.
6. Apsley Cherry-Garrard, *The Worst Journey in the World*, p154.
7. Cherry-Garrard, quoting Henry 'Birdie' Bowers, p183.
8. *Ibid*, p186.
9. *Ibid*, p196.
10. Scott, diary 3 March 1911.
11. Gran, diary, 1 March 1911.
12. Polar Record, 3 (17): 78–79, SPRI (1939).
13. Scott, diary 19 April 1911.
14. Cherry-Garrard, p217.

Chapter 8
1.   Tryggve Gran, *The Norwegian With Scott*, p89.
2.   *Ibid*, p114.
3.   Robert Scott, diary, October 1911.

Chapter 9
1.   Edward Wilson, *The Diary of the 'Terra Nova' Expedition*, 29 October, 1911.
2.   William Lashly, diary 1 November 1911, SPRI.
3.   Robert Scott diary, 1 November 1911.
4.   *Ibid*, 31 October 1911.
5.   E.R.G. Evans, *South With Scott*, p200.
6.   Wilson, diary 9 December 1911.
7.   Henry Bowers diary, 14 December 1911.
8.   Scott diary, 14 December 1911.
9.   Roald Amundsen, *The South Pole*, Vol II, p121.
10.   *Ibid*, p122.
11.   Patrick Keohane, diary 21 December 1911, SPRI.
12.   Apsley Cherry-Garrard, *The Worst Journey in the World*, p425.
13.   Scott, diary, 21 December 1911.
14.   *Ibid*.
15.   Lashly, p430.
16.   Evans, p231.
17.   Tryggve Gran, *Kampen on Sydpolen*, p158.
18.   *Ibid*, p158.
19.   Gran, *The Norwegian With Scott*, events recorded after discussions with Crean, p200.
20.   *Ibid*.
21.   *Ibid*.
22.   Evans, *South With Scott*, p235.
23.   Scott diary, 3 January 1912.
24.   *Ibid*, 4 January 1912.

Chapter 10
1.   E.R.G. Evans, *South With Scott*, p236.
2.   *Ibid*.

3. An incident recalled by Hon. Broke Evans from conversations with his father.
4. Evans, *South With Scott*, p239.
5. *Ibid.*
6. Evans, *The Last Supporting Party*, SPRI.
7. William Lashly, diary 17 January 1912.
8. Evans, *South With Scott*, p243.
9. Evans quoting Crean, p246.
10. Evans, pp246–7.
11. *Ibid*, p249.
12. Lashly, diary 22 January 1912.
13. Evans, *South With Scott*, p252.
14. Lashly diary, 3 February 1912.
15. *Ibid*, 3 February 1912.
16. *Ibid*, 7 February 1912.
17. Evans, *South With Scott*, p253.
18. Reginald Pound, *Evans of the* Broke, p117.
19. Lashly, diary 17 February 1912.
20. *Ibid*, 18 February 1912.
21. Evans, *South With Scott*, p253.
22. Evans, *Adventurous Life*.
23. Evans, *South With Scott*, p253.
24. *Ibid*, p254.
25. Lashly diary, 17 February 1912.
26. Evans, *South With Scott*, p254.
27. Apsley Cherry-Garrard, *The Worst Journey in the World*, p463.
28. Evans in address given to Royal Geographical Society, July 1913
29. Cherry-Garrard, p463.
30. *Ibid*, p471.
31. *Ibid*, pp462–3.
32. Crean, letter to unknown person, 26 February 1912.
33. Crean, letter to James Kennedy, 18 January 1913.
34. Evans, *Adventurous Life*, p80.

Chapter 11
1. Robert Scott, diary 5 January 1912.
2. *Ibid*, 15 January 1912.
3. *Ibid*, 17 January 1912.
4. *Ibid*, 17 January 1912.
5. *Ibid*, 18 January 1912.
6. *Ibid*, 30 January 1912.
7. *Ibid*, 16 February 1912.
8. *Ibid*, 3 March 1912.
9. *Ibid*, 11 March 1912.
10. *Ibid*, 29 March 1912.

Chapter 12
1. Tryggve Gran, interview Ontario Educational Communications Authority, 1974, SPRI.
2. Charles Wright, papers, SPRI.
3. Edward Atkinson, papers SPRI.

Chapter 13
1. Apsley Cherry-Garrard, *The Worst Journey in the World*, p481.
2. Tryggve Gran, *The Norwegian With Scott*, p183.
3. Roland Huntford, *Scott & Amundsen*, p468.
4. Frank Debenham, *Polar Record*, 3 (17): 78–79 (1939) SPRI.
5. Gran, p205.
6. Debenham, *The Quiet Land*, 5 May, 1912.
7. Gran, p215.
8. Gran, interviews, Ontario Educational Communications Authority, 1974, SPRI.
9. Thomas Williamson, diary, SPRI.
10. Crean letter to J. Kennedy, January 1913, SPRI.
11. From recollections by Crean's daughters, Mary O'Brien and Eileen O'Brien.
12. Crean letter to Captain R.H. Dodds.
13. Gran, p216.
14. Robert Scott diary, March 1912.
15. Crean letter to Capt Dodds, 3 September 1918.
16. Patrick Keohane diary, 13 November 1912, SPRI.

17. Edward R.G.R. Evans, *South With Scott*, p314.
18. Cherry-Garrard, p631.

Chapter 14
1. Apsley Cherry-Garrard, *The Worst Journey in the World*, p637.
2. *Ibid*, p638.
3. Sir Peter Scott, quoted in notes and references to *Scott of the Antarctic and Cardiff*, p69.
4. Tom Crean letter to Peter Scott, 1935.
5. Kathleen Scott, letter to Sir Francis Drake, 12 August 1912, SPRI.
6. Citation for Albert Medal, July 1913.
7. Hugh R. Mill, *The Geographic Journal*, May 1912.
8. Edward R.G. Evans, Royal Geographic Society address, 21 May 1913.
9. Oriana Wilson letter to Tom Crean, 23 February 1913.

Chapter 15
1. Tom Crean, RN service record.
2. Margery and James Fisher, *Shackleton*, p300.
3. Agreement between Tom Crean and Sir Ernest Shackleton, 1914.
4. Roland Huntford, *Shackleton*, p401.
5. Sir Ernest Shackleton, *South*, p22.
6. *Ibid*, p28.

Chapter 16
1. Sir Ernest Shackleton, *South*, p38.
2. *Ibid*.
3. Frank Worsley diary/papers, SPRI.
4. *Ibid*.
5. *Ibid*.
6. *Ibid*.

Chapter 17
1. Frank Worsley, diary, SPRI.
2. Roland Huntford, *Shackleton*, p477.

3.   Worsley, diary, SPRI.
4.   Sir Ernest Shackleton, diary, SPRI.
5.   Worsley, diary, SPRI.

Chapter 18
1.   Frank Hurley, *Argonauts of the South.*
2.   *Ibid.*
3.   Sir Ernest Shackleton, *South*, p104.
4.   *Ibid.*

Chapter 19
1.   Harry McNeish, diary, ATL.
2.   Sir Ernest Shackleton, *South* quoting Frank Hurley, p110.
3.   Frank Worsley, diary, SPRI.
4.   McNeish, diary, ATL.
5.   Worsley, diary SPRI.
6.   Shackleton, p116.
7.   Worsley, diary, SPRI.
8.   *Ibid.*

Chapter 20
1.   Frank Worsley, diary ,SPRI.
2.   *Ibid.*
3.   *Ibid.*
4.   *Ibid.*
5.   *Ibid.*
6.   *Ibid.*
7.   *Ibid.*
8.   Sir Ernest Shackleton, *South,* p127.
9.   Worsley, diary.
10. Shackleton, *South,* p128.
11. Worsley, diary.

Chapter 21
1.   Harry McNeish, diary, ATL.
2.   *Ibid.*
3.   Frank Worsley, diary, SPRI.

4.   *Ibid.*
5.   Frank Worsley, *Endurance*, p154.
6.   *Ibid.*, p156.
7.   Sir Ernest Shackleton, *South*, p145.
8.   Worsley, diary, SPRI.
9.   Shackleton, *South* p149.

Chapter 22
1.   Duncan Carse, *The Times*, 16 March 1956.
2.   Frank Worsley, *The Great Antarctic Rescue*, p214.
3.   Frank Worsley, *Endurance*, p165.
4.   Sir Ernest Shackleton, *South*, p150.
5.   John Knightly, from personal recollections of his father, Bob Knightly.
6.   Hugh R. Mill, *The Life of Sir Ernest Shackleton*, pp245–6.
7.   T.S. Eliot, *The Waste Land*, from Collected Poems 1909–62.

Chapter 23
1.   Frank Worsley, *The Great Antarctic Rescue*, p216.
2.   *Ibid.*, p216.
3.   Frank Worsley, *Endurance*, p166.
4.   Sir Ernest Shackleton, *South,* p152.
5.   Shackleton, letter to Emily Shackleton, 3 June 1916, SPRI.
6.   *John Bull*, 22 July 1916, BL.
7.   *Ibid.*
8.   Tom P. Jones, *Patagonian Panorama*, p80.
9.   Tom Crean, letter to Hazel Marston, 3 July 1916, SPRI.
10. Shackleton, *South,* p155.
11. *Ibid.*

Chapter 24
1.   Tom P. Jones, P*atagonian Panorama*.
2.   *Magellan Times*, 7 September 1916, BL.
3.   *Ibid.*

Chapter 25
1.   Admiralty letter to Sir Ernest Shackleton, 30 December 1916.

2. Tom Crean letter to Apsley Cherry-Garrard, 2 September 1917, SPRI.
3. Shackleton family papers.
4. Margery and James Fisher, *Shackleton*, p414.
5. Shackleton letter to Emily Shackleton, October 1916, SPRI.
6. Royal Navy specimen Examination Paper.
7. Shackleton, letter to Tom Crean, 27 June 1917.
8. Emily Shackleton, letter to Crean, 12 November 1916.
9. Admiralty Certificate of Qualification for Warrant Officer, 17 August 1917.
10. Shackleton letter to Crean 27 June 1917.
11. Royal Navy service record.
12. HMS *Fox*, Log book, April 1919, PRO.
13. Admiralty Certificate for Wounds and Hurts, 28 April 1919.
14. Admiralty Certificate of Conduct, HMS *Fox*, 31 October 1919.
15. Ministry of Defence service record.
16. Admiralty Certificate of Conduct, HMS *Hecla*, 4 March, 1920.

Chapter 26
1. Ministry of Pensions letter to Tom Crean, 16 March 1922.
2. Crean letter to Kathleen Scott, 26 Augus, 1920, SPRI.
3. *Ibid*, SPRI.
4. Crean letter to Capt R. H. Dodds, undated but probably written in 1918.
5. Correspondence between The Admiralty and Sir Ernest Shackleton, regarding a new expedition, 1920, PRO.
6. Recollections of Mary and Eileen (Crean) O'Brien.
7. *Ibid*.
8. *Ibid*.
9. Recollections by Broke Evans, son of Teddy Evans.
10. John Knightly, recollections of Crean from his father, Bob Knightly.

Bibliography

PUBLISHED SOURCES

There are a considerable number of works about the history of Polar Exploration and the following list is meant to show those which were the most helpful to my background and understanding of the subject. It is, of course, a personal choice.

Alexander, Caroline: *The Endurance*, Bloomsbury Publishing, 1998
Amundsen, Roald: *My Life as an Explorer*, Wm. Heinemann 1927
Amundsen, Roald: *The South Pole*, C. Hurst, 1976 (First published John Murray, 1912)
Armitage, Albert: *Two Years in the Antarctic*, Arnold, 1905
Barry, Denis: *Polar Crean*, Capuchin Journal, 1952
Bernacchi, Louis: *A Very Gallant Gentleman*, Thornton Butterworth, 1933
Bernacchi, Louis: *Saga of the* Discovery, Blackie & Son, 1938
Campbell, Victor: *The Wicked Mate*, (Ed. H. G. King), Bluntisham Books, 1988. (Original diary: Memorial University, Newfoundland Library)
Carse, Duncan: *The Times*, 16 March 1956
Cherry-Garrard, Apsley: *The Worst Journey in the World*, Constable, 1922
Debenham, Frank: *Tom Crean: An Appreciation*, Polar Record, 1939
Debenham, Frank: *In the Antarctic*, John Murray, 1952
Debenham, Frank: *The Quiet Land: The Antarctic Diaries of Frank Debenham*, Bluntisham Books/Erskine Press, 1992
Dunnett, Harding: *Shackleton's Boat, The Story of the* James Caird, Neville & Harding, 1996

Evans, Lord Mountevans: *Adventurous Life*, Hutchinson, 1946

Evans, Lord Mountevans: *South With Scott*, Collins, 1924

Evans, Lord Mountevans: *The Antarctic Challenged*, Staples Press, 1955

Evans, Lord Mountevans: *The Last Supporting Party*, (publication unknown) 1913

Fisher, James & Margery: *Shackleton*, Barrie, 1957

Gran, Tryggve: *Mitt Liv Himmel og Jord*, Ernest G. Mortensens Forlag, 1979

Gran, Tryggve: *The Norwegian with Scott – Tryggve Gran's Antarctic Diary 1910–13*, (Ed. Geoffrey Hattersley-Smith), HM Stationery Office, 1984

Gregor, Gary: *Swansea's Antarctic Explorer – Edgar Evans, 1876–1912*, Swansea City Council, 1995 (Now: West Glamorgan Archive Service)

Gwynn, Stephen: *Captain Scott*, The Bodley Head, 1929

Hallock, Judith Lee: *Profile: Tom Crean*, Polar Record, 1984

Hanssen, Helmer: *Voyages of a Modern Viking*, G. Routledge, 1936

Harrowfield, David: *Icy Heritage – Historic Sites of the Ross Sea Region*, Antarctic Heritage Trust, 1995

Headland, Robert: Place Names in the Antarctic after Thomas Crean of Anascaul, *The Kerry Magazine*, No 4, 1992

Huntford, Roland: *Scott & Amundsen*, Hodder & Stoughton, 1979

Huntford, Roland: *Shackleton*, Hodder & Stoughton, 1985

Hurley, Frank: *Argonauts of the South*, G.P. Putnam's Sons, 1925

Hussey, Leonard: *South With Shackleton*, Sampson Low, 1949

Huxley, Elspeth: *Scott of the Antarctic*, Weidenfeld & Nicolson, 1977

Johnson, Anthony: *Scott of the Antarctic and Cardiff*, University College Cardiff Press, 1984

Jones, A.G.E: *Polar Portraits*, Caedmon of Whitby, 1992

Jones, Tom C: *Patagonian Panorama*, Outspoken Press, 1961

Lansing, Alfred: Endurance: *Shackleton's Incredible Voyage*, Hodder & Stoughton, 1959

Lashly, William: *Under Scott's Command, Lashly's Antarctic Diaries* (Ed. by A. R. Ellis), Gollancz, 1969

Limb, Sue and Patrick Cordingley: *Captain Oates – Soldier and Explorer*, B.T. Batsford, 1982

MacDonogh, Steve: *The Dingle Peninsula*, Brandon Book Publishers, 1993

Markham, Sir Clements: *Antarctic Obsession – The British National Antarctic Expedition 1901–4*, Bluntisham Books/Erskine Press, 1986 (Original manuscript material: SPRI)

Mason, Theodore K: *The South Pole Ponies*, Dodd, Mead & Co, 1979

Mill, Hugh R: *The Life of Sir Ernest Shackleton*, Heinemann, 1923

Mill Hugh R: *Geographic Journal*, May 1912

Mills, Leif: *Frank Wild*, Caedmon of Whitby, 1999

Mountfield, David: *A History of Polar Exploration*, Hamlyn 1974

Ponting, Herbert: *The Great White South*, Duckworth & Co, 1921

Pound, Reginald: *Evans of the* Broke, Oxford University Press, 1963

Pound, Reginald: *Scott of the Antarctic*, Cassell & Co, 1966

Priestley, Raymond: *Antarctic Adventure – Scott's Northern Party*, McLelland and Stewart/C. Hurst & Co, 1974 (First published T. Fisher Unwin)

Ross, Sir James Clark: *A Voyage of Discovery & Research in the Southern and Antarctic Regions, 1839–43*, John Murray, 1847

Savours, Ann: *The Voyages of the* Discovery, Virgin Books, 1992

Scott, Robert F: *The Voyage of the* Discovery, Smith Elder & Co, 1905

Scott, Robert F: *Scott's Last Expedition, The Journals*, Smith Elder & Co, 1913

Scott Robert F: *The Diaries of Captain Robert Scott*, (Facsimile Edition) University Microfilms Ltd, 1968

Seaver, George: *'Birdie' Bowers of the Antarctic*, John Murray, 1938

Seaver, George: *Edward Wilson of the Antarctic*, John Murray, 1933

Shackleton, Sir Ernest: *South*, Century Ltd, 1991 (First published by William Heinemann, 1919)

Taylor, Griffith: *With Scott: The Silver Lining*, Smith, Elder & Co, 1916

Thomson, David: *Scott's Men*, Allen Lane, 1977

Thomson, John: *Shackleton's Captain: A Biography of Frank Worsley*, Hazard Press, 1999

Wild, Frank: *Shackleton's Last Voyage*, Cassell & Co, 1923

Wilson, Edward: *Diary of* Discovery *Expedition to the Antarctic 1901–4*, Blandford Press, 1966

Wilson, Edward: *Diary of the 'Terra Nova' Expedition to the Antarctic 1910–12*, Blandford Press, 1972

Worsley, Frank: *The Great Antarctic Rescue*, Times Books 1977 (First published Folio Society)

Worsley, Frank: *Endurance*, Philip Allan, 1931

Wright, Charles: Silas: *The Antarctic Diaries and Memoir of Charles S. Wright*, (Ed. C. Bull and P. Wright), Ohio State University Press, 1993

Films

90 degrees South, Herbert Ponting, National Film and Television Archive, 1933

Scott of the Antarctic, Ealing Studios, 1948

The Last Place on Earth, Central Television, 1985

Archive Sources

Admiralty Library, Ministry of Defence, London, UK (AL)

Bank of England (BoE)

British Library, Newspaper Library (BL)

The Library, Dingle, Kerry, Ireland (DL)

Dundee Heritage Trust, Dundee, UK (DHT)

Kerry County Library, Tralee, Ireland (KCL)

McManus Galleries, Dundee, UK (McMG)

Ministry of Defence, UK (MoD)

Public Record Office, London, UK (PRO)

Royal Geographical Society, London, UK (RGS)

Scott Polar Research Institute, Cambridge, UK (SPRI)

Alexander Turnbull Library, Wellington, New Zealand (ATL/NLNZ)

The Gilbert White/Oates Museum, Selborne, Hampshire, UK (WOM)

NEWSPAPERS, PERIODICALS

Note: A large number of contemporary newspapers and periodicals
were consulted, including:

John Bull, Falkland Islands, BL
Cork Examiner, Cork, BL
Daily Express, London BL
Daily Mirror, London BL
Daily Sketch, London BL
Daily Telegraph, London BL
Kerry Champion, Tralee, BL
Kerry Evening Post, Tralee, BL
Kerry News, Tralee, BL
The Kerryman, Tralee, BL
Magellan Times, Punta Arenas, BL
Reader's Digest
The Times, London, BL

UNPUBLISHED DIARIES, JOURNALS, RECORDS

Armitage, Albert	*Discovery* journals, 1901–4, SPRI
Barne, Michael	*Discovery* diaries, journals, 1901–4, SPRI
Bernacchi, Louis	*Discovery* journals, 1901–4, SPRI
Crean, Mary and Eileen	Interviews with author, 1997; Family papers
Duncan, James	*Discovery* diary, 1901–3, McMG
Evans, Lord Mountevans	Antarctic journals, papers, letters, 1910–3, SPRI
Fisher, J. and M.	Papers, letters re: *Shackleton*; SPRI
Ford, Charles	*Discovery* journal, 1901–4, SPRI
Gran, Tryggve	Ontario Educational Communications Authority, transcript of interviews, 1974, SPRI
Hare, Charles	*Discovery* diary, 1901–3 SPRI
Keohane, Patrick	Antarctic journals, 1910–2 SPRI
Lashly, William	Antarctic diary, 1911–2, SPRI
McNeish, Harry	*Endurance* diaries, 1914–6, NLNZ

Marston, George	Antarctic papers, letters, 1914–7, SPRI
Oates, Lawrence E.G.	Fragments of diary, 1911–2, letters, WOM
Scott, Robert F.	Letters of Proceedings, No 4; No 5; *Discovery* expedition, December 1901, RGS
Shackleton, Sir E.	*Endurance* diaries, letters, papers, 1914–6, SPRI
	Correspondence, papers, etc, to Admiralty relating to proposed expedition 1920, PRO
Wild, Frank	Antarctic papers, SPRI
Williamson, Thomas	Antarctic journals, 1901–4; 1910–3; SPRI
Worsley, Frank	*Endurance* diaries, papers, documents, 1914–6, SPRI
Wright, Charles	Antarctic diaries and papers, SPRI

Ships' logs:

RRS *Discovery*	RGS
HMS *Fox*	PRO
HMS *Hecla*	PRO
HMS *Inflexible*	PRO
HMS *Ringarooma*	PRO

Documents:

Tom Crean – Service documents

Royal Navy service record, 1893–1920: Copy collated by A.J. Francis for Navy Departmental Record Officer, dated 25/11/1975, RN;

Copy produced for the author by RN Departmental Records Office, 21/7/1997, MoD

Certificates of Appointment Various

Certificate of Service or Conduct Various

Gunnery and Torpedo History Sheet Various

Certificate of qualification for Warrant Officer, 11/8/1917

Certificate for Wounds and Hurts 28/4/1919

(Many of Tom Crean's original service documents are in the possession of Gerard O'Brien, Crean's grandson. Copies are lodged with the Kerry County Library, Tralee, KCL)

Letters:

Admiralty to Sir Ernest Shackleton, 30 December1916

Crean Thomas to Robert Scott, 10 October 1905 SPRI

Crean, Thomas to (unknown) 26 February 1912

Crean, Thomas to J.P. Kennedy, 18 January 1913

Crean, Thomas to Hazel Marston, 3 July 1916

Crean, Thomas to Apsley Cherry-Garrard, 2 September 17

Crean, Thomas to Capt H. R. Dodds, (undated); 3 September1918

Crean, Thomas to Kathleen Scott, 26 August 1920, SPRI

Paymaster General's Office: to Tom Crean, re: Disability Retired Pay

Pensions, Ministry: to Tom Crean, re: pension award, 16 March 1922

Perris, Ernest to Tom Crean, 2 January 1917

Scott, Kathleen to Sir Francis Drake, 10 August 1912, SPRI

Scott, Peter to Tom Crean, 1935

Scott Robert F to Tom Crean, 23 March 1910

Shackleton, Sir Ernest to Tom Crean (Agreement for employment on Imperial Trans-Antarctic Expedition) 1914; 27 June 1917

Shackleton, Emily to Tom Crean, 12 November1916; 29 March 1917; 23 August 1917

Wilson, Oriana to Tom Crean, 23 February 1913

Index

Also by Michael Smith:

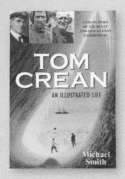

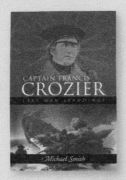